MONEY CREATION 101

CHANGE OUR MONEY – CHANGE OUR WORLD

NICK EGNATZ

Money Creation 101 / Nick Egnatz

June 2023.

Published by Nick Egnatz.

www.nickegnatz.com

Contents

People, Planet & the Power of Money Project

Change Our Money — Change Our World

The *People, Planet & the Power of Money Project* is a public education initiative undertaken to give the basic facts on how our money is presently created and how it easily could and should be created. This is basic information that we all should have, but the vast majority of us lack. With this information we can tackle both the environmental and inequality crises that confront us today. Without this information we can expect our society to continue to stumble along, unable to find the money necessary for the known challenges of the day and the unknown challenges that are sure to confront us in the future.

The project initially consists of three books:

> Book 1: *Money Creation 101*
> Book 2: *History of Money 101*
> Book 3: *Spaceship Earth 101*

I am upfront about my lack of academic standing in taking on the economics establishment. The book titles reflect the one economics course I did take, Econ 101. In this course the class was informed that only a handful of people in the entire country were capable of understanding how our money is created within the Federal Reserve System, so the entire class would be spared from studying that which we were not smart enough to understand—how our money is created. It was only decades later that I happened across the answer of how our money is created in my reading and research as an antiwar, social justice and environmental activist.

These are not boring textbooks about economic theories and formulas, but rather the basic, necessary information we all need as citizens to determine what type of money system we should have and who should create this money—our government or private entities. Please trust your instinct when reading. Our present money system was not created to be easily understood. Rather it was designed to completely baffle and hide the truth from us so that we would never be able to challenge its legitimacy.

The *People, Planet & the Power of Money Project* uses academic, historical, government, and journalism sources to present the case for publicly created money. The phrase *Change Our Money – Change Our World* has been used by the Alliance For Just Money of which I am a member. It perfectly tells us what we must do.

The bibliography contains numerous sources that are available online to all, in addition to some histories that are difficult to find. An effort was made to use as many easy to find sources as possible. The entire bibliography is available at my website: NickEgnatz.com.

DEDICATION

The People, Planet & the Power of Money Project would never have been possible without my beloved wife, Sue, our children, Erin and Nick, and our five grandkids, Tristan, Kedzie, Harrison, Maddie and Leo, without whom I would be a lost soul and quite incapable of researching, writing about and ultimately challenging the current debt-money system.

Whatever level of understanding this book is able to add to our knowledge of our money system is the direct result of the loving, nurturing environment that my parents, Louise and Nicholas Egnatz, MD, provided for me and my seven rambunctious brothers, Mike, Alex, Tom, Joe, Chris, John and Bill, and our wonderful sister, Lisa.

The People, Planet & the Power of Money Project is dedicated to the people and the planet we inhabit and derive our sustenance from, all of whom desperately need a better money system.

PREFACE

The *People, Planet & the Power of Money Project* is an educational outreach to everyday citizens, advocating for a system of publicly created money. It started as a single book, but eventually became three shorter books to properly tell the story of how our money is created to those of us with no formal economics training. But why on Earth should a project about how our money is created be of interest to those of us outside the academic community?

Because in 2018 a fifteen-year-old girl in Sweden, Greta Thunberg, took it upon herself to skip school and stand outside Parliament with a sign that read "School Strike for Climate."

We are told that we do not have enough money to address the crises of climate change, dying oceans and plastic everywhere including our hearts and brains. Nor do we have the money to ensure that all of our citizens have a decent social safety net to get by on if a robot, a pandemic or another financial flimflam scam like that behind the Global Financial Crisis/Great Recession decides to take our jobs. As citizens we are expected to accept this limitation of what our money system can do, without being told the truth about who really creates our money and how they do it.

Book One: *Money Creation 101* directly answers the question of who creates our money. It also takes the economics profession to task for being unable or unwilling to tell us who creates our money and how they create it. We hear from a Federal Reserve economist, university professors and others who have difficulty answering the question of who creates our money. We also listen to the pleas of economics students beseeching their university programs to simply teach the truth about who creates our money so that they will be properly equipped to respond to the existential crises facing humanity that they will be asked to solve after they graduate. After reading *Money Creation 101* you will be better informed on the question of who creates our money and how they create it than the two respected economists from top university programs, who were interviewed anonymously at their own request, for the *People, Planet & the Power of Money Project*.

Book Two: *History of Money 101* takes us back to our civilization's birthplace—the Fertile Crescent, then to ancient Greece, Rome, the American colonies, the U.S. Revolution and the U.S. Civil War, examining examples of publicly created money that successfully met the challenges of their time. A basic understanding of this history makes it much easier for us as citizens as we decide whether or not we want to keep our present system of bank-created debt-money or change to a more democratic system of publicly created money. This short book is chock-full of the type of monetary history that economics students across the globe are now begging their own university programs to include in their education.

Book Three: *Spaceship Earth 101* owes its title to American economist Kenneth Boulding's 1966 paper *The Economics of the Coming Spaceship Earth.*[1] Dr. Boulding defined the American economy of the time as a *cowboy economy*, symbolic of the seemingly limitless American plains and associated with exploitative, reckless, violent and romanticized conduct. In sharp contrast, he coined the term *Spaceship Earth*, in which Earth was viewed as a closed single spaceship, devoid of unlimited resources that would allow us to extract and pollute indiscriminately. Within the concept of *Spaceship Earth*, humanity must find its place in a cyclical ecological system that we now casually refer to as a sustainable lifestyle. The *Spaceship Earth 101* model looks at the Earth as a closed system powered by the sun, with finite resources. It expands the discussion to include the political and economic systems that the monetary system operates within, arguing that just as publicly created money rose to meet the challenges of the past, it can provide the necessary money to meet our environmental and social crises of today and tomorrow.

Author's Note: the *People, Planet & the Power of Money Project* was written in 2020 during the COVID pandemic. The first rough draft was given to a group of test readers who provided a much-needed reader's view and critique: Jeffrey Hopkins, Mishel G. Salazar, Derek Scott Calum Sayer, Marie Rose daSilva, Nicholas Summers, Kristen Waller and Laura Wilson. With the phenomenal help of developmental editor Morgan Day, copy editor Johanna P. Leigh, proofreader Christine LePorte, and designer Tammy Falkner it has been rewritten, refined and rewritten again and again over the course of 2021, 2022 and into 2023. Our daughter Erin Werley, a bestselling author in her own right, then took charge of the crucial publishing process. I am deeply in debt to all of these wonderful, talented individuals for their yeoman's efforts in helping me present it to you.

Climate disasters and social issues may be commented on as they have occurred when writing and rewriting. By mentioning this now, it will hopefully avoid confusion if you see a reference to something mentioned in 2021, 2022 or 2023 but being placed earlier in the text than other things that may have occurred in 2020.

Climate change, dead zones in the ocean, nitrogen and phosphorus cycles run amok and plastic pollution everywhere, including our bodies, are global problems, as is the tremendous level of inequality within human society. While individual nations may have their own money systems, we are all part of a global money system. America must lead and that is the immediate focus. However, the change must extend across the planet and those who live outside the U.S. are encouraged to advocate for reform in their respective countries. The information within these pages pertains to you and should be helpful to your understanding of a money system that was not designed to be understood, no matter what country or part of the globe you reside in.

The three separate books are all interrelated and you are encouraged to read all three. As your tour guide, I thank you for entering the world of the *People, Planet & the Power of Money Project.*

Prologue: You're No Dummy

Have you ever wondered where our money comes from? Or how it is created? I didn't when I was in college, but I certainly should have. My penance for not caring about where our money comes from is that in some uncanny way karma has now entrusted me with the task of helping you to understand how our money is created. I know it may sound crazy, but I believe that nothing less than the future of our people and planet hangs in the balance. Perhaps after reading the *People, Planet & the Power of Money Project*, you may agree.

In 1965, I was sitting in a college classroom. The subject was Econ 101, a beginning course on economics. My second chance at higher education was at St. Joseph Community College in East Chicago, Indiana. It went no better than the first opportunity at Indiana University in Bloomington. My crimes in academia were serious. At Indiana, I was put on disciplinary probation for starting a shaving cream fight in our dormitory and soon found myself hitchhiking home. At St. Joe's I cut too many classes so I could play poker and soon enough found myself as a member of the U.S. Air Force on a midnight flight to Vietnam to help protect U.S. capitalism from Vietnamese peasants.

Back to that Econ 101 class. My idle daydreaming was interrupted by our econ instructor saying that we would skip the upcoming chapter in our textbook on the Federal Reserve System since there were only a few people in the country capable of understanding how our money is created. I should have jumped up and taken issue with him, calling it an absolute outrage. How dare he deny us the opportunity to understand how the Federal Reserve System operates to create our money! Instead, I'm quite sure I had a smile on my face as I left the classroom, completely oblivious to where our money comes from and how our money system operates.

I would certainly like to take this opportunity to thank you for investing in and reading *Money Creation 101*. Especially considering the fact that in an earlier attempt at writing it I had latched onto the title *Monetary Reform for Dummies*. But I meant no disrespect, for we are all ignorant until we gain some knowledge. You must be thinking, *First, he wanted to call me a dummy, then he kind of takes it back and says I'm ignorant. And I'm still reading?*

Let's switch the subject for a second. What is the most important thing, the most necessary thing we need to survive in today's world? I remember being taught that we absolutely need food, shelter and clothing. True. We also can't survive without clean air and water. Also true. But is there one thing that makes it possible for us to get the food, shelter, clothing and to a degree clean air and water? *Money*—and I have every confidence that you will agree. We must have money to exist. It is the most important thing in our lives. Some might say God is more important and others may say love is more important. Perhaps, but there isn't a church around that can exist without money being collected by the ushers, and even those of us who fall in love have to buy a marriage license. Then with love in our hearts, marriage licenses in our hands, and often children to follow, we are consigned to a lifetime of bills to pay, all accomplished with money.

I've used words like *dummy* and *ignorant*, but what does that make me? I'm the one who was silent when my college instructor said that the American people were not smart enough to understand how our money is created. And while my teacher was the one who inferred that we are all dummies, I am the one who brought up the word *ignorant*. But being ignorant doesn't mean we are dumb, it simply means we don't have knowledge on a subject, such as how our money system works.

We are told that we are not smart enough to understand how our money is created. It doesn't matter if our politicians say that there isn't enough money to pay for food for the hungry, housing for the homeless, jobs for the jobless and safeguards for the environment. And now that we are in the midst of the COVID-19 global health pandemic/depression, it certainly might be helpful for us to have knowledge about how the money system works in America so that we can make sure that we are able to get money into the hands of those of us who can't afford food, rent, car payments, credit card bills and other necessary things while jobless, or to get money in the hands of small businesses so that they can stay afloat until they can safely reopen. But it doesn't stop there. Even before COVID-19 emerged, the Financial Health Network reported that as of 2019, 70% of Americans said they struggled with at least one aspect of financial stability, such as paying bills or saving money.[1][2]

It is essential for us to know how our money is created and how our money system operates. The fact that as a lousy student I was silent on the subject more than fifty years ago is the reason I am writing this book. It is something I owe to you and everyone else in the country. There I was in 1965, a wise guy, a young man who took a principled stand and refused to pay $5 for each class I had cut to stay in school because I thought that it was an injustice. Yet, I couldn't find the voice to object when I was told that I and everyone else in the entire country, save a handful of exalted intellectuals, were not smart enough to understand how the most necessary thing in our lives was created.

While you may be temporarily ignorant of how our money is presently created, as I was before I began my research, you won't be ignorant for long. You will learn about the ancient lost power of publicly created money that can be created and spent into existence in sufficient quantities to ensure that none of us in our country fall through the cracks without the wherewithal to pay for life's necessities in addition to creating the infrastructure to tackle climate change and the other existential threats to our environment that presently challenge us. This means that you are certainly no dummy!

Chapter 1

Introduction: Modern Money as Easy as 1, 2, 3

Most of us understand the following:

1. Our federal government creates our money.
2. Banks loan us money that has already been created by our federal government.
3. The Federal Reserve Banks are a part of our government.

We've known these facts since we were old enough to earn money cutting grass, caddying or babysitting. If not, then certainly when we got our first full-time job and eventually moved on to independent living and raising families. We earned and spent money that the government created. We borrowed money for a house, car, and a few things that we probably shouldn't have purchased. For most of us, the Federal Reserve is an impossibly complex entity that oversees the entire money system. The *People, Planet & the Power of Money Project* is here to demystify this system. We are all capable of understanding the basics of our present money system and the alternative system we propose here.

What is false are the three facts listed above. We believe that they are true because they should be. But they aren't, since those of us who stayed awake in class during the reading of Shakespeare's *Hamlet* know, "Something is rotten in the state of Denmark," and that rotten something is our U.S. money system. The reality is that:

1. Our federal government only creates a tiny sliver of our money.
2. Banks only loan us money that they create out of thin air, right on the spot as they make us loans. That is where almost all our money comes from.
3. The 12 Federal Reserve Banks are all 100% privately owned by the private banks in their districts.

When my wife and I bought our house and took out a mortgage, I asked myself a question I'd never considered before: *Where did the money come from?* Though I'd never thought about it before, I assumed that the bank had an account for mortgage loans and other loans. *But where did that loan account come from?* I thought it came from previous earnings, or money that people invested in the bank that was then loaned to other people, and they then shared in the profits.

Just grasping the concept that private banks create our money out of thin air is difficult at best to understand. When I first heard it, I began to read and research on the subject. It was not easy to find material about money creation. Even today, not much exists. *Web of Debt* by Ellen Hodgson Brown described the bank-created debt-money system in a very entertaining and informative manner.[1] Ms. Brown documents the classic American fairytale *The Wonderful Wizard of Oz* written by L. Frank Baum in 1900 as a parable about our national search for a functional and just system of money. I absolutely loved her book when I read it more than a decade ago.

Ms. Brown's proposed solution at the time was for our individual states to each create a state bank. But the solution of creating state banks would leave the present bank-created debt-money system functioning and just add state banks to the mix. It was not until I discovered the American Monetary Institute that I began to get information on not only the present bank-created debt-money system but also the proposed solution of a publicly created money system, the NEED Act, which was introduced into Congress in 2011.[2] The NEED Act, which will be covered in detail in Chapter 7, is an alternative to the current system of bank-created debt-money.

The three necessary reforms that will bring about a system of publicly created money are:

1. Our federal government will become the sole creator of our money.
2. Banks will only loan us money that has already been created by our federal government. Bank creation of money as debt will be decisively stopped.
3. The Federal Reserve System will be slimmed down and put into our government.

I also tried to find the answer to "who creates our money?" in articles written by Federal Reserve economists. I was surprised that I couldn't find any articles that addressed the question I had. I went directly to the source and sent an email to 11 Federal Reserve (Fed) macroeconomists. I mentioned the 2014 Bank of England paper *Money creation in the modern economy*, which clearly states that "the majority of money in the modern economy is created by commercial banks making loans,"[3] and ended my email by asking, "Who creates our money?" Ten of the Fed economists ignored my inquiry. I was delighted to hear from the one Fed economist who did answer, and whose identity I'll keep anonymous, even though his response gave me little to work with.

Dear Mr. Egnatz,

I will forward your inquiry to our public affairs office when I get back to [location redacted] next week. They would be best suited to point you to any official position policymakers may have taken on this issue.

As a researcher, I can tell you that the topics upon which your comment touches are important and that several people within the Fed system participate in this academic debate. On the issue of 100% reserve banking [economist's description of publicly created money], an important reference is the following:...

The Federal Reserve economist then referenced a couple of quite technical articles that could help my understanding. Now after over a decade of research into our money system, I'm still baffled that an organization that employs hundreds of economists is unable to answer a simple question about who creates our money. As I was working on this book in 2020, I sent another letter to a similar group of Federal Reserve macroeconomists who did not yield a single reply to the question, "Who creates our money?" One might also wonder why the one PhD Federal Reserve macroeconomist who took the initiative to answer my letter would direct the question to the Federal Reserve public relations department instead of answering the question himself. I am still waiting for the public relations department to provide an answer.

EXPERT WITNESS: BANK OF ENGLAND (BoE)

Throughout the book, I reference expert witnesses, sources of high importance and utmost relevance. Established in 1694, the United Kingdom's Central Bank should be an expert enough witness in the court of *Who creates our money?* It was my next source for understanding how our money system operates in the U.S. today. While we use the United States as our example throughout this book, it is important to understand that basically all countries have the same banking and money system that we have here in the U.S. More or less, what is said here pertains to all countries across the globe. The one major difference is that almost all foreign governments have a nationally owned central bank, while our central bank, the Federal Reserve, is privately owned. The Federal Reserve does take its overall direction from our Congress. But if our Congress members do not themselves have the knowledge about how our money is created, how can they properly offer direction to this huge monolith in charge of creating it?

Arrayed against this international banking system that controls and creates almost all the money in the world is an International Movement for Monetary Reform (IMMR) with member organizations in 27 countries.[4] In the U.S. the Alliance For Just Money[5] is the U.S representative organization in the IMMR. Also in the U.S. is the American Monetary Institute[6] that began the modern movement for monetary reform in 1996. The American Monetary Institute is a think tank that holds an annual conference on monetary reform every fall. These conferences have brought people from all corners of the globe together to then go back to their own respective countries and begin to educate and advocate for monetary reform. It might seem that trying to change a monolith that oversees the creation of money worldwide is a little like David taking on Goliath, but David prevailed and so can we.

For both the UK under the Bank of England and the U.S. under the Federal Reserve and the entire world:

> The majority of money in the modern economy is created by commercial banks making loans...most money takes the form of bank deposits. But how those bank deposits are created is often misunderstood. The principal way is through commercial banks making loans. Whenever a bank makes a loan, it simultaneously creates a matching deposit in the borrower's bank account, thereby creating new money...[7]
>
> — BANK OF ENGLAND, 2014, *MONEY CREATION IN THE MODERN ECONOMY*.

Clear enough—a majority of our money is created by banks making loans. They create this new money by conjuring up out of thin air a matching deposit in the borrower's bank account, completely unknown to the borrower, at the exact time they make the loan. Not only do we not know that these deposits exist in our accounts, but we also have absolutely no access to them.

Martin Wolf is the Chief Economics Commentator for the *Financial Times*, London, and in 2000 was named by the UK government the Commander of the British Empire "for [his] services to financial journalism." Wolf has bluntly said that we should "strip private banks of their power to create money." He continues:

Printing counterfeit banknotes is illegal, but creating private money is not. The interdependence between the state and the businesses that can do this is the source of much of the instability of our economies. It could – and should – be terminated.... Banks create deposits as a byproduct of their lending. In the UK, such deposits make up about 97 per cent of the money supply. Some people object that deposits are not money but only transferable private debts. Yet the public views the banks' imitation money as electronic cash: a safe source of purchasing power.[8]

Why does it seem that the British are ahead of us in admitting how our money is created? If all the central banks are in this together, why is the Bank of England willing to come clean and admit to bank creation of money and the Federal Reserve not willing to admit it? When I sent my inquiry to the Federal Reserve economists, I did point out that the Bank of England had written *Money creation in the modern economy* and asked why I could not find any papers or articles written by Federal Reserve economists commenting on the Bank of England's statements about money creation.

MONEY POWER

When I started this project about our money system, I did so with the intent of presenting things in an understandable manner. The title *Money Creation 101* clearly states my intention to tell the story in a way that we can all understand. Economists have their own language, and the only way I can describe it is as a guaranteed headache. In the language of economists, most of their writing and speaking is directed to others at their own level. The money creation system is complex and indecipherable. This makes it extremely difficult for those of us outside the economics intelligentsia to understand.

Like other professions, economists have the need for their own technical jargon or language. But if the economics professionals are either unable or unwilling to also take an occasional step outside academia, so as to explain money creation in understandable language to those of us not literate in their language, then we have a problem. If money is the most necessary thing for survival in modern society, is there not a need for us to be able to understand who creates it and how they do so? Can our democracy properly function if we have no idea who creates our money or how they do it? If the answer is that it is just too complicated a system for the people to understand, then perhaps those of us who do the voting need to tell those whom we put in office with our votes that this is simply unacceptable. My intention has been to present what our money system should be, in a way that you can easily grasp and follow. Yet explaining the present bank-created debt-money within the umbrella of the Federal Reserve System is much more of a challenge because it was created to be opaque and inscrutable, not to be easily understood. The 1913 creation of the Federal Reserve System will be explained in much greater detail in Book Two: *History of Money*.

What is the greatest power in our society? Some might say it is democracy—our power to vote and ultimately determine the course of society. While a good argument can be made for democracy, let's also consider something called the Money Power or the power to create money. Democracy vests society's decision-making power with the people. Yet what good is the power to make decisions for society if the power to create the most necessary thing to survive in society—money—is in private hands and not the people's? Putting the power to publicly create our money back with the people through our elected government is absolutely necessary to democratic governance. Over the last century the Money Power has used 7 tactics to keep the bank-created debt-money system in power.

Money Power's 7 Tactics to Stay in Power:

1. The first line of defense used to ensure the continuation of a toxic money system is to keep the people confused and in the dark about the present system of bank-created debt-money and the democratic alternative—publicly created money.
2. The second line of defense is to tell us we are too stupid to understand it.
3. The third line of defense is to create textbooks that lie to us about how our money is created.
4. The fourth line of defense is to stop teaching monetary history, even in the most prestigious economics programs.
5. The fifth line of defense is to simply ignore papers critical of the debt-money system or supportive of publicly created money.
6. The sixth line of defense is to control economics journals so that they will not publish papers critical of the debt-money system or supportive of publicly created money.
7. The seventh line of defense is to make it clear to up-and-coming young economists that for them to buck the debt-money system is career suicide.

Little wonder that we, the people, are ignorant of how our money is created. While it might seem that I certainly must be exaggerating in describing the above seven tactics used by the Money Power to keep us ignorant about money creation, ample support for all seven tactics or charges will be provided throughout the *People, Planet & the Power of Money Project*.

Money is an ancient lost power that belongs to a people through its legal system. Money is necessary for society to exist and thrive. That makes it a power like no other. As such, the creation of money (Money Power) is the absolute power and it must reside with the people through their government and legal system and not with a group of private banks, its true nature hidden from the people by misinformation, double-talk and outright deception. Reclaiming this ancient lost power of money for the people will allow us to be able to create the money needed, debt-free, to take care of the financial needs of our unemployed workers and devastated small businesses from the COVID-19 depression and at the same time to put our unemployed to work combating climate change and tackling the other environmental crises that confront us. People and planet need relief and only a system of publicly created money can deliver it.

While I personally advocate for strong government action to reduce and draw down the level of harmful greenhouse gasses in our atmosphere causing climate change and other environmental crises confronting humanity which will be discussed in *Spaceship Earth 101*, I understand that everyone in our country does not share my level of concern for these issues. The same can be said for personally supporting a living wage for all workers and other government social programs to ensure that no one in our country falls behind. I also believe in democracy and that if we are to fund these programs, it must be done through the democratic process with a majority of our country's people supporting the reforms.

Who creates our money, private banks or the people through our government, is an entirely separate issue. We should never allow money creation to be used to divide us. It is simply too important whether you consider yourself a conservative or a progressive. Publicly created money will give conservatives a sound fiscal system that will repay the federal debt as it comes due. Repayment of the federal debt and a sound fiscal system are completely impossible under the present debt-money system. Instead, the debt-money system relies on periodically bailing out the same private banking entities that have been given the power to create our money. Publicly created money can provide for debt-free funding for programs like an all-inclusive national health care program, while also funding climate action and remediation for climate-induced destruction from hurricanes, tornadoes, floods, droughts, and wildfires. Whether or not we as a society choose to fund these issues is a matter for us to determine through our democratic process. Whichever side of the political aisle you reside in though, publicly created money is for you.

Stanford University professors Robert N. Proctor and Londa Schiebinger edited a book in 2008 titled *Agnotology—The Making & Unmaking of Ignorance*. They coined the term for the study of ignorance "agnotology." *Agnotology* examines societal ignorance across a wide spectrum of subjects, including "global climate change, military secrecy, female orgasm, environmental denialism, Native American paleontology, theoretical archaeology, racial ignorance and more."[9] What is missing from that laundry list of subjects is our societal ignorance of how money is created. We might go so far as to say that our ignorance of who creates our money is so great that even those academics who have taken up the mantle of studying ignorance are ignorant that we as a society are ignorant about how our money is created.

Ignorance of money is not an option though. The very values our country was founded on—liberty, equality and democracy are impossible if we continue to allow ourselves to be kept ignorant of money. Telling us that we are not capable of understanding how our money is created is simply unacceptable. Tell us the truth and let us decide if we want to continue the present money system or switch to a more functional system that can pay for the infrastructure necessary to battle the crises that confront us. Our present bank-created debt-money system has shown itself to be completely unable to deal with the massive unemployment of the COVID-19 depression without increasing federal debt. It has thus far proven itself to be incapable of funding real climate action. Other huge issues such as Artificial Intelligence (AI) replacing us in the workplace hover over us. Expecting the bank-created debt-money system to be able to properly fund them is a dereliction of our duty as citizens.

In the midst of a global pandemic, if we had a system of publicly created money we could tell our Congress to create whatever money is necessary to then distribute to our people for food, rent, mortgage payments, bills, etc. We could determine that small businesses must receive funds to pay their expenses so that they can survive while being forced to close for reasons of public safety. Much of my working career has been in the hospitality industry. I sold hot dogs at a golf course stand as a child. Later, I worked in the kitchen and behind the bar and waited tables. I've worked as a business owner, paying bills to try and keep a restaurant and golf course open for people to exercise, relax and enjoy themselves. Even with that background, I absolutely cannot imagine the challenges small business owners are facing during this COVID-19 pandemic and depression.

Before COVID-19 hit us like a ton of bricks in 2020, we as a people were finally starting to take seriously the results of our addiction to carbon fossil fuel. We were beginning to realize the havoc that climate change has already wreaked on Earth and its ecosystems and starting to imagine what our future life might be like on the planet. Climate action to change to clean renewable energy will require lots of money. Only publicly created money can provide the funds necessary to properly address both the environmental crises and the people crises. Why? Because only publicly created money can put millions of people to work changing to a climate-friendly energy system without increasing our debt. And while some workers in the present energy sector will lose their jobs in the change to clean renewable energy, they should be among the first employed by the new jobs created. If they are not immediately reemployed, publicly created money can be used to provide money for them, along with all our other workers who continue to be unemployed due to COVID-19, until they are all properly reemployed. While we can do all this with publicly created money, we don't have to do these things. Making that decision will be up to all of us as a society through our democratic process.

Money is an invention of society. Money does not exist naturally as a rare metal in the Earth; instead, it is a creation of a country's legal system. Book Two: *History of Money 101* will demonstrate that money creation was specifically assigned to the people's representative, Congress, in the Constitution and cannot be given away to private banks. Stripped down, money is a social invention that enables society to function. As such, the responsibility to create it rests with our legal government, doing so to benefit society as we, the people, deem necessary, while the private bank-created debt-money system has a responsibility, not to benefit society, but to generate the greatest return to the banks' ownership.

Over the last two decades, I have had the honor of demonstrating with fellow citizens in the cause of peace and social justice. When people call out for "power to the people," they may not realize it, but they are making the strongest of statements for publicly created money. Money creation is the ultimate power, and that power belongs to the people.

The *People, Planet & the Power of Money Project* demonstrates that the Money Power (power to create money) belongs to the people in a democracy. The U.S. Constitution assigns it to the people through our elected Congress. In a democracy, it is imperative that the people understand and approve of the money system we have. Reclaiming the ancient lost power of publicly created money will return the Money Power to the people, giving us what we need to properly care for our people and planet. Publicly created money is money created by our federal government for the needs of the people and planet as determined by our representative, Congress. Under this system of publicly created money, banks will be decisively stopped from creating our money as debt, and the Federal Reserve System will be slimmed down and put into the Treasury Department of our federal government.

To tell our story, which includes a money system that has been kept at least somewhat secret from us, the history of money which has also been kept at least somewhat secret from us, and solutions to our present and future problems of which our present money system is structurally incapable of funding, the *People, Planet & the Power of Money Project* presents the information in three books:

Book One: *Money Creation 101* explains what economists and textbooks have been reluctant to do—tell us how our money is created out of thin air by banks when they make loans. The banks can only do this because all the other banks are also doing this and because the Federal Reserve Banks, after bank money creation has already taken place, move reserve funds around to keep the books balanced. We take you behind the curtain of secrecy at the Federal Reserve System to reveal that which it has been more than reluctant to explain—how our money is created. Economics professors and students are given their chance to speak up and the tremendous cost of the debt-money system is revealed. Publicly Created Money in Action: the NEED Act is examined in stark contrast to the financial shenanigans and the absolute domination of the debt-money system. Publicly created money is defended and a plea is made to the economics profession to join the struggle for publicly created money.

Book Two: *History of Money 101* looks at the first money systems in the birthplace of civilization, the Fertile Crescent. It traces the history of money and its ties to human slavery in the past and debt slavery today. It also looks at an alternative system originating in ancient Greece and Rome that rejected the gold and silver system and began to create money as a function of the law and society. We will look at the American colonies that were denied a functioning system of money by England and out of necessity stumbled across the ancient lost power of publicly created money. They used it to build colonial infrastructure and when told to stop, they used the ancient lost power to fight and win the American Revolution. Fourscore and seven years later the young country again turned to the ancient lost power to fight another war, this time to save our country by ending the scourge of human slavery. The American people were quite happy with the publicly created money used to save the union. The private banking interests were then successful in deceiving the American people into believing that under the proposed Federal Reserve System the Money Power would be with the people. Unfortunately for us all, the creation of the Federal Reserve System instead represents the triumph of the bank-created debt-money system.

Book Three: *Spaceship Earth 101* looks at our political, economic and monetary systems through the lens of the values our country was founded on—liberty, equality and democracy. The capitalist/socialist divide is revealed for what it is, a method to control us by putting us into two separate camps with no hope of ever considering the merits of the opposing camp. We examine the breakup of the Soviet Union and how publicly created money would have produced a more peaceful outcome, especially in relation to Russia's invasion of Ukraine. *Spaceship Earth 101* agrees with the consensus evaluation by the scientific community of human-caused climate change and other environmental crises confronting our people and planet. As such, we demonstrate how publicly created money and only publicly created money can fund the myriad of programs and solutions required to heal both the crises confronting our planet and the financial crises facing our people from pandemic depressions and job loss due to artificial intelligence. We also recognize that support for these programs must come from the will of the majority in a democracy.

CHAPTER 2

THE FEDERAL RESERVE SYSTEM

Changing our money system to one that's better for people and planet can only be brought about through education. That education begins with an understanding of how our current money system came to be. People and planet are completely dependent on our money system working for us rather than against us. The people need a monetary system that delivers a full employment economy at a living wage. Anything less is unacceptable. Meanwhile, our fragile planet, our very mother, is dependent upon humanity awakening to and ending the destruction on multiple fronts that threaten the very future of life as we know it.

The banking profession and economics professions have successfully muddied the waters about money for centuries. The creation of the Federal Reserve System (Fed) in 1913 has continued this dissemination of disinformation. But understanding our present monetary system and what a reformed system would be like is not a difficult concept.

The Money Power, or power to create our money, belongs to the people, the new sovereigns in America that in 1776 replaced King George in England. The American people specifically placed the Money Power in our Constitution with our elected Congress. In

1913 our elected Congress voted to give this Money Power to the private banks that would be overseen by a newly created entity that was not a part of our government but certainly sounds like it is—the Federal Reserve System. In Book 2: *History of Money 101* we will make the argument that Congress does not have the power under the Constitution to give the Money Power away by legislation. It can only be done by amending the Constitution. These 12 Federal Reserve Banks are owned not by our federal government, but by the very same private banks that the Federal Reserve is in charge of overseeing.

The Bank of England was the model for the Federal Reserve when the Fed was created in 1913. The Bank of England was created in 1694 as a private bank that was given the right to create the nation's money and then loan it back to King William III so that he could finance his Nine Years' War against France. William almost certainly did not realize that the Bank of England was creating the money out of thin air, or he would have simply done it himself as the king. At the time, gold and silver were the only money and when the Bank of England issued banknotes, they were representing that they had the gold or silver in their vault to back up all the notes issued. The dirty little secret is that they didn't. Today, this practice is called fractional reserve lending. They generally issued banknotes for about ten times whatever precious metal (gold and silver) they had in their vault.[1] Describing the Bank of England's activities, 18th-century merchant and financier Sir Francis Baring said, "Very few foreigners have understood the Bank.... They have always considered their notes as Government paper."[2] This means that the money (banknotes) issued by the Bank of England was mistakenly thought of as being issued by England (now the United Kingdom), when in fact they were issued by the private Bank of England.

Just as the Bank of England was a private bank of issue (central bank authorized to issue banknotes) that masqueraded as a government bank, the Federal Reserve by its very name also falsely implies that it is a government institution. Previous central banks were also private banks of issue whose very names gave the illusion that they were government institutions: First Bank of the United States (1791–1811) and Second Bank of the United States (1817–1837). They were preceded by the Bank of North America (1781–1789), which was named before our country was named.

Adam Smith, whose 1776 book *The Wealth of Nations* is considered as a Bible by the modern economics profession, completely misunderstood the Bank of England's role in privately creating the banknotes that it then loaned to the Crown at interest: "The stability of the Bank of England is equal to that of the British Government.... It acts...as a great engine of state."[3] The Bank of England was merely a private bank that had been given the power to create the nation's money. Mr. Smith should have said that the Bank of England acts as *if* it is a great engine of state [creating the nation's money], while in fact it is not a great engine of state, but merely a private bank that had been given the power to create the nation's money. Former Director of the American Monetary Institute Stephen Zarlenga provided a different view than Adam Smith's view of the Bank of England: "The bank's main protection was that its complexity kept people from understanding the true source of its power—the money creation process."[4] Exactly the same thing can be said today about the Federal Reserve System.

The Bank of England was a privately owned bank as were the Federal Reserve Banks that were created in its likeness. But the first half of the 20th century was tough for the British; two world wars sandwiched around the Great Depression, all intensified by the bank-created debt-money system. Historically it has been very profitable for banks to create and loan money at interest to their governments for militarism and war. One need look no further than our own bloated military budget, euphemistically called a defense budget, for an example of out of control military spending, enriching the banks that ultimately make the loans.

After the conclusion of World War II, the British Labour Government, supported by the 1942 statement of the Archbishop of Canterbury William Temple that "banking had become the master when it should be the servant of society," led to the nationalization of the Bank of England in 1946.[5] It could have become a great engine of state, as Adam Smith had mistakenly claimed it was, if only the Brits had been astute enough to understand at the time to keep the money creation power with the Bank of England after nationalization. And the big difference between becoming an engine of state and a great engine of state was unfortunately not achieved. Prior to nationalization, the BoE created much of the nation's money as debt. After nationalization, this practice ceased, and other private English banks then took up the slack and began to create the vast majority of the nation's money as debt. The BoE now creates only the nation's coin and paper money, representing just 3% of the nation's money, with the other 97% created by the nation's private banks.[6] Even this is slightly better than the American system, in which only coins are created by our government. Our paper currency is physically made by the Department of Engraving and then shipped to the Federal Reserve Banks, who in turn pay us only for the cost of making or engraving the currency. Currently, in 2021, we are paid only 14 cents for each $100 bill.[7]

The British were successful in relating the World Wars and Great Depression to the banking system when they nationalized the Bank of England in 1946. We weren't. If we had been able to make the connection, perhaps we too would have nationalized our central bank as they did. The nationalizing and shrinking down of the Federal Reserve is one of three necessary monetary reforms we propose.

The Federal Reserve has been quite successful for the last century in keeping us in the dark about what it does and where our money comes from, but occasionally even the Fed allows the truth to see the light of day. Before the Federal Reserve was created Americans were well aware that the banks in our country needed federal control. But when the Federal Reserve Act was passed and became law in 1913, the American public was led to believe that the Federal Reserve was a government entity and would be creating our nation's money. They failed to understand that the newly created Federal Reserve was a private entity and that under its supervision the banks' private creation of debt-money would continue. The American people were given the short end of the stick, instead of the reform of the banking system and actual publicly created money that were desperately needed and that the people thought they were getting in 1913. Chapter 10 in Book Two, *The Federal Reserve – The Triumph of the Debt-Money System*, reveals the secretive conditions under which the Federal Reserve System was created, as told from the Fed's own history website.

The Federal Reserve does claim to be independent: "The Federal Reserve, like many other central banks, is an independent government agency but also one that is ultimately accountable to the public and the Congress."[8] Congress within the Federal Reserve Act does have the power to direct the Federal Reserve's actions. But there is little evidence that Congress members understand the bank-created debt-money system any better than the American people. As a result, Congress has been cowed into silence and inaction. Whether or not we have been kept intentionally in the dark about its secrets is a point of contention.

Private banks create our money out of thin air. While that is true, there is a little more to it than that. The banks create our money out of thin air when they make loans. But they can only do so because they are a bank in cahoots with all the other banks, and because they have a Federal Reserve System put in place in 1913 by an act of Congress that is able to move around reserve money and balance the books on the reserve end of the operation after the banks have already created the money. When we later discuss the U.S. Constitution we will argue that bank creation of our money within the Federal Reserve System is unconstitutional and that the Money Power (power to create our money) belongs to the people through our elected Congress.

The concept of the Federal Reserve system was confusing and inscrutable, not just to the American people but also to virtually everyone involved with the new system, with the exceptions of Paul Warburg, partner at Kuhn Loeb & Co. Investment Bank and ally of the European Rothschild banking family, and Benjamin Strong, 1st President of the New York Federal Reserve Bank.[9] Former Director of the American Monetary Institute Stephen Zarlenga quotes New York Federal Reserve Bank President Benjamin Strong admitting in a private letter that amongst the entirety of officers for the 12 Federal Reserve Banks, only he and Paul Warburg had the slightest clue of how they would operate:

> "In 1914 when these 12 [Federal Reserve] banks were organized, a large staff of officers were gathered from all parts of the country and to them was delivered...just exactly what is contained in the Federal Reserve Act – and no more. With the exception of Paul Warburg and the writer, there was not one man in the entire organization who ever had the slightest experience in foreign banking, nor the opportunity to study the methods and policies of the banks of issue of Europe,"[10] such as the Bank of England.

The entire Federal Reserve money system was created to be absolutely baffling. We know from the Bank of England that the "majority of money in the modern economy is created by commercial banks making loans."[11] This majority of money in the money supply amounted to 97% of the amount in circulation when *Money creation in the modern economy* was written in 2014.[12] We also know that banks can only create our money supply if they all do so working together, as Nobel laureate in economics Paul Samuelson described in his best-selling textbook *Economics*:[13] "The banking system as a whole can do what each small bank cannot do!"[14] The Federal Reserve then moves around reserve money as necessary to ensure that all the private banks in the system have the necessary amount of reserves. We will take a closer look at Dr. Samuelson's work in the next chapter.

There are two separate money loops in this mass of debt-money creation confusion. The two loops don't mix either. In 1913, I doubt whether anyone outside of Paul Warburg and Benjamin Strong understood this. For a more advanced understanding, let us go over a brief overview of split-circuit reserve banking:

Expert Witness: Joseph Huber, Martin Luther University, Halle, Germany

Split-circuit reserve banking – functioning, dysfunctions and future perspectives

Real-World Economics Review, Issue #80, 2017.

Throughout *The People, Planet & the Power of Money Project*, I use brackets to, in my own words, clarify the meaning of words or terms used by various experts. I use either quotation marks or indented block quotes to quote our experts and will use brackets within the quotations to in my own language help the reader with understanding. When I quote Dr. Huber below, the parentheses are his and the brackets are mine. Below I have tried to put Professor Huber's technical explanation into an understandable text for non-academics. What he calls *bankmoney* is simply the money [dollars/Federal Reserve Notes/computer accounting entries] we use in our everyday lives that I refer to throughout the book as bank-created debt-money.

Split-circuit reserve banking means the Federal Reserve System has two different and distinct classes of money:

1. Public circulation of *bankmoney* [bank-created debt-money]. This is the money in the economy that we use every day. It is the only money that we have any contact with at all.
2. Interbank circulation of reserves among banks—these payment reserves are liquid excess reserves for making interbank payments to reconcile cashing checks from other banks, etc. These liquid payment reserves are in contrast to the basically illiquid minimum reserves requirements.

Huber explains: "Reserves and bankmoney represent two distinct classes of money that cannot be exchanged for one another. Customers never obtain reserves in their current accounts, and bankmoney [bank-created debt-money] cannot be transferred into a bank's central bank account. Customer deposits (bankmoney) thus cannot be used by banks to make interbank payments, and cannot be lent by banks to whomsoever; only customers themselves can spend, or invest, or lend their deposits (bankmoney) to other nonbanks."[15]

Basically what Dr. Huber is saying is that there are two separate classes of money. The first class, *bankmoney*, is what we have called bank-created debt-money. The other class is the reserve money that stays within the Federal Reserve Banks. These two classes of money are separate, distinct, and generally never mixed. Within the Federal Reserve Banks, there are also two classes of money that stay within the Federal Reserve System. Federal Reserve Banks keep illiquid minimum reserve amounts in each bank. The Fed Banks also have more liquid payment reserves that are moved from bank-to-bank accounts at the Fed to account for the transfer of funds from one bank to another via checks cashed at one bank and drawn at another. It's okay if you are unable to make heads or tails out of all this right now. Remember that this system was not designed for us to understand it, but rather to keep us confused so that we do not rise up and demand a system of publicly created money.

SOVEREIGN MONEY & SEIGNIORAGE

Now let's see what Dr. Huber has to say about what we refer to here as publicly created money, what he refers to as sovereign money:

Sovereign money gives a nation-state, or community of nation-states, monetary sovereignty. This includes three monetary prerogatives:

1. Determining the *currency* of the realm, the monetary unit of account.
2. Creating and issuing *money*, the means of payment denominated in that currency.
3. Benefiting from the *seigniorage*, the gain that accrues from the creation of money.[16]

On the one hand we have the mysterious and almost incomprehensible bank-created debt-money system in which our money is created by private banks when they make loans to us putting us in debt. While the fortunate few may get out of debt, many more must remain in debt for us to have money so that society can function. It is basically a system of debt slavery to the private Money Power. On the other hand we have what Huber calls sovereign money—a system of that most necessary thing for survival in modern civilization. The nation state accepts the responsibility for determining what this currency of the realm is. It creates and issues this currency that is necessary for our survival. The gain that comes from the creation of this thing that we all need is called *seigniorage.* In a representative democracy such as our country, this gain or *seigniorage* belongs to the people through their representative government. It is our choice which system we want and if we do not presently have the system we think we should have, it is up to us to fight to get it.

Comparing the Bank of England and the Federal Reserve

Former director of the American Monetary Institute Stephen Zarlenga's book *The Lost Science of Money* gives a tour de force history of money and monetary systems. His chapters on the creation of the Bank of England and the Federal Reserve System are must-reads for an understanding of the two central banks. Zarlenga offers the following parallels between the Bank of England (BoE) and the Federal Reserve:[17]

1. Secret efforts surrounded the formation and passage of both institutions. The Bank of England was quietly passed as a rider on a nondescript bill on shipping tonnage. Book Two: *History of Money 101* uses the Federal Reserve's own history to provide a detailed description of the secrecy around the creation of the Federal Reserve.
2. The Federal Reserve legislation was originally written as a Republican bill championed by international bankers. After it failed to pass as a Republican bill, it eventually became an alleged progressive reform Democratic bill under President Woodrow Wilson. Republicans in Congress who had originally supported almost exactly the same thing a few years earlier then publicly opposed it. This Republican opposition then gave the

Democratic Congressional majority the political cover to support and pass The Federal Reserve Act that the vast majority of its supporters mistakenly believed was putting the power to create our money with our federal government.

3. Both laws rested heavily on sophisticated, wealthy foreign supporters and organizers. The structuring of the Federal Reserve came from the Kuhn Loeb bankers connected with the European Rothschilds, supported by J.P. Morgan and America's financial establishment.

4. Both institutions were complex to the point of being indecipherable. I have related my own personal observation while in college and taking Econ 101. When we came to the chapter on the Federal Reserve, our instructor announced that we would skip the chapter because, according to him, only a few people in the entire country understood how it worked. And now, years later when retelling this story, I have had numerous individuals say that similar things happened to them. Those desiring further evidence that the Federal Reserve is indecipherable should ask a banker, politician, university professor or Federal Reserve official to explain who creates our money and how it is created.

5. Both the BoE and the Federal Reserve were privately owned but masqueraded as government institutions. The Bank of England and Federal Reserve System: the very names imply that they are part and parcel of their respective governments, and most citizens mistakenly believe they are.

6. The Bank of England, after 252 years of private ownership, was nationalized in 1946. But because the UK did not stop other private banks from creating money, money creation simply morphed over to those other private banks. These other banks now create about 97% of the UK's money (bank-created debt-money).

The UK central bank, the Bank of England (BoE) only creates coins and paper notes, representing approximately 3% of their money supply.

7. Important early supporters condemned both institutions. William Paterson, one of the founders of the BoE, later opposed it and published a book calling for the repayment of the national debt.[18]

8. William Jennings Bryan was one of the most influential politicians of his time. He was the Democratic Party nominee for president three times, 1896, 1900 and 1908. Later he was Secretary of State under President Woodrow Wilson in 1913 and an important early proponent of the Federal Reserve legislation who was key to bringing Democrats on board in support of it. He mistakenly thought that within the proposed Federal Reserve System legislation, the government would be creating the money. Bryan wrote: "The provision in regard to the Government issue of notes to be issued by the banks is the first triumph of the people in connection with currency legislation."[19] Bryan and the populists both wanted our money to be created and issued by our federal government—publicly created money. With such statements as above, Bryan assuaged populist fears that money would not be created by the government. However, Bryan, the populists and the rest of the country were duped into supporting the Federal Reserve Act that instead of giving us a system of publicly created money, gave us a system of government guaranteeing bank-created debt-money under the umbrella of the Federal Reserve System. Bryan was able to deliver progressive and populist support for the legislation, exactly because they all mistakenly thought that the federal government issuing notes (money) meant that the federal government would be creating the notes (money) and benefitting from the *seigniorage*

accrued from creating it. Instead, the federal government physically made the notes and then gave them to the banking system, which then created them as debt when the banks loaned them to the people, charging us all interest for their privilege.

9. Both the Bank of England and the Federal Reserve gave the impression that their notes were backed by gold. Originally, the Federal Reserve's notes, not its created deposits or debt-money, were backed by gold, but that soon changed.

10. After the creation of the BoE and the Federal Reserve, both countries were almost immediately launched into war, Britain with the Dutch and French, and the U.S. into World War I.

In the depths of the Great Depression and out of absolute necessity, the convertibility of Federal Reserve Notes (bank-created debt-money) to gold was stopped by the Gold Reserve Act of 1934. It was the culmination of President Franklin Delano Roosevelt's controversial gold program. "Among other things, the Act transferred ownership of all monetary gold in the United States to the US Treasury and prohibited the Treasury and financial institutions from redeeming dollars for gold."[20] Both Roosevelt and Congress ignored the *Chicago Plan* [explained in Chapter 7] advocated by top level university economists to switch to publicly created money and instead in 1934 made the convertibility of the Fed Notes to gold illegal for U.S. citizens. In 1971 President Richard Nixon again surrendered to the reality that there was not enough gold in the vault to back the Federal Reserve Notes and stopped the international convertibility of our money to gold in 1971.[21] From that time forward, the U.S. dollar has officially been a fiat currency. The major problem with our money is not its fiat status, but the fact that it is privately created and not publicly created by our government.

The Federal Reserve refers to itself as an independent government agency: "The Federal Reserve, like many other central banks, is an independent government agency but also one that is ultimately accountable to the public and the Congress."[22] One might ask, independent of whom? All 12 Federal Reserve Banks are owned by the private banks in their respective districts. The Federal Reserve chairman and board of governors are appointed by the president and confirmed by the Senate. The board of governors, the president of the New York Federal Reserve Bank, and four of the remaining eleven presidents of Federal Reserve Banks form the twelve-member Federal Reserve Open Market Committee[23] that determines policy. All these stalwart individuals are either members of the Wall Street inner circle or university economics intelligentsia who have been thoroughly vetted in supporting the status quo of the present bank-created debt-money system. Indeed, the Federal Reserve is independent—of the American people.

While I take issue with the 1976 Nobel Prize in Economics recipient Milton Friedman on many fronts, he too, was not enamored with the Federal Reserve System: "The Federal Reserve System therefore began operations with no effective legislative criterion for determining the total stock of money.... The discretionary judgment of a group of men was inevitably substituted for the quasi-automatic discipline of the gold standard. Those men were not even guided by a legislative mandate of intent (except the title of the act)."[24]

The U.S. Court of Appeals for the Ninth Circuit in 1982, *Lewis vs. U.S.*, ruled that Federal Reserve Banks for the purposes of the Federal Tort Claims Act "are not federal instrumentalities," but "are independent, privately owned and locally controlled corporations."[25] While, "after paying its expenses, the Federal Reserve turns the rest of its earnings over to the U.S. Treasury,"[26] the private banks that own the Federal Reserve Banks keep all the net proceeds they enjoy from the money creation process.

The constitutionality of the Federal Reserve Act has never been challenged or affirmed by the nation's Supreme Court. We will examine this in the discussion of the U.S. Constitution in Book Two: *History of Money 101*. But it is a bridge too far for this observer to imagine in any way that our founding fathers and those who voted to ratify and thus make the Constitution the law of the land, in any way intended that the power to create money, our nation's very lifeblood, would reside almost entirely within the nation's private banks. Especially since these private banks charge us interest for their privilege to create this money by loaning it to us and that this process would be expedited by an ambiguous entity with the title of Federal Reserve, which is owned by these same banks. The rumbling sound that we are hearing is our founding fathers rolling over in their graves!

AND THE PROPER DESCRIPTION FOR BAMBOOZLING & BEFUDDLING US ABOUT OUR MONEY IS...

At one point, the Federal Reserve released a pamphlet intended to educate citizens on the Federal Reserve system. *Modern Money Mechanics* is a booklet published by the Federal Reserve Bank of Chicago from 1961 till 1994. The text below is from the last revision in 1992. It explains how the process called fractional reserve lending originated with goldsmiths or early bankers writing receipts or notes for more gold than they held in their vaults. The rationale behind banks creating our money supply out of thin air is a direct result of this practice, also known as "fractional reserve lending" or the "money multiplier," as described by the Federal Reserve below:

Who Creates Money?

...In the absence of legal reserve requirements, banks can build up deposits [bank-created debt-money] by increasing loans and investments so long as they keep enough currency on hand to redeem whatever amounts the holders of deposits want to convert into currency. This unique attribute of the banking business was discovered many centuries ago. It started with goldsmiths. As early bankers, they initially provided safekeeping services, making a profit from vault storage fees for gold and coins deposited with them. People would redeem their "deposit receipts" whenever they needed gold or coins to purchase something, and physically take the gold or coins to the seller who, in turn, would deposit them for safekeeping, often with the same banker. Everyone soon found that it was a lot easier simply to use the deposit receipts directly as a means of payment. These receipts, which became known as notes, were acceptable as money since whoever held them could go to the banker and exchange them for metallic money. Then, bankers discovered that they could make loans merely by giving their promises to pay, or banknotes to borrowers. **In this way, banks began to create money**. More notes could be issued than the gold and coin on hand because only a portion of the notes outstanding would be presented for payment at any one time. Enough metallic money had to be kept on hand, of course, to redeem whatever volume of notes was presented for payment. Transaction deposits are the modem counterpart of banknotes. **It was a small step from printing notes to making book entries crediting deposits of borrowers, which the borrowers, in turn, could "spend" by writing checks, thereby "printing" their own money.** [27] [Emphasis mine.]

— *MODERN MONEY MECHANICS*, FEDERAL RESERVE BANK OF CHICAGO

In other words, the entire system is based on a fraud beginning with early bankers/goldsmiths issuing receipts, notes and paper money, allegedly backed by gold in their vaults, in amounts vastly greater than the actual gold in their vaults. Their only justification for this was that because everyone would not want to redeem their notes at once, they could get away with doing so. The people in the goldsmiths' time were not informed that "there is not enough gold to back up the note" when they left their gold for alleged safekeeping. Presently the same deception exists; when you or I walk into a bank and fill out a loan application or just carry a balance on our credit card, we are not told that "we are creating this money that you are borrowing from us out of thin air and then charging you interest for allowing us to do so."

The fraudulent system described is called fractional reserve lending or the money multiplier: banks loaning out more receipts/notes (money) representing gold than they have gold sitting in their vault to give to people when they present such a note or receipt for redemption. Traditionally, the amount of gold kept in reserve was only about 10% of the notes issued. A fraudulent, unsound system if there ever was one; but also a system that is based on money being a commodity—in this case, gold.

Most of us know the story of King Midas that was told by the Roman poet Ovid. King Midas had everything anyone could desire. The god Dionysus granted him a wish to reward Midas for a good deed. Midas had plenty of gold and thought that more might be a good idea. He asked that everything he touched would turn into gold. When his wish was granted, he soon discovered that his food and water turned to gold and the simplest of everyday tasks became impossible. Even his beloved daughter Marigold turned into gold when he touched her. Eventually, Dionysus took pity on Midas and reversed the golden touch that had become a curse. Most of us are accustomed to thinking of the King Midas story as a warning against greed. Just perhaps though, it is also a monetary warning against idolizing gold and making gold or any other precious commodity our money.

The first time a sane person hears about the debt-money system, the natural reaction is incredulity, the inability or unwillingness to believe that it is true. But understanding the debt-money system is not rocket science. The justification for the present debt-money system is based upon money being a commodity such as gold. The bankers then say that they will loan you paper money based on the fact that they have gold in their vaults in amounts that, in fact, they do not actually possess. While banks no longer claim to have gold to back up their notes, the United States government backs them up now and the banks continue to create our money using the same logic.

If we define money as gold or debt that is created by bankers, we will be consigned to unending debt slavery. If instead of defining money as gold, we define money as an abstract legal power of the state that acts as a store of value and a final means of payment, thus providing for the common good by enabling society and commerce to function smoothly, we can have a free and prosperous people in a free and prosperous nation.

Of course, there are apologists for the debt-money system who use terms like "stocks" and "flows," and who will be quick to point out that there does not have to be enough money in the system to repay all the debts because this has never been done. We as a society have never tried to repay all debts. Of course, it has never been done or even tried because any significant repayment of the overall level of indebtedness within the present bank-created debt-money system would result in a crash of the system. The system is designed to keep us in debt, not to allow us to repay our debt. The system is designed for debt slavery, not freedom from debt.

For 33 years, from 1961–1994, the Chicago Federal Reserve printed *Modern Money Mechanics* and the Federal Reserve rather proudly claimed to create money via fractional reserve lending. Back to that Econ 101 classroom in 1965, our economics instructor could have easily used this account to explain how the banking system under the umbrella of the Federal Reserve fraudulently creates our money. Our economics instructor was either unaware of *Modern Money Mechanics* or did not understand it. In any case, the Federal Reserve abandoned this pamphlet and explanation after 33 years in 1994 and has basically been silent on money creation for the 26 years that have followed.

FRAUD

Merriam-Webster defines fraud as: DECEIT, TRICKERY, intentional perversion of truth in order to induce another to part with something of value or to surrender a legal right; an act of deceiving or misrepresenting: TRICK; a person who is not what he or she pretends to be: IMPOSTOR.[28]

The banks create our money out of thin air when they make loans. But they can only do it because they are a bank in cahoots with all the other banks, and because they have a Federal Reserve System put in place in 1913 by an unconstitutional act of Congress that is able to move around reserve money and balance the books on the reserve end of the operation after the fact of bank money creation has already taken place.

This is a fraudulent system. If it wasn't fraudulent, we would know about it. Even the economics textbooks that you and I and our economists have been trained with don't tell the truth or properly represent the system. We can't sugarcoat it—if the creation of our nation's very lifeblood, our money, has been misrepresented, largely by the Federal Reserve System that dominates and controls the economics profession, that is fraud.

Within the present Federal Reserve Banking System, virtually all of what we use for money is created and comes into existence as debt when banks make loans (Bank of England, *Money Creation in the Modern Economy*).[29] When the loans are repaid, the money is extinguished on the bank's computer accounting ledger and therefore no longer exists, meaning that almost our entire money supply (97% or more) exists only as debt.[30] The problem is compounded because only money for the principal amount of the loans is created, however temporarily, and nothing is created for the significant interest that we must pay over the life of the loans. Because repaying the loans erases the money, it is necessary that huge unmanageable levels of debt be carried by individuals and the government, or else there will not be enough money in the system for society to function.

Our federal government makes our currency but does not create our money. The Bureau of Engraving physically makes our currency (paper money) and sends it to the Federal Reserve. The U.S. Mint physically makes our coins and sends them to the Federal Reserve. The private Federal Reserve then repays us, our public federal government, for the cost of engraving the paper money, 6.2 cents for a $1 bill and 14 cents for a $100 bill in 2021.[31] This money then becomes a part of our bank-created debt-money within the banking system.

The private Federal Reserve repays us, our federal government, for the full face value of all coins produced and shipped to the Fed. These coins then also become a part of the bank-created money within the banking system. The difference between the coins and paper money is that we, the people, through our government benefit from the difference between the cost of production and face value in our coins [Dr. Huber referred to this as *seigniorage*], thus making the coins in our pockets the only real publicly created money in our dysfunctional money system. After subtracting expenses and dividend payments made to its private bank owners, the Federal Reserve system does return all profits it makes to the federal government. Within the system though, the private banks are allowed to keep all profits made from their private creation of our money.

IS THE BANK-CREATED DEBT-MONEY SYSTEM CAPABLE OF CONTROLLING INFLATION?

Within conventional economics wisdom, interest rates have an adverse effect on the supply of money—with higher rates discouraging us from borrowing, thus shrinking the supply of money and reducing economic growth; and lower rates encouraging us to go deeper into debt, thus increasing the supply of money and increasing economic growth. This is the very reason in the summer of 2022 that the Federal Reserve is raising interest rates— to attempt to reduce inflation by reducing the supply of money. According to the Federal Reserve Bank of Cleveland, "The Federal Reserve seeks to control inflation by influencing interest rates."[32] This is an unproven economic assumption that interest rates have an adverse effect on economic growth and that raising interest rates will slow down growth and reduce inflation. It is the bitter medicine that we are told we must take to reduce inflation. The conventional economic thinking is that if enough of us lose our jobs or maybe just get our hours cut in half, then we won't be able to afford to buy luxuries like food and gas or pay our rent or our mortgage and the prices will just come tumbling down for those of us fortunate enough to still be working.

Since inflation is very real in the summer 2022 and into the spring of 2023, this is an important subject. Professors Richard Werner and Kang-Soek Lee wrote a 2018 academic paper that there is no adverse relationship between interest rates on economic growth and that there are no economic studies that support this adverse relationship that the Federal Reserve has used in the past and is now using to justify their raising interest rates.[33] This is a scholarly paper and is a challenging read for the average person, but Professor

Werner has a very understandable 20-minute interview on YouTube in which he explains his research to us: "Professor Richard Werner, interest rates do not drive the economy".[34] If Werner and Lee are correct that there is no adverse relationship between interest rates and economic growth, this takes away the only tool the Federal Reserve claims to have to fight inflation within the bank-created debt-money system. In other words, the Federal Reserve–led bank-created debt-money system is incapable of controlling inflation.

Within a system of publicly created money interest rates would have no effect on the supply of money. Instead of banks creating our money supply by loaning it to us at interest, our government would create it by spending it into existence for the programs we deem necessary. As we are rewriting in the summer of 2022 and into early 2023, inflation is very much on the minds of the American people. Inserting this section here, which directly questions the ability of the Federal Reserve bank-created debt-money system to control inflation by raising interest rates, seems appropriate. Evidence shows that the inflation that began in 2021 is largely the result of supply chain backlogs as a result of the slowing down and then speeding up the economy because of the COVID Pandemic,[35] Russia's War on Ukraine disrupting world food supplies[36] and some good old-fashioned corporate price gouging.[37] Raising interest rates will change none of the three major causes of this inflation. Instead it will punish poor and working class people both here in the U.S. and across the globe.

CHAPTER 3

THE NITTY-GRITTY ON DEBT-MONEY CREATION

Here we offer empirical proof from a respected economist that banks create money out of thin air. Understanding this cornerstone of the bank-created debt-money system will give us the proper foundation to understand publicly created money and ultimately to choose which system we want.

EXPERT WITNESS: RICHARD A. WERNER

Chair International Banking, University of Southampton, UK

Director of its Centre for Banking, Finance and Sustainable Development[1]

German economist and expert on central banking Dr. Werner published *A lost century in economics: Three theories of banking and the conclusive evidence* in 2015. Professor Werner is one of the few economists who has been courageous enough to publicly take on the entrenched debt-money system in any way. Tough job, but he does it very well. His empirical test is based on observing factual evidence without regard for system or theory. His findings prove that what he refers to as the "credit creation theory of banking" [bank-created debt-money system] is how our money is created. And that anyone representing another viewpoint [Federal Reserve?] is misinforming us.

Although Dr. Werner proves the credit creation theory of banking is the one being used, it does not mean that Werner supports its use. He is merely the bearer of bad news. Werner as an academic provides us with the facts. Using his research, we conclude that a dysfunctional, fraudulent and evil system of money creation controls society. Now it's time to wade into the murky water of debt-money creation.

A LOST CENTURY IN ECONOMICS: THREE THEORIES OF BANKING AND THE CONCLUSIVE EVIDENCE

During the past century, three different theories of banking were dominant at different times:

---

(1) *Financial Intermediation Theory* of banking, currently prevalent, says that banks collect deposits and then lend these out. [In other words, they don't create money.]

(2) *Fractional Reserve Theory* of banking says that each individual bank is a financial intermediary without the power to create money, but the banking system collectively is able to create money through the process of 'multiple deposit expansion.' [Also referred to as the money multiplier in the out-of-print Federal Reserve pamphlet, *Modern Money Mechanics*.]

(3) *Credit Creation Theory* of banking, predominant a century ago, does not consider banks as financial intermediaries that gather deposits to lend out, but instead argues that each individual bank creates credit and money newly when granting a bank loan.[2] [In other words, they create money out of thin air.]

Before we wade into Dr. Werner's explanation and ultimately his test proving that the Credit Creation Theory of Banking is currently in use, please be clear in understanding that this means that the bank-created debt-money system is currently in use. The Financial Intermediation Theory of Banking is most certainly not in use.

If you are wondering what system of money creation would be representative of a system of publicly created money, the answer is none of the above. Publicly created money stands apart and is representative of none of the above theories. The Financial Intermediation Theory says banks don't create money, but loan out money from our savings and checking accounts. While publicly created money would absolutely not allow banks to create money, it also would absolutely not allow banks to loan out savings and checking account money without our knowledge or permission. They would only be able to loan money that they actually owned, or had the authority to loan from the owner of the money through some mutual agreement to share in the profits, or loan money that they had borrowed from the federal government. Chapter 7: *Publicly Created Money in Action—The NEED Act* describes such a system.

Who knows exactly what theory of banking or money creation the Federal Reserve purports to be in use? Internet searches for "Federal Reserve financial intermediation theory of banking" yield articles by the Fed, but the ones we can find all deal with non-bank financial institutions acting as financial intermediaries, an entirely different animal than whether or not actual banks create our money. The Fed does answer the question, "What is the economic function of a bank?" The Fed's response: "As a key component of the financial system, banks allocate funds from savers to borrowers in an efficient manner..."[3] Allocate means distribute or apportion the money that savers have entrusted to the banks to borrowers as loans. In addition to this being patently false,[4] this statement also indicates that the Federal Reserve claims the Financial Intermediation Theory of Banking is in effect—banks loaning money from savers to borrowers. One is still left wondering why the Federal Reserve does not come out and simply admit to the Financial Intermediation Theory of Banking if that is their official position. And if they do subscribe to it, who creates our money if the Federal Reserve and the private banks are simply moving around already created money? We know the federal government doesn't create our money, because if it did it would not be borrowing it from private sources to the tune of $28.4 trillion federal debt as of June 3, 2021.[5]

An important distinction to make here is that no one who advocates for publicly created money thinks that banks should be allowed "to distribute or apportion the money that savers have entrusted to them to borrowers as loans,"[6] what the Federal Reserve claims is the economic function of a bank. This should never be done. Under a system of publicly created money, we would be able to deposit money in bank safekeeping accounts, in which the bank would be required to do just that—keep them safe and not invest them in any way. Banks would be able to charge us for this service and we could decide whether or not it was reasonable, whether we would rather put it in a different bank or perhaps just put it under the mattress. We would also be free to voluntarily invest our money into accounts in which the bank would lend it out and we would share in the proceeds from the loans in an agreed manner, but also assume a degree of risk if the loans are not repaid.

Bank Money Creation

Banks have asset and liability columns on their bookkeeping. These columns must always balance or equal the same amount. When you take out a loan, your promise to pay the loan is an asset to the bank. Let's say you take out a home mortgage loan of $200,000. You sign a promissory note to pay $200,000 and this $200,000 promise is entered as an asset of the bank, increasing the asset column by $200,000. If nothing else happens the bank's books would not balance, because the asset column would be $200,000 greater than the liability column. If the bank was loaning money that already existed and not creating it out of thin air, the $200,000 that the bank had just loaned you would have to come from somewhere, such as cash on hand. And this cash on hand also in the asset column would diminish by $200,000 at the moment the loan papers were signed, and you were handed the $200,000 check to turn over to whomever you had just bought your new house from. This is how most of us intuitively think bank lending works.

BANK BALANCE SHEET UNDER A PUBLICLY CREATED MONEY SYSTEM:

Assets		Liabilities	
Cash on hand before loan	$1,000,000.00	Check/Saving Deposits	$1,000,000.00
Loan amount taken from cash on hand is subtracted	-$200,000.00	No new deposit created with your loan	$0.00
Cash on hand after loan	$800,000.00		
New loan added to assets	$200,000.00		
Total Assets remain	$1,000,000.00	Total Liabilities become	$1,000,000.00

With a publicly created money system above, both Total Assets and Total Liabilities remain $1,000,000 and no new money has been created with the loan.

But the balance sheet below is how the bank-created debt-money system actually operates. Immediately when the $200,000 loan is entered into the bank's computer program, a like amount, a $200,000 deposit, is automatically credited to your checking account. This is all done completely unbeknownst to you, and you will never have access to what the bank has created and placed in your account and had the gall to call it a deposit of $200,000. But the bank's books balance and the $200,000 deposit entered into your account did not come from bank reserves or deposits or anywhere else. It was created out of thin air. You are never told that there exists a deposit of $200,000 in your account and you have absolutely no access to that money.

BANK BALANCE SHEET UNDER THE PRESENT BANK-CREATED DEBT-MONEY SYSTEM:

Assets		Liabilities	
Cash on hand before loan	$1,000,000	Check/Saving Deposits	$1,000,000
Loan amount taken from cash on hand	$0	New deposit created with your loan	$200,000
Cash on hand after loan remains	$1,000,000		
New loan added to assets	$200,000		
Total Assets increased to	$1,200,000	Total Liabilities	$1,200,000

In the above example under the bank-created debt-money system, the bank has created $200,000 out of thin air. Calling bank money creation "deposits" is a great example of the misinformation about who creates our money. When most people hear the term "deposit," they immediately think of their own savings or checking accounts and the hard-earned paychecks they deposit into these accounts. It takes a truly Machiavellian system to create money out of thin air when they make loans to us, charge us interest for their privilege, and then call the creation of the money a "deposit" so no one will know what the hell is going on.

Professor Werner was able to prove this bank money creation in a previous empirical test, but critics said that because modern banking has transactions that take place around the clock, you can never be sure if the test was not interfered with by those other transactions. Bank Director Marco Rebl of the Raiffeisenbank Wildenberg, a cooperative bank in Lower Bavaria, Germany, came to the rescue. Director Rebl thought of a way to completely control external transactions. All Bavarian cooperative banks use two parallel IT (informational technology) systems. The first empirical test described used only the daily balance sheet and reporting software, "BAP Agree." A second software system, "HJAP," is used for the compilation of the formal annual accounts of the banks that are submitted to the bank auditors and the regulatory authorities. The HJAP system contains all the bank accounting rules, functions and conforms with all the bank supervisory, prudential and legal requirements, regulations and procedures (which may not necessarily be relevant or enforceable on a daily basis as applied by BAP Agree in everyday use). HJAP also conforms to the more stringent annual reporting requirements and has other functions useful for regulators.

At year-end all transactions are put into HJAP for the annual accounts. Transactions in BAP Agree automatically feed into HJAP. It is possible that a transaction—because of the holidays or for another reason—would not make it into the BAP Agree system in the calendar year. (This is the very reason that detractors of Werner's first empirical test objected, because other transactions could also be taking place along with the test.) In such a case the bank directors can manually put the transaction into the HJAP software even after the end of the calendar year. The empirical test involved manually adding a 200,000-euro loan into the HJAP software for the year 2013 after the BAP Agree year-end report. Therefore, there were no other transactions or externalities that could confuse the results.

The result was consistent with the credit creation theory of money creation(bank-created debt-money system). Bank assets increased by 200,000 euro as a result of the manual entry of the loan into the asset column. Bank liabilities also instantly and automatically increased by a like 200,000 euro, although nothing was entered here. The bank software automatically created a deposit to balance the books, in effect creating 200,000 euro that did not come from cash, reserves or any other asset of the bank.[7]

Simply put, banks create what we use for money from nothing when they make loans. As stated before, they can only do this because all the banks are in league together doing exactly the same thing, and because the Federal Reserve Banks (and central banks in other countries) move reserve funds around after the loan has been made to take care of the bookkeeping. This way, all the banks will have the required amount of reserves on hand to cover or underwrite each individual bank's loans, even though this is all done after the loans have already been made. There can only be one reason why this is not common knowledge. The financial establishment does not want us to know their dirty fraudulent secret.

PAUL SAMUELSON'S *ECONOMICS*

Dr. Paul Samuelson is from Gary, Indiana, just ten miles or so from my home. His textbook *Economics,* published from 1948–1995, "immediately became the authority for the principles of economics courses"[8] and became the nation's best-selling economics textbook for three decades.[9] He won the 1970 Nobel

Prize in Economics "for the scientific work through which he has developed static and dynamic economic theory and actively contributed to raising the level of analysis in economic science."[10] I can only wonder what grade he would give me if I had taken his class.

As a less than successful college student, I have no status to critique Dr. Samuelson. I'll let someone vastly more qualified take a look at Dr. Samuelson's position on bank creation of money. Dr. Richard A. Werner does just that in *A lost century in economics: Three theories of banking and the conclusive evidence.* Let me preface this by stating that I believe Dr. Samuelson would reconsider his position on bank creation of money if he were still alive today. I do not think Dr. Samuelson was doing anything but trying to put lipstick on a pig, i.e., explain a dysfunctional money system. It is unfortunate that instead of trying to come up with an explanation for how our dysfunctional system functions, he did not spend some time looking into an alternative system that would not require both people and government to carry huge debt loads for society to have money to exist. Since Dr. Samuelson is no longer with us now, perhaps other economists will answer the challenge in his absence.

The simple fact of the matter is that the economics profession has almost completely ignored the discussion of publicly created money. I cannot find papers written by economists critiquing Dr. Werner's research, the NEED Act, a system of publicly created money put into Congress in 2011, but ignored, Stephen Zarlenga's book on the nature of money, *The Lost Science of Money,* or other papers in support of publicly created money (all of which are discussed later). Internet searches for critiques from the Federal Reserve yield nothing despite having an estimated 348 macroeconomists on their payroll. One would think they would be anxious to shoot down opposing opinions on money creation. The entire economics establishment has ignored a discussion of what should be a healthy dialogue between those who support the present bank-created debt-money system and those who support a system of publicly created money. But we can't have a healthy discussion when only one side shows up at the public square to debate.

Before venturing into Dr. Samuelson's explanation of bank money creation, please don't feel that there is something wrong with yourself if you do not understand him. The system was not designed to be understood. It was designed more for us to scratch our heads and say to ourselves that the gentleman with the Nobel Prize certainly must know what he is talking about, and I'll just accept what he is saying as true. Dr. Werner has just offered an empirical controlled experiment objectively proving that what Dr. Samuelson describes below is not how banks create money. The Bank of England agrees with Dr. Werner, yet Dr. Samuelson's explanation below is largely what the economics profession has hung its hat on since it first came out in 1948. Personally, Dr. Samuelson's explanation made no sense to me when I first read it a decade ago and it still leaves me scratching my head.

DR. WERNER EXAMINES DR. SAMUELSON'S *ECONOMICS*:

Werner acknowledges that Samuelson's *Economics* was "the most influential post-war textbook in economics." Samuelson's first edition in 1948 dismisses the Credit Creation Theory of banking [bank-created debt-money system]. Dr. Samuelson takes a clear position against what he calls "false explanations still in wide circulation." He explains:

According to these false explanations, the managers of an
ordinary bank are able, by some use of their fountain pens,
to lend several dollars for each dollar left on deposit with
them. No wonder practical bankers see red when such
behavior is attributed to them. They only wish they could
do so. As every banker well knows, he cannot invest
money that he does not have; and any money that he does
invest in buying a security or making a loan will soon leave
his bank.[11]

Samuelson supports the Fractional Reserve Theory of banking,
believing a bank must first gather funds before it can make loans
in excess of the funds gathered. Samuelson states that individual
banks do not create money, but that the banks acting together in
the banking system create money. He uses the example of a "small
bank" that has a 20% reserve requirement (meaning that the bank
must keep reserves on hand equaling at least 20% of their total
loans) and looks at the balance sheet accounts of the bank in
which the bank asset and liability columns must always be equal.
Under the Federal Reserve System which was certainly in effect in
1948, reserve funds are separate and held in Federal Reserve Banks
and a $1,000 deposit put into a bank customer's savings or
checking account could not be used as a bank reserve. We can
assume that Dr. Samuelson used an example in which a bank held
its own reserves to simplify his explanation. "What can the bank
now do?" Samuelson asks if this bank receives a new cash deposit
of $1,000, "Can it expand its loans and investments by $4,000 so
that the change in its balance sheet looks as shown in Table 4b?[12]

Samuelson, Table 4b. Impossible situation for a single, small bank: [This example starts with zero assets and zero liabilities.]

Assets		Liabilities	
[cash deposit of $1,000 entered below]			
Cash reserves [are now]	$1,000	Deposits [become]	$5,000
Loans & investments [are made of]	$4,000		
Total [assets become]	$5,000	Total [liabilities become]	$5,000
(Samuelson, 1948, p. 325.)			

(Samuelson, 1948, p. 325.) [Authors note: Dr. Samuelson has a plus sign in front of all the money figures in his three diagrams we show beginning here. It seems logical that these plus signs are meant to convey the action that takes place. For some strange reason we are unable to reproduce this plus sign in our renderings of his diagrams. As such, we have added our own bracketed words to convey the meaning of Dr. Samuelson's plus signs.]

Samuelson continues, "The answer is definitely 'no'. Why not? Total assets equal total liabilities. Cash reserves meet the legal requirement of being 20% of total deposits. True enough. But how does the bank pay for the investments or earning assets that it buys? Like everyone else it writes out a check – to the man who sells the bond or signs the promissory note.... The borrower spends the money on labor, on materials, or perhaps on an automobile. The money will very soon, therefore, have to be paid out of the bank ... A bank cannot eat its cake and have it too. Table 4b gives, therefore a completely false picture of what an individual bank can do."[13]

Because all the money lent out will leave the bank, Samuelson argues that after the loan has been extended, the bank's true balance sheet after receiving a new deposit of $1,000 will look as follows:[14]

Table 4c. [Previously mentioned bank from Table 4b that again begins the process with zero assets and zero liabilities. It receives a $1,000 cash deposit and loans out $800 of the deposit so that it still had $200 cash on hand to cover the bank's reserve requirement of 20%.]

Assets		Liabilities	
[$1,000] Cash reserves [become]	$200.00	Deposits are created]	$1,000.00
[When] Loans & investments [are made of]	$800.00		
Total [assets are now]	$1,000.00	Total [liabilities are now]	$1,000.00
Samuelson, 1948, p. 326			

(Samuelson, 1948, p. 326.)

Samuelson's position is that although individual banks cannot create credit [money] out of nothing, the banking system acting together does so. "As far as this first bank is concerned, we are through. Its legal reserves are just enough to match its deposits. There is nothing more it can do until the public decides to bring in some more money on deposit....[15] The banking system as a whole can do what each small bank cannot do!"[16] [Create money out of thin air. Notice that Dr. Samuelson mentions when "loans & investments" are made. This tells us that banks also create money when they make investments, in addition to when they make loans.]

Samuelson proceeds to describe a process he calls a "chain of deposit creation." He lays out an example in which money from a new loan from one bank is being deposited in a second bank, loaned out again and deposited in a third bank, then a fourth bank, a fifth bank, and so on. This process results in $5,000 of total deposits in the banking system, which are the direct result of the original $1,000 deposit, with its aforementioned 20% reserve requirement giving the system a money multiplier of 5 times. In Samuelson's example, the banking system creates $4,000.

Theoretically, the banks might claim that they only created $4,000 in credit and destroyed the same $4,000 as the loans were repaid to them. True enough, but the credit-money [debt-money] is almost the only money in our system. So, we are forced to use this money or there will be almost no money in the system and everything, jobs, commerce, and industry, will grind to a halt without money.

Table 4i below: [Samuelson shows the consolidated balance sheet of the entire banking system. [17] This example, as did Table 4b, starts with zero assets and zero liabilities.]

Assets		Liabilities	
Cash reserves [added]	$1,000	Deposits [are created]	$5,000
Loans & investments [made]	$4,000		
Total [becomes]	$5,000	Total [becomes]	$5,000

(Samuelson, 1948, p. 329.)

"If the reader will turn to Table 4b previously marked *impossible*, he will see that the whole banking system can do what no one bank can do by itself. Bank money has been created 5 for 1 – and all the while each bank has only invested and lent a fraction of what it has received as deposits!"[18]

Table 4b, an impossible situation for a single small bank, is identical to Table 4i, which is what the entire banking system can do. [What Dr. Samuelson has said is impossible for one bank to do above, becomes the standard for all banks to do together below.][19]

This is what Samuelson calls "multiple deposit expansion." The "money multiplier" is a synonymous term. Both are interchangeable with the Fractional Reserve Theory of money creation as supported by Samuelson in the following excerpt. "All banks can do what one can't do alone." This is the same heading used to describe the process in all of Samuelson's textbook editions through 1995. The major difference is that the reserve requirement in the example had been reduced from 20% to 10% in the 1995 edition [still a vastly overstated number].[20]

Werner goes on to compare the 1948 edition to the 1995 text-book, noting several differences. In 1995, the amount of space given to the topic of bank money creation is much smaller. The 1995 textbook provides a clearer explanation of the Fractional Reserve Theory: the central bank-created reserves are used by banks "as an input" before being "transformed...into a much larger amount of bank money [bank-created debt-money]."[21]

It is important to understand that what Dr. Samuelson describes above is not what actually happens. Instead of banks loaning multiples of central bank-created reserves, Dr. Werner has proven that banks create the money first when a loan is made, and Dr. Huber concurs that the Federal Reserve then moves around reserve money so that all the banks have whatever percentage of reserves the Federal Reserve is requiring from them.[22]

The very thought of an individual bank creating deposits [bank-created debt-money] is entirely omitted by the 1995 edition of *Economics*. The 1948 edition said that an individual bank might also be able to "create deposits" despite the potential for quick losses, a stance that can be interpreted to support the Credit Creation Theory, but that they just didn't do this.[23]

Also omitted from the 1995 edition was an important section titled "Simultaneous expansion or contraction by all banks," which described the possibility that each individual bank could, after all, create deposits [bank-created debt-money], if all banks created the same amount at the same time (the outflows being canceled by the inflows). The modern textbook omits this significant admission.[24]

To conclude, Dr. Samuelson claims that banks cannot create money (deposits) alone. Instead, they can create money (deposits) [fast and furious] as long as they do so in concert with all the other banks, all with the help of the Federal Reserve System moving reserve funds around from bank to bank in order to justify the bank money creation that has already taken place. Dr.

Samuelson never considered an alternative to banks working together to create what we use for money (credit or debt-money). Or that our federal government should create money and that the Constitution gave it the legal power to do so: "The Congress shall have Power...To coin [create] Money, regulate the Value thereof." Art. I, Sec. 8.[25] [The legal argument for publicly created money is presented in Chapter 6 of the *History of Money 101*.]

Dr. Samuelson's Explanation Turns Actual Bank Money Creation "on its head"

Deputy Chief of Modeling at the International Monetary Fund Michael Kumhof, along with colleague Jaromir Benes, published an International Monetary Fund Working Paper in 2012, titled *The Chicago Plan Revisited*. They decisively state that bank lending creates money and argue that the money multiplier (deposit multiplier/fractional reserve) theory of banking that Samuelson subscribes to turns the actual way banks create money "on its head":

> Bank reserves held at the central bank...do not play any meaningful role in the determination of wider monetary aggregates [larger supply of money]. The reason is that the 'deposit multiplier' [money multiplier/fractional reserve theory of money creation] of the undergraduate economics textbook, where monetary aggregates [money used in the economy/bankmoney/money supply] are created at the initiative of the central bank, through an initial injection of high-powered money [reserve money] into the banking system that gets multiplied through bank lending, turns the actual operation of the monetary transmission mechanism [how money is created] on its head.[26]

Kumhof and Benes then reference a 1990 Federal Reserve Working Paper by Nobel Prize winning economists, Norwegian Finn E. Kydland and American Edward C. Prescott that shows that bank-created debt-money leads the economic cycle [money creation cycle], while central bank reserve money lags the economic cycle, stating that central bank reserves impose no constraint, and the deposit multiplier is a myth.[27] Therefore, "Private banks are almost fully in control of the money creation process."[28]

Let's take a look at one term that, as Kumhof and Benes say, turns the entire system "on its head"—deposits. When people hear the term "bank deposit" they automatically think of the deposits we make into our savings and checking accounts. But we have also discovered that the money banks create when they make a loan is called a "deposit" and that these deposits are put into our checking accounts during the bank money creation process even though they do not show up on our monthly statements, and we have no access to that money in any way.

It might be helpful here to look at a group discussion that took place at one of the American Monetary Institute's Annual Conferences on Monetary Reform in 2014 as related in my pamphlet "Linking Social Justice to Monetary Reform."[29]

DO BANKS REALLY CREATE MONEY OUT OF THIN AIR WHEN THEY MAKE LOANS?

Monetary reformers claim they do, and most bankers and economists will claim they do not. Both statements are somewhat true. The monetary reformers' statement that banks create money is technically incorrect, but actually offers a more correct picture of reality than the bankers' claim that they don't create money. Stephen Zarlenga, Director of the American Monetary Institute, said it best: "Banks do not create money, they create what we use as money when they make loans."

What we use for money is not real money, although we call it "money." Almost the entirety of what is used for money in the U.S. is bank-created debt-money, also referred to as credit, created by banks when loans are made and then extinguished into the ether of the atmosphere when the loan is paid, except for the interest we pay on the loans, which goes into the pockets of the banks. The bank simply makes two accounting entries, a credit and a debit balancing each other, the loan check is issued, and the money is created from thin air. As the loan is paid off the accounts are reduced and with the final payment, the money is completely extinguished.[30]

Professor Werner's 2015 empirical test proved beyond any doubt that the credit creation theory of money is how what we use for money is created. The Federal Reserve ignored Dr. Werner's test and refuses to publicly tell us how our money is created. In contrast to this mass of confusion within the debt-money system of who creates our money and how it is created is a completely ignored system of publicly created money that would be spent into existence, debt-free, for the needs of the nation as determined by the people, existing free and clear of debt. The American people individually and through our government would not have to be in debt for publicly created money to exist, providing us our society's very lifeblood.

This does not mean that there would be no debts in society. We would still be free to borrow money to buy homes, cars, and the many things necessary to live in a modern society. Under a system of publicly created money, loans will be made borrowing money that already exists. The system will be exactly what most of us mistakenly think it is now. Such a system of publicly created money was put into Congress as the NEED Act in 2011[31] and will be presented in Chapter 7. It could easily be revised for the COVID-19 and climate change crises and be resubmitted to Congress as *The NEED Act Revisited* today.

Throughout the *People, Planet & the Power of Money Project*, the term *publicly created money* is used to describe the alternative to the bank-created debt-money system. Monetary reform colleagues at the Alliance For Just Money, referencing the concept of justice, use the term *just money* to describe exactly the same thing. When the Alliance For Just Money settled on the term *just money*, I supported and voted for it because invoking justice is important. Professor of Economic Sociology Joseph Huber uses the term *sovereign money* to describe the same thing. Professor of Economics Kaoru Yamaguchi uses the term *public money system*. My mentor in monetary reform, Director of the American Monetary Institute Stephen Zarlenga, used the term *money by law*. They all mean exactly the same thing. I chose to use *publicly created money* in this book because I felt that it best describes the difference between the public system we are fighting for and the privately created bank debt-money system that we want to get rid of. *Publicly created money* also describes what we must do and that is publicly create our money. They are all great ways to illustrate our goal. I finally settled on *publicly created money* because I thought it would be the most descriptive term to use for readers who are taking their first look at what kind of money system we should have.

All of the above terms depict a money system that is created and issued by our government's legal system, as a function of our democracy. Another term for this is fiat money. Fiat means an official, legal order of the state that must be followed. Fiat money is a creation of a country's legal system. Proponents of gold-backed money use the term fiat money as a pejorative, inferring that there is something wrong with a money system that is a function of a country's legal system vs. money that is based on a commodity such as gold or silver. They fail to take into account that gold and silver money systems were based on slave labor extracting the gold and silver from the Earth for the country's king or emperor. They also ignore the fact that gold and silver money systems never had enough gold and silver to go around for all the people. In Book Two: *History of Money 101*, we will show that as soon as gold or silver was allegedly backing money, those banks always issued the paper money in vastly greater quantities than they had gold or silver in their vaults that allegedly backed this paper money.

CHAPTER 4

ECONOMICS PROFESSORS ON HOW OUR MONEY IS CREATED

The first draft of *The People, Planet & the Power of Money Project* did not include direct input from economists who opposed the concept of publicly created money. The beta readers who had read the first draft desired to know why economists opposed publicly created money. Those of us who have been trying to get the concept of publicly created money out to the American public would also like to know why economics professionals oppose it. But the broad community of economics professionals has quite simply ignored the concept of publicly created money. I had already reached out to local economics professors hoping to start a dialogue on the subject and my entreaties were all left unanswered. Just as the papers and books written by supporters of publicly created money have all been largely ignored by the economics professionals. Rather than ask again what they thought of publicly created money, I decided to make another attempt at just getting economics professors to state how our money is created. One would think that professors at our nation's top-rated economics programs would be able to tell us how our money is created.

As described in the introduction, I had previously sent emails to Federal Reserve economists describing publicly created money and asking them who creates our money. This time, I decided to focus on economics professors from top-rated economics programs, along with professors from local universities. I composed a short email stating that I was in the editing phase of my forthcoming book and was looking for feedback from economics professionals. They were given the choice of answering the questions anonymously or using their names.

I did not ask them for their opinions on publicly created money. Instead, I asked them to say which of the three theories most accurately describes how our money is created— Financial Intermediation Theory, Fractional Reserve Theory or Credit Creation Theory. Then I asked them which theory the Federal Reserve System uses to describe how our money is created and to also provide a Fed paper or article that supports this conclusion.

I also asked if they believed that money was necessary for survival in modern society, if the nation's citizens having an understanding of how money is created was necessary for democracy, and finally if they, the economists, would be interested in reading *People, Planet & the Power of Money* prior to publication. [It was to be just a single book at the time.]

I sent the questionnaire out to 104 university economists, who all taught at top ten ranked economics programs as listed by *U.S. News & World Report*, and another 8 from local universities. I received two replies from the top ten professors and none from the local professors.

PROFESSOR A'S RESPONSE

The first response was from Professor A, a former department chair at a prestigious university. His reply indicated that he favored the Fractional Reserve Theory of banking and he sent me an article he had co-written that was largely indecipherable to anyone lacking a high degree of formal economics training. The article was about interest rates and their effect on the supply of money.

Professor A's scholarly article was not an explanation of how the Federal Reserve creates money, be it via fractional reserve or any other method. While he had originally said I could use his name, I didn't feel it was appropriate to do so. He responded to me with what he considered the best of intentions. He obviously had no idea that I might actually know anything about money creation and using his name would not be fair to him, especially in light of his later response in which he specifically requested that I not use it after initially saying that I could use it.

Professor A did go on to tell me that he had had extended discussions with another economist who did believe that our money was created via the Credit Creation Theory. Professor A stated, "My best guess, though, is that the Fractional Reserve Theory is the right one." The economist that he referred to was none other than Michael Kumhof, formerly of the International Monetary Fund and now with the Bank of England. I found this quite remarkable considering Dr. Kumhof is one of the relatively few high-level economists who have come out in support of publicly created money. I have had the pleasure of meeting Dr. Kumhof at a couple of American Monetary Institute Conferences. He co-authored *The Chicago Plan Revisited*, which concludes that publicly created money would completely eliminate bank runs, stabilize business cycles, and dramatically reduce both public and private debt, all while seeing the economy grow at a rate of 10% yearly with zero inflation. The computer modeling used for their study was the same one used by the Federal Reserve, the Dynamic Stochastic General Equilibrium (DSGE).[1] We referred to Dr. Kumhof in the previous chapter and will take a closer look at *The Chicago Plan Revisited* in Chapter 9.

Professor A was extremely courteous and I mean no disrespect to him, but it is bewildering to me that a learned economist who has written books and published papers in top economic journals, served as chairman of a top economics program and had a decades-long relationship within the Federal Reserve System could only say that it is his "best guess" that money is created through Fractional Reserve Lending. In Professor A's words: "My best guess, though, is that the Fractional Reserve Theory is the right one."

He did mention that Fractional Reserve Lending was built into models used in his research for policy simulations with other economists. But he did not say that these simulations in any way proved or intended to prove that Fractional Reserve Lending was how our money is created.

Professor A went on to say that it is not necessary for people to know how our money is created. Let us, for now, accept his premise that it is too complicated for mere mortals like you and me to understand how our money is created, exactly what my Econ 101 instructor told our class 56 years ago. Professor A went on to say that the market allows us to focus on what we do individually. [This does not take into account the periodic recessions, depressions and panics that have occurred in our country under the watchful gaze of the free market.] Professor A said that when the market fails, we have our democratically elected officials to provide the necessary oversight.

In my response to Professor A, I mentioned that the United Kingdom monetary reform group Positive Money polled the UK Parliament Members in 2017 and found that 85% of them did not know how money was created.[2] There is no reason to believe that our own Congress has any more insight into how our money is created than their counterparts in the UK. [In fact, how can anyone be expected to know how our money is created if a distinguished and accomplished economist cannot definitely state that he himself understands? I neglected to put this into my first reply to Professor A because I had not initially grasped that it was only his "best guess" that Fractional Reserve Lending was how our money is created. It was only after later rereading our dialogue that it really struck me.]

I also mentioned that Richard Werner's empirical test clearly shows that private banks create out of thin air what we use for money as debt when they make loans. The Federal Reserve does whatever bookkeeping is necessary by moving reserve funds from bank to bank, after the banks have already created the money, to justify the process. If I can understand this after having only one Econ 101 course fifty-some years ago, I think that the majority of the American people can, too. We are very much capable of understanding this basic system. What we definitely have difficulty wrapping our heads around is that banks create the very money that we need to exist out of thin air and charge us interest for the privilege. No wonder that we have a vastly unequal society and there never seems to be enough money to go around for everyone.

I stated that my research has found that the Federal Reserve System has about 348 macroeconomists whose jobs should include analyzing and writing about how our money is created, providing arguments about the pros and the cons of our current system, addressing books, papers, and proposed legislation that would support publicly created money or any other proposed money systems. Yet, using internet searches I can find nothing from Federal Reserve economists critiquing the system of publicly created money that the NEED Act (National Emergency Employment Defense Act),[3] put into Congress in 2011 by Dennis Kucinich and John Conyers, would give us. Or the Bank of England's *Money creation in the modern economy*,[4] Stephen Zarlenga's *Lost Science of Money*,[5] Richard Werner's *A lost century in economics: Three theories of banking and the conclusive evidence*,[6] Kumhof/Benes' *The Chicago Plan Revisited,* Joseph Huber's

Split-circuit reserve banking – functioning, dysfunctions and future perspectives,[7] or Kaoru Yamaguchi's research and modeling *Workings of A Public Money System of Open Macroeconomies – Modeling the American Monetary Act.*[8] These papers and books all demonstrate the structural flaw in the debt-money system. Why have the Fed macroeconomists failed to comment on the morality of bank-created debt-money or the many mentioned papers by academics on the subject?

The net result of our money being created as debt, and existing only as debt, is that we, the people, and our government must be in debt forever or society will grind to a halt.

Money is only created by the banks for the principal amount of the loans, nothing is created for the substantial interest that we must pay over the life of the loan. This means that there is never enough money in the system to repay the loans. The gap between the money supply and the overall debt must forever widen because of the absence of money created to pay the interest due. While a system of publicly created money would give us the positive results that Kumhof/Benes and Yamaguchi have modeled in their studies.

PROFESSOR B'S RESPONSE

The second and final response came from Professor B:

> Dear Nick,
> Just two comments:
> (1) The "money system" has nothing to do with the movement toward or away from inequality. The sources of inequality of income and wealth are numerous, for instance different levels of education and the resulting demand for labor, the relative share of labor and capital, inherited wealth, movements in the stock market, and many others.
> (2) A simple google search will provide you with an explana-

tion of money creation at any level of detail you want. In about two seconds I found the following explanation in plain English. Money creation is NOT complicated, whatever your textbook in the 1960s misled you to believe.

He attached a link from his two-second search to a 2020 commentary piece on Federal Reserve money creation. It describes the Federal Reserve creating money as it puts more money into circulation by buying assets from banks with money the Federal Reserve creates by a keystroke on its computer.

Professor B's credentials are beyond reproach as a respected member of the economics profession. Mentioning some of his distinguished achievements might give up his identity, so we will refrain from doing so. His two comments and the above link were all in bold type. I'm assuming this was to emphasize his point that inequality has nothing to do with our money system and that the explanation for how our money is created is right there in plain English for all to read. I answered his first point that creating our money as debt must lead to an indebted people and government, and that indebted people are on an unequal footing with those who own the banks.

"Money creation is NOT complicated, whatever your textbook in the 1960s misled you to believe." He obviously skimmed through what I had to say, or he would have realized that our class so many years ago was not misled by our textbook about how money is created, but rather spared from showing our inability to grasp a subject that our instructor said we were not capable of understanding. If only Professor B had been our instructor, perhaps we would have all become economists just like him.

The article that he referenced in his comments was "How the Federal Reserve Literally Makes Money"[9] by economist William J. Luther, posted on the CATO Institute website in June 2020. The Federal Reserve System's initial policy in response to COVID-19 provided up to $2.3 trillion in lending support to households, employers, financial markets, state and local governments. According to the article, "Very little of the Fed's money actually comes from taxpayers or sales of government bonds. Most of it, in fact, emerges right out of thin air.... To put more money into circulation, the Fed typically purchases financial assets—in much the same way that it plans to spend that $2.3 trillion....The Fed does not print money to buy assets because it does not have to. It can create money with a mere keystroke.... So as the Fed buys treasuries, mortgage-backed securities, corporate debt, and other assets over the coming weeks and months, money will rarely change hands. It will just move from one account to another."[10]

This would seem to support the Financial Intermediation Theory of banking, currently prevalent, which says that banks collect deposits and then lend them out. And that presumably any money creation that takes place does so at the Federal Reserve level. If you read the article, I hope you are able to follow that better than I was the first couple of times I read it. It brings to mind a saying my mother had to describe her inability to impart some wisdom unto her nine children who were all so anxious to grasp it. She would say, "Clear as mud?" and we would all nod our heads in agreement.

I have no reason to doubt that the Federal Reserve was creating money as Professor B and Dr. Luther claim, but that is hardly the entire story in the money creation game. The described action of the Fed was at least in part the creation of money by keystroke to buy up toxic assets that had made our big banks insolvent. It was the bailout of the big banks. Chapter 8 will take a closer look at these bailouts. Remember the Bank of England's statement: "This article explains how the majority of money in the modern economy is created by commercial banks making loans."[11] What about the money created, not just in response to a national financial crisis but as an everyday occurrence by banks making loans? In June of 2020, the U.S. Money Supply was $18.18 trillion[12] before the Fed promised the $2.3 trillion in lending support. Who created that money?

I had hopes that both professors would begin a dialogue to help my understanding. I was polite in my responses to them and asked them to continue the discussion. Professor A did respond: "Dear Nick: Thank you for not using my name. Please do not use it in the future."

In my email to both of our responding professors, I provided them a copy of the above transcript for this chapter which I said would be included in my book, along with this request, "Please let me know if you think it is a fair representation of your position and answers." Neither professor responded further, indicating that it was a fair representation of their views.

Professor A had said it best himself: "My best guess, though, is that the Fractional Reserve Theory is the right one." A learned, distinguished professor at one of our nation's top economics schools is not sure how our money is created. And a second respected, equally distinguished professor, also at one of our nation's top economics schools, does not seem to care if the American public is provided a clear answer on the subject. Whether or not this second professor understands that almost the entirety of our money is created as debt by private banks when they make loans is also unclear.

What this entire exercise demonstrates is that the economics intelligentsia, whether they are employed by the Federal Reserve or the nation's top university economics programs, are at the very least partially ignorant about money creation and disinterested in a serious discussion of publicly created money. Blithely ignorant on money creation and far too content with the present bank-created debt-money system, our economics intellectuals have proven themselves structurally incapable of being able to fairly consider an alternative publicly created money system. All this regardless of the inability of the bank-created debt-money system to adequately fund the planetary crises of climate change, dying oceans, unchecked plastic pollution, COVID-19 and artificial intelligence —all of which we will examine in detail in Book Three: *Spaceship Earth 101.*

Chapter 11 of this book covers economics student initiatives in getting their curriculums changed to represent reality instead of some of the fantasies that are the staple of whatever passes for economic wisdom from the economics establishment. Perhaps a way for students to break the ice and begin a discussion with their own professors is to ask them if they are either Professor A or B in *Money Creation 101*, who were either unable or unwilling to correctly tell us how our money is created.

CHAPTER 5

THE COST OF THE DEBT-MONEY SYSTEM

"We must make our choice. We may have democracy, or we may have wealth concentrated in the hands of a few, but we can't have both."[1] [2]

— LOUIS BRANDEIS, U.S. SUPREME COURT
JUSTICE, 1916–1939

The debt-money system is dysfunctional, fraudulent, unconstitutional and immoral. There are big winners in this system, but they come at the expense of the rest of us. The system of publicly created money proposed in the NEED Act is functional, legal, constitutional and moral. Publicly created money will reduce public and private debt loads dramatically (Kumhof & Benes).[3] A system of publicly created money will also improve the lives of our people and greatly increase the level of liberty, democracy and equality in our country. In sharp contrast, the current debt-money system is structurally incapable of giving us liberty, equality and democracy while demonstrating that it is quite capable of giving us guaranteed endless debt.

When we reviewed Professor Werner's discussion on the three theories of banking and money creation, he told us that in the early 1900s, just before the Federal Reserve System was created, there was a much greater understanding among political economists (those who preceded today's economists) that money was created by banks as debt than there is among today's economists. Henry Macleod's 1856 textbook *The Theory and Practice of Banking* explained the working of the mysterious system quite simply:

> The business of banking is not to lend money, but to create Credit.... And all these Credits are in the ordinary language and practice of commerce exactly equal to so much cash or Currency.... These banking Credits are, for all practical purposes, the same as Money.[4]

Now, more than a century and a half later, our money is still created by banks when they make loans, only now done under the umbrella and protection of the Federal Reserve System. A basic awareness of bank money creation existed a century ago. This does not mean that political economists then supported bank money creation; it merely means that some of them were more aware of its existence. Today, as a result of the economics profession's failure to inform us about how our money is created, few members of the general public understand how our money is created. We can only assume that today's economists are either confused by the money creation process, do not want us to know how our money is created, or are content to allow the complexity of the system to act as a shield to public knowledge. The event most responsible for the decline in the American people's knowledge about money creation was the passage of the Federal Reserve Act in 1913. Book Two: *History of Money 101*, Chapter 10: *The Federal Reserve System—The Triumph of the Debt-Money System* uses the Federal Reserve System's own history to tell the story of the secrecy and deception that enabled its creation.

NOT FOR THE FAINT OF HEART

We cannot enter the realm of the Federal Reserve with a faint heart. Even if you don't initially understand, please proceed with a brave heart. It is vital that we American citizens figure out what has been done with our country's lifeblood. Only when we as a people begin to grasp the depravity of the bank-created debt-money system will we then be able to demand that we change to a system of publicly created money. And only a system of publicly created money can create the amounts of money necessary to move forward and tackle the myriad of crises affecting us. Providing a just system of money is the people's responsibility. Within our democracy, the people's representative Congress is entrusted by the Constitution with this duty. Our country was founded on the principles of liberty (freedom), equality and democracy. The cost of the debt-money system cannot be measured in dollars alone. The cost of the debt-money system is the loss of our liberty, equality and democracy.

Indiana University Northwest Professor of Minority Studies Raoul Contreras teaches an advanced level class on participatory democracy. Every year since 2009, at the conclusion of the semester in April, the class holds an annual two-day IUN *Democracy Is in the Streets Participatory Democracy Conference*. I've attended and participated in each conference, and for years I also audited and sat in on the class. Professor Contreras is an ardent believer in exposing his students to community members and activists and vice versa.

At some point during the semester, Dr. Contreras asks everyone to write out the one word that embodies being an American. By a landslide margin every time, the students would choose one of two words that have the same meaning—freedom or liberty. As important as freedom is to Americans, it is impossible to have freedom when the thing that is most necessary for our survival—money—is created and controlled by private bank corporations for profit. How can we say we are a free people when we have to be in debt for there to be money in existence so that our society can function?

DOES THE DEBT-MONEY SYSTEM CAUSE INEQUALITY?

Professor B, whom we met in the previous chapter, is an extremely distinguished economist at a top-10 university economics program. He seemed almost incredulous that I would even suggest that the debt-money system might in some way be responsible for the level of inequality in our country. His response to my questionnaire contained two comments, neither of which answered any of my questions. But who am I to complain? I am just a citizen with no formal economics training.

"The 'money system' has nothing to do with the movement toward or away from inequality. The sources of inequality of income and wealth are numerous: different levels of education, demand for labor, the relative share of labor and capital, inherited wealth, movements in the stock market..." Of course Professor B's listed items contribute to inequality, but to discount the bank creation of our money as debt as also a cause of inequality seems contrived. Perhaps if Professor B was aware of what type of money system we actually have, he would have made a different assessment of whether or not our money system is a cause of inequality. Let's call in an expert witness to give the other side of the story on money creation and inequality.

EXPERT WITNESS: LINO ZEDDIES

Pluralist economist and consultant for transformation, self-organization and utopia development at *Reinventing Society – Center for Real Utopias.*

Master of Economics, Free University Berlin.

Mr. Zeddies' 2018 article "Money Creation and Inequality – An Underexposed Topic for Monetary Reformers"[5] begins by stating that all public debate about inequality has been focused on existing money and wealth. Professor B's above statement illustrates that at least some of our economics professionals are not interested in how and why our money is created. According to them, inequality and money creation have nothing in common.

Lino Zeddies on how the current debt-money system expands inequality:

Boom/Bust Credit Cycles. The boom creates huge profits for banks, financial markets and the rich. In a fair world, the same players who benefit from the boom would suffer in the bust. But because the banks create our money supply and we need a money supply to simply exist, society cannot allow them to fail when the economy goes bust. Thus, the banks and those who own them are bailed out by the Central Bank [Federal Reserve in the U.S.] as they buy up the banks' toxic assets to save the entire system. The rest of us during the Great Recession were left to sink or swim with homes that were no longer worth what we owed to the banks, homes which we had mortgaged our lives to pay for. Because tax money is used to bail out the banks, the Central Bank is forced to increase public debt and the government is thus forced to cut public infrastructure and services. All of these factors increase inequality.

Big Corporations Have a Competitive Advantage: Because of the "too big to fail" nature of the present monetary system, big loans for big businesses are easier to get than small or mid-sized loans for smaller businesses. Big corporations are able to set up their own in-house banks, giving them an advantage over their smaller rivals. Central Banks with quantitative easing policies have bought more corporate bonds, government securities and other financial instruments than ever before, benefitting the big banks and corporations. [As illustrated by the Federal Reserve over the last year increasing its portfolio of assets by 60% from $4.7 trillion in March 2020 to $7.9 trillion in April 2021.[6]] The cheap interest environment, combined with the above factors, provides the perfect financial climate for megamergers and takeovers, squeezing out small and mid-sized companies.

Whoever Has Some Will Be Given More: Within the debt-money system, the "haves" get more and cheaper credit than the "have-nots" [and the "have-nots" are well aware of this].

Growth Imperative and Underemployment: The system of bank-created debt-money results in a structural scarcity of money in circulation. This necessitates a continuous growth imperative, thus increasing lending and the supply of money in circulation. Whenever the growth slows down or stops it results in defaults, economic depression and structural unemployment. Workers are left with low wages and weak unions.

Mr. Zeddies concludes, "To sum up, money being created as bank credit systemically results in a multitude of direct and indirect factors that concentrate the distribution of power, wealth and income in the hands of few." Mr. Zeddies goes on to describe how a sovereign money system [publicly created money] will alleviate inequality: "Where the financial sector is back in its proper role as a servant of the real economy."[7]

Recovery from the Great Recession

The recovery from the Great Recession amounted to a tremendous increase in wealth in America. U.S. wealth increased from $58.9 trillion 2008 year-end[8] to $113.5 trillion 2019 second quarter,[9] an increase of $54.6 trillion in 10 1/2 years (Federal Reserve figures). With a U.S. population of 329 million, the increase in wealth translated to $166,000 per person. That is the recovery from the Great Recession, $166,000 for every person in the country, almost a doubling of the wealth that existed in 2008. The once typical family of four should have seen their wealth increase $664,000. For those of us who didn't get their share of this loot, remember that someone else at the top of the heap most certainly did get their share and your share too. That's inequality, made possible by the bank-created debt-money system.

Readers are invited to compare their own financial situations with the national average of $166,000 increase in wealth. Using the above figures, the average net wealth of all Americans at the end of 2019 was $345,000 per person. The average net wealth for the traditional American family of four in 2019 was $1,380,000. While these averages are wonderful, they are just that, averages. "The bottom half of Americans combined have a negative net worth" (an assessment of economist Gabriel Zucman).[10] [11] That's 165 million people with no combined net worth. And that is all one needs to know about American inequality. Paraphrasing the Bandito leader in the iconic 1948 film *The Treasure of Sierra Madre*,[12] "It means the stinkin' rich are even richer than we thought they were." Or as film critic Edwin Schallert says of the film, "That gold changes the character of men who are fortunate enough to find it is the central thesis of this curiously powerful production."[13] One can certainly surmise that this classic film represents that historically equating gold with wealth has spawned greed and inequality. The same can be said of a bank-created debt-money system which originally claimed to be backed by gold.

FEDERAL RESERVE TACKLES INEQUALITY WITH THE $400 QUESTION

Anyone who watched the 2020 Democratic Party presidential primary campaign must remember hearing practically every candidate mention that nearly half of all Americans could not afford a $400 emergency expense without borrowing the money. Four hundred dollars is a trip to the dentist or new tires on a very small car. Four hundred dollars is very little money unless you don't have it... then it is everything.

Federal Reserve Reports on Economic Well-Being of U.S. Households:

Over the four years 2013–16, the Federal Reserve continued to ask the question on a hypothetical emergency expense costing $400. The responses gradually declined a modest one percent per year from 48% not being able to pay the expense without borrowing or selling something in 2013 to 44% in 2016.[14] [15] [16] [17] Beginning in 2017, for whatever unknown reason, the question and answers were phrased slightly differently, resulting in only four in ten (40%) in 2017 not being able to cover the unexpected expense of $400,[18] to 27% would borrow or sell something and 12% would not be able to cover the expense at all. That should equal 39% but the answer was not given that way in 2018,[19] to finally 16% of adults were not able to pay all of their current month's bills, and another 12% said they could not pay an additional $400 expense, giving a 28% total but not stated as such in 2019. The 2019 Q&A added the following, "If faced with an unexpected expense of $400, 63% of [2019] adults said they would cover it completely using cash or a credit card paid off at the end of the month—an improvement from half who would have paid this way in 2013."[20]

Who knows what the correct percentage is for adults who cannot pay for an unexpected $400 trip to the dentist or a very minor car repair without borrowing? We do know that for the first three years it dropped from 48% to 44% or 1.33% per year. Then they started to word the answer options differently. Perhaps they also worded the question differently. Or perhaps the people answering started to hear the politicians talking about it on TV and didn't want to appear too poor in their answers. At any rate, the number of people admitting that they couldn't buy tires for the car without borrowing went down yearly from 48% to 47% to 46% to 44% to 39% to 37%.

People struggle with debt and bills in America. It is quite likely that many of these people are not in the mood to be too candid with strangers asking them personal questions over the phone. Juggling credit cards to pay the bills each month is an activity that far too many Americans participate in with great regularity.

EXPERT WITNESS ON AMERICAN POVERTY: LINDA TIRADO

Author of *Hand to Mouth – Living in Bootstrap America*

Linda Tirado is an American woman with two kids and two jobs. Several years ago, she wrote an essay that ended up going viral at the *Huffington Post*, *The Nation*, and several other publications. The essay, read by more than six million people, is titled "Why I Make Terrible Decisions, or, Poverty Thoughts." Linda did not start out poor. She was a staffer working in political campaigns when she was injured in a traffic accident. Medical and dental bills from her accident put her in a financial debt hole that she couldn't dig herself out of. In her 2014 book, *Hand to Mouth – Living in Bootstrap America*, Linda tells us what it is like to be working and poor in America:

Poverty is when a quarter is a f**king miracle. Poor is when a dollar is a miracle. Broke is when five bucks is a miracle. Working class is being broke, but doing so in a place that might not be run-down. Middle class is being able to own some toys and to live in a nice place – and by 'nice', I don't mean fancy; I mean that you can afford to buy your own furniture and not lease it and that while you still worry about bills, you aren't constantly worried about homelessness. And rich is anything above that.[21] When you never have enough money it ceases to have meaning.... Poverty is bleak and cuts off your long-term brain.[22]

On May 30, 2020, Linda Tirado was shot in the left eye by what she believes was a police rubber bullet. She was in Minneapolis as a member of the press covering the equality movement protests that began with the killing of George Floyd by a Minneapolis policeman. George Floyd gasped, "I can't breathe" as the policeman applied a knee to his neck for 9 minutes and 29 seconds.[23] Days later Linda Tirado was on TV when a Minneapolis police officer applied a rubber bullet to her eye.

Incredibly Linda Tirado was back to work as a freelance photojournalist shortly after being shot and losing the sight from her left eye. "No worries, I've been back at work for five hours now. My job is to witness, and they only got my left eye. My right one is good to go."[24] A year later, Linda had a lawsuit dragging through the court system that will hopefully allow her to pay her tens of thousands in medical bills incurred from the shooting.[25] Linda is fortunate that she shoots her camera with her right eye so she can continue to work. My heart goes out to Linda. A freelance photojournalist in the wonderful gig economy means no benefits and no security. It is the fervent hope of those who struggle to fix our money system that we give Linda and her kids and the millions upon millions of other struggling American families hope, joy and a future. The good-paying jobs with benefits that publicly created money would provide the funds for would help to level the playing field, giving these families a decent shot at financial stability.

DEBT

The most obvious and direct result of the debt-money system is debt. To get money into the system, we must indebt ourselves to private banks. Money is created as debt. Money exists only as debt. Within the dead-end, bank-created debt-money system we can either have a society without money and the resulting depression and anarchy that would follow, or we must be in debt to have any sort of society at all.

What does debt equal? Debt = poor people. Yes, there is a direct correlation between a huge level of debt and a large number of poor people. The definition of "poor" is lacking money or material possessions. If you are in debt, that means that someone else has a claim on your material possessions. Therefore, in a sense, you are poor. But that doesn't mean it is your fault—as we have been conditioned to believe. It is a structural failure of the debt-money system that a huge, ever-increasing amount of debt must be carried by our people and our government for our society to function. Sure, a lot of rich people carry large amounts of debt, but they can always sell off assets to repay their debts when forced to do so. Poor people need their houses and cars to live in, so selling off their meager assets is not an option.

And the level of debt must increase. The money is created when we take out a loan. Our promise to repay the loan is an asset to the bank. When the bank enters our promise to pay into the asset column in their system, at the very same time a computer accounting entry automatically pops up for the amount of the loan on the liability side of the bank's computer accounting system. Professor Werner's previously described test proved this without a doubt.[26] What magically appears is a deposit in your account equal to the amount of the loan. You have no access to this deposit, and you are never told it exists. As you make principal payments on the loan, the deposit in your account is reduced by a like amount. When you have completely repaid the loan, the deposit is also reduced to zero. It exists only while you are in debt, and for the amount of principal for which you are in debt.

Nothing is created when the loans are made for the significant amount of interest you will have to pay over the life of the loan. What this means is that we, as a society, always owe more money than there is money available with which to repay our debts. As interest adds up over time, the difference between the amount we owe and the lesser amount of the money available from which to pay it grows progressively greater. As the song "Sixteen Tons" laments, "Another day older and deeper in debt." Yet we also know that a simple $400 emergency expense, such as a trip to the dentist or a new set of tires, cannot be paid for without going further into debt by almost half of our fellow Americans.

DEBT STAT SHEET

Government Debt:		
Federal Debt:	$28.6 trillion	7/25/2021
State Gov Debt:	$1.2 trillion	7/25/2021
Local Gov Debt:	$2.1 trillion	7/25/2021
Government Debt Total:	$31.9 trillion	7/25/2021

US Debt Clock, https://usdebtclock.org/

Repaying the government debt, which is an absolute duty within the Constitution, is not possible within the debt-money system. Yet repayment is required by the Constitution:

"The validity of the public debt of the United States, authorized by law...shall not be questioned."[27] What our government does is repay the old debt with new debt, thus always keeping our government in ever-increasing debt.

Household Debt:	
1st Quarter, 2021	
Student Debt:	$1.6 trillion
Credit Card Debt:	$.8 trillion
Auto Debt:	$1.4 trillion
Other:	$.3 trillion
Mortgages:	$10.2 trillion
Home Equity:	$.3 trillion
Total Household Debt:	$14.6 trllion

Federal Reserve Bank of New York,"Microeconomic Data, 2021, Q1, Quarterly Report Household Debt & Credit," released May 2021, https:// www.newyorkfed.org/medialibrary/interactives/householdcredit/data/pdf/ HHDC_2021Q1.pdf

US Corporate Debt* $11.2 trillion[28]

* Nonfinancial debt of U.S. large corporations, 1st Quarter, 2021

Total Debt:		
Total Gov. Debt	$31.9 trillion	
Total Household Debt:	$14.6 trillion	
US Corporate Debt:	$11.2 trillion	
Total US Debt:	$57.7 trillion	
US Money Supply M2:	$20.1 trillion	May of 2021

FRED—Federal Reserve Economic Data, "M2 Money Stock, Updated June 22, 2021," Federal Reserve Bank of St. Louis, https://fred.stlouisfed.org/ series/M2SL

Amount Debt is greater than Money Supply: $37.6 trillion June 2021

. . .

Our present debt-money system is dysfunctional. There is no other word for a system that requires us to repay a total of $57.7 trillion with $20.1 trillion in money. It is quite simply an impossibility. The only way to repay our total of $57.7 trillion in debt is to increase the money supply. That can only be done by creating more debt, and creating more debt can in no way decrease the overall level of debt.

We would have to almost triple the money supply to repay our debt. Even then, we would still be in debt, because repaying old debt with new debt simply changes the name of the creditor that we owe money to. Remember that when money is used to repay a loan, it is destroyed. It cannot repay other loans after it has been destroyed. The debt-money system is a nightmare that requires our government and people to be in steadily rising debt forever.

Debt Stat Sheet:			
U.S. federal debt per person		$85,885	July 1, 2021
State & local gov. debt per person		$9,910	July 1, 2021
Private debt per person		$12,012	July 1, 2021
Private mortgage debt per person		$30,630	July 1, 2021
Total debt per person		$138,437	July 1, 2021

This debt must not only exist but continue to increase to keep our bank-created debt-money system operating. As the level of government debt increases, our politicians are much less likely to advance money for programs like food assistance, rent support, Medicare for all, unemployment benefits, climate change, etc. While one of our political parties is much more likely to support funding these people-oriented and planet-oriented programs, many from the opposing party are also mindful of curtailing spending because of our federal debt of $28.6 trillion on July 25, 2021 and now $31.6 trillion on March 13, 2023. Changing to a system of publicly created money is the only way we can both repay our federal debt and finance the legislative programs to properly address the needs of people and planet.

CHAPTER 6

DEMANDING CHANGE

"Over time, whoever controls the money system, controls the nation."[1]

— STEPHEN ZARLENGA (1941–2017)

The Occupy Movement in 2011 brought all sorts of disparate individuals together to discuss how we could make our country better and live up to the promise of liberty, equality and democracy for all. Among them was the world's leading expert on publicly created money and an anti-war, social justice and environmental activist whose monetary education was just beginning.

Our country was founded on the statement that "All men are created equal." A nation's money system belongs to its people. Giving it away to private bank corporations is a moral crime of the highest order. It took the Occupy Movement in 2011, inspiring thousands of people occupying the public square in every major city in our nation, to even begin a public discussion of America's massive financial inequality. Before the Occupy Movement you could watch cable news for weeks on end and never hear the word "inequality." Publicly created money is a huge step toward addressing this inequality. It reclaims the creation privilege of money away from the private banking corporations and returns it to the people. It gives the people the power to create our money for the programs that will heal and benefit both ourselves and our planet.

On September 17, 2011, an estimated 1,000 people, fed up with a system that produced tremendous economic inequality went to the heart of the U.S. financial system in New York City—Wall Street. They protested and many stayed on, occupying Zuccotti Park, a small park nearby. Within days simpatico protests popped up across the country. Before long every major U.S. city had an occupy encampment. Occupy Chicago began within a week after Occupy Wall Street. I saw an article in the newspaper when it first started, and I was there the next day. When one becomes involved in a just cause, it is so powerful, energizing and joyful to find others who share your passion. I talked with the young lady who was said to have started the occupation. From my recollection, she was not a hardcore activist at the time, just someone who was so absolutely upset with the system and so inspired by the actions in New York that she just had to do something.

The Chicago location was in front of the Federal Reserve Bank at the corner of Jackson and LaSalle. After the Occupy Movement disbanded, a few friends and I would go to the same corner across from the Federal Reserve every Wednesday and hold our own vigil for monetary reform. Eventually, we had a contingent from the American Monetary Institute's Annual Conference do the same. The Occupy Chicago site differed from most of the other sites across the country in that there was no permanent or semi-permanent encampment. While there was no encampment, there was a permanent presence throughout the occupation. Twenty-four hours a day, people were present. The police did not allow sitting, lying down, or standing still, rendering the occupation a constant sidewalk movement in solidarity against a system that produced inequality.

This was a deep commitment from many people. A few of the major actions had numbers in the thousands while some of the smaller marches had only a hundred activists or even less. Although I went many times and joined in many of the marches through the downtown area, I never stayed overnight or did anything that would have put that level of abuse on my aging body. But others did, and I commend all the Occupy Chicago protesters for their dedication and sacrifice, as well as all others across the country who stood, marched and occupied for a more equal society. After a month of occupying the Federal Reserve Bank site, Occupy Chicago, on October 16 and October 22, 2011, twice set up a permanent encampment several blocks away in the public Grant Park. Both times the camps were broken up by the Chicago police with arrests made.[2] [3]

Similar camp breakups happened at all the major city occupations across the country. They were coordinated by our federal government and the very big banks that we were protesting against. "The crackdown, which involved, as you may recall, violent arrests, group disruption, canister missiles to the skulls of protesters, people held in handcuffs so tight they were injured, people held in bondage till they were forced to wet or soil themselves—was coordinated with the big banks themselves,"[4] reported author Naomi Wolf. The Partnership for Civil Justice Fund detailed, "FBI documents just obtained by the Partnership for Civil Justice Fund (PCJF) pursuant to the PCJF's Freedom of Information Act demands reveal that from its inception, the FBI treated the Occupy movement as a potential criminal and terrorist threat even though the agency acknowledges in documents that organizers explicitly called for peaceful protest and did 'not condone the use of violence' at occupy protests."[5]

Merriam-Webster Dictionary in 2012 named "socialism" and "capitalism" as the joint words of the year. The Occupy Movement had stimulated the American people to look for answers that they were not getting from the status quo. Finally the word "inequality" began to pop up on TV news shows and in political speeches and campaigns, mentioned in context to the disparity between those at the top of the heap and the rest of us.

During the 2011 Occupation, I stood across the street from the Chicago Federal Reserve Bank describing the debt-money system to a group of occupiers. A woman who had been walking by stopped to listen to my talk. After I finished speaking, she asked me if I knew Stephen Zarlenga, Director of the American Monetary Institute. I said that I had talked with him on the phone a few years earlier but had never met him. She then called him and took me to personally meet Stephen, who was nearby retrieving his car from a parking garage. I had first talked with Stephen Zarlenga a year or two earlier, after reading about the bank creation of our money as debt and finding it to be an incredible injustice. I then read about an upcoming Monetary Reform Conference that was to be held in Chicago and hosted by the American Monetary Institute. At the time I was immersed in anti-war and social justice activism. I was just beginning to get a grasp on the destructive nature of the debt-money system and I knew nothing about an alternative publicly created money system.

I thought it would be a good idea that those attending the Monetary Reform Conference walk over to the Chicago Federal Reserve Bank, which was only a few blocks away from University Center where the conference was being held. We could then do a demonstration there, activists and economists together, united in front of the Federal Reserve Bank. I called the American Monetary Institute and pitched my idea to its director, Stephen Zarlenga.

He thought it was a good idea, and so I began to recruit activists to take part. I didn't have much luck; many of those I contacted had so much on their plate with the wars and social justice issues that they were unable to see what I was beginning to see—that the present debt-money system had a role in both our proclivity for war and the inequality in our society. I did have a few close friends in the movement who would normally go anywhere with me, as I would with them. But even with some of them, it was difficult to get a commitment. Eventually, Stephen decided that he just couldn't make the time in the tightly packed conference schedule for the demonstration. Since I had been unable to get commitments from very many activists, we jointly decided that we wouldn't do the action at the Fed. Stephen was very gracious and did invite me to attend the conference, but I declined. I could not see myself with a bunch of economics PhDs. A couple of years later, I would discover how wrong I was to turn down that invitation.

Over the winter of 2012, Chicago was chosen to hold two huge summits in May 2012 for NATO and the G8, the world's eight top economic powers: the United States, United Kingdom, France, Germany, Japan, Italy, Canada and Russia. Currently, it is the G7, as Russia was expelled for its unlawful 2014 action in annexing the Ukraine Peninsula and Donbas Region in eastern Ukraine. With the more recent Russian interference in the 2016 and 2020 U.S. elections, Solar Winds computer hacking, the refusal of Russia to go after ransomware computer pirates and most recently the 2022 invasion of Ukraine, it doesn't look like they will be leaving the penalty box any time soon either.

Full disclosure: at the time I was sympathetic to some of Russia's claims in Ukraine. In retrospect after witnessing Russia's brutal assault and the brave resistance of both Ukraine-speaking and Russian-speaking Ukrainians to the invaders, I can now see that I was mistakenly influenced by the massive Russian propaganda campaign in the U.S. alternative media that I often visit. Despite whatever previous historical claims Russia had in Ukraine, there can be absolutely no justification for their present invasion to literally wipe Ukraine off the map and kill all its people for the greater good of Putin's Russia. This is all discussed in greater detail in *Spaceship Earth 101*. On March 17, 2023 Vladimir Putin was indicted by the International Criminal Court over Ukraine war crimes that included the abduction of children in Ukraine and their resettlement in Russia.[6]

China is also not a member of the G8/7 and I am unable to find a reason for this exclusion by the G8/7, at least that is publicly admitted. The G8/7 economic powers get together every year to foster consensus on global issues like economic growth, crisis management, global security, energy and terrorism. This may seem all well and good, and you might be wondering why the anti-war movement and Occupy Chicago organized to protest NATO and the G8 in Chicago.

Former U.S. Congresswoman and Green Party 2008 candidate for president Cynthia McKinney tells a story of former World Bank Director James Wolfensohn's speech to Stanford University Business School graduate students. In the speech, he described the 80/20 rule that he grew up with. He carried a paper in his back pocket with the 80/20 rule on it in his travels across the globe for the World Bank so that he would never forget it. The rule was that 80% of the world's GDP (gross domestic product) was to be enjoyed by 20% of the world's people, while the other 80% of the people were meant to get by on 20% of the world's GDP.[7] This 80/20 rule that Director Wolfensohn carried in his pocket was not an official rule of any country or organization. It was more of an unwritten rule, whose very real results were and continue to be manifested in the Global South/Third World countries. In Chicago we protested NATO and the G8 in support of a more even local and global playing field for all.

The Occupy Movement began, in part, because of a Canadian magazine ad that showed a female dancer posed on top of the Wall Street bull with a hazy background of protestors underneath the question, "What is our one demand?"[8] Years later and my answer to the question is that Occupy's one demand was for a more equal society.

Someone from President Obama's staff thought that holding two mega summits in Chicago at the same site in the same week would be a good idea. There were plenty of us in the anti-war and social justice communities along with others who disagreed. This early opposition over the winter did lead the Obama White House to move the G8 Summit to the secure and secluded Camp David Presidential Retreat in Maryland, due to concerns over huge protests. Moving the G8 protest to the secluded military presidential retreat site would keep those who did not believe in the 80/20 rule from physically protesting the G8 Summit on site. But we still had the NATO Summit at McCormick Place in Chicago as the site to protest the actions of both organizations.

Stephen Zarlenga told me about The Other Economic Summit (TOES) that began in 1984 as a counter to the G7 Economic Summit in London. Bringing together community activists, outside the box economists, and environmentalists, TOES summits were held as near as the activists could get to the G7/G8 Summits for about the next 20 years.[9] But in 2012 they were no longer being held. Stephen and I tried to get an alternative economic summit for Chicago in 2012, somewhat along the lines of what the TOES summits had been, in which we could spread the word about how publicly created money in the U.S. could be the first step in ending the debt-money system globally. We had finally secured a venue at a church near the NATO McCormick Place Convention Center. Then about two weeks before the conference I was informed by the church that they had to cancel our reservation for their meeting facility because the city of Chicago was not allowing meetings anywhere near the downtown area during the NATO conference.

Although Occupy Chicago had failed to get an outside permanent encampment, they did get some funding from a well-off angel and rented warehouse space over the winter about two miles from the Federal Reserve Bank. It was a space for meetings and congregating. Of course, the city and the banks were happy because the occupiers would be out of sight. Occupy Chicago held a People's Summit at their warehouse location during the NATO Summit. Stephen and I attended all the planning meetings for the People's Summit but were unable to convince the group to have an individual economic summit within the larger People's Summit, which mainly consisted of individual groups holding workshops about a wide range of important social justice and anti-war issues. Our reason for wanting to hold the Alternative Economic Summit was to demonstrate the role of the debt-money system in both our aggressive foreign military interventions and our inability to fund desperately needed social programs at home. Part of the reason we failed to get the Alternative Economic Summit was simply logistical because there were plenty of individual rooms for workshops but no area suitable for a large economic summit. But also within Occupy, there was a commitment to ruling with consensus. While great in theory, it is next to impossible to get a large group to completely agree on anything. Lacking consensus, without a large space at the warehouse and losing the church site, our hopes of an Alternative Economic Summit near the 2012 Chicago NATO Summit ended.

Stephen would never have been considered a member of Occupy, even though there was no membership. But he was a champion of justice and equality, and the Occupy Movement was certainly searching for a way to achieve them both. They used what was called the people's microphone. When addressing the group, the person speaking would say a short sentence or phrase and then pause. Those at the farthest point of earshot would then repeat the phrase to those further out. In very large groups, this process was duplicated until everyone had heard. It was ingenious, democratic and absolutely exasperating to use because the person speaking had to stop after saying a phrase or short sentence so that it could be repeated. I remember a large meeting in Grant Park where Stephen was given a chance to say in a couple of minutes what took him 750 pages in his book *The Lost Science of Money* to document. And they used the infernal people's microphone. Stephen was an accomplished public speaker, but he also had trouble hearing. Within the cumbersome system of the people's microphone, he was unable to effectively explain the present debt-money system and the publicly created money system adequately in the couple of minutes he was allotted.

A major benefit of all the planning meetings that Stephen and I attended was that we got to know each other. He encouraged me to write. I had written lots of online articles and letters to the editor in my local newspaper advocating social justice and against militarism, war and empire. After meeting Stephen, much of my writing began to be about changing our money system.

In 1991 Stephen Zarlenga, who had spent years in the world of finance, securities, insurance, mutual funds and futures trading, realized that something was not right with our money system. So he did what any red-blooded American would do—he went to work on the problem. First, he needed knowledge. He had a lifetime career of dealing with money and finance. But did that give him knowledge of our money system? Actually, no. He confided to me some years ago that when he originally began his quest for monetary knowledge, he thought all money should be backed by gold. He had built the distribution network for a leading American mutual fund concentrating in gold shares. It is to Stephen's credit and the good fortune of posterity that when he went to work on the money issue, he was able to abandon his gold-bug premise that money should be gold when it was proved wrong by the evidence he subsequently uncovered.

For the next eight years, Stephen researched and wrote. He asked questions. What is wrong with our money system? Why is it unable to deliver what society needs? Should money be gold? Why is there so much inequality in society, especially in the United States? Does the money system play a role in our inequality? And above all, what is the nature of money? If we can just figure out what money's true nature is, then we can construct a money system that conforms to that nature.

While he was researching and writing, Stephen split his time between a cabin in upstate New York and New York City, with access to the New York City Library. He helped to establish the American Monetary Institute in 1996 to further the cause of monetary research. When he finished his historical examination of money, he was unable to find a publisher willing to go against the monetary establishment and publish it in English. Conzett Verlag of Zurich, Switzerland, stepped up to the plate. He translated it into German and published it in 1999. Finally, in 2002, the American Monetary Institute was able to publish the expanded English language version of *The Lost Science of Money*.

A year after the NATO/G8 protest, I had not attended the American Monetary Institute's Annual Conference on Monetary Reform, nor had I read *The Lost Science of Money* either. One day Stephen asked me why I had not attended the conference. I told him that I considered myself an activist and I would be out of place in an academic conference. He laughed and said that while certainly academics did attend and make important presentations, the majority of conference attendees were ordinary people interested in monetary reform from all walks of life. He offered me what he referred to as a free scholarship to attend the 2013 Conference, with but one stipulation. I had to read *The Lost Science of Money* before attending.

I read *The Lost Science of Money* and attended my first monetary reform conference in the fall of 2013 in Chicago. I was shocked as

I began to read. It was not the dry book about economics that I had thought it was. Instead, it was a treatise on how to achieve social justice through reclaiming the ancient lost power of publicly created money. Stephen drew on monetary principles from ancient Greece and Rome all the way forward to the present bank-created debt-money system of the Federal Reserve. Studying Muslims, Jews, church scholars, Venice, Knights Templar, Bank of Amsterdam, Bank of England and the Federal Reserve, Stephen traced the history of money. He had discovered that, above all else, money is power. A system that conforms to money's true nature would put that tremendous power to work for the betterment of society, while a system that is contrary to money's true nature has done quite the opposite.

The challenges we face today are vastly different from those that the ancients faced. In *The Lost Science of Money*, Zarlenga looked at how the ancient religions and societies treated money. Examining the Old Testament in the Bible, the Koran, the ancient Celtic law book *Senchus Mor*, the Code of Hammurabi, Spartan King Lycurgus' Constitution, 1,500 years of Roman law, Code of Justinian, Laws of Charlemagne, Magna Carta, Aristotle and the church scholastic scholars, Stephen Zarlenga discovered a common thread: these ancients all understood that the structural misuse of society's money system was a foundational wrong. All of the above ancient texts, both religious and secular, either forbade the taking of interest for the use of money or sharply curtailed its use. The church scholastic scholars, such as Thomas Aquinas, in the 13th and 14th centuries referred to Aristotle's assertion that money by nature is sterile. It does not beget more money the way fields grow grain or cows beget more cows. The charging of interest or usury on money is contrary to the nature of money (created by society as a medium of exchange). Believing that monetary and economic questions are in essence completely moral issues, the scholastic scholars were successful for centuries in holding back the deluge of usury.[10]

Much the same as Aristotle, who used the term "chrematistics" for the manipulation of society's money system, Zarlenga believed that the misuse of a society's money system is on a par with genocide and deserves its own name. Following the lead of Aristotle and the church scholastics, Zarlenga's contention is that the term usury was never meant to be just a high rate of interest. Usury is the structural misuse of the society's monetary system and today's system of bank-created debt-money fits that original definition of usury.[11]

It was Jeremy Bentham's 1787 book *In Defence of Usury* that completely turned the definition of usury on its head. The word usury which had previously been used in a much broader context was reduced to the taking of a greater rate of interest than is usual or than the law allows. Later in the U.S., operating under Bentham's misdefinition, most of our U.S. states developed usury laws that limited the rate of interest. Laws limiting the rate of interest are not a bad thing. But by labeling usury as simply a high rate of interest, we had completely lost sight of the structural misuse of our money system. That is the Money Power in private hands, creating our very lifeblood as debt and with this lifeblood existing only as debt, thereby consigning our society to endless debt slavery to the Money Power.

When I grew up in the 1950s and '60s the individual state usury laws against high interest rates were in full effect. These all went out the window when the U.S. Supreme Court ruled in 1978 that nationally chartered banks could charge the legal rate of interest in the state they are chartered, regardless of the borrower's state of residence. Congress followed in 1980 passing the Depository Institutions Deregulation and Monetary Control Act that exempted federally chartered savings banks, installment plan sellers and chartered loan companies from state usury limits.

While your state may have a usury limit of 18%, it does not apply to banks or credit card companies that have a location in another state with a higher rate or no limit at all. This effectively voided all state usury laws. "In effect, what that really meant is that there are virtually no interest rate limits that are applicable to any type of bank, anywhere in the country, anymore,"[12] according to University of Utah law professor and usury law expert Christopher L. Peterson. Eliminating governmental limits on interest rates has put the public at the complete mercy of the Money Power. First by allowing the banks to create our country's lifeblood via the Federal Reserve System of bank-created debt-money, and then for those of us fortunate enough to have a few bucks left, to squeeze that out of us with sky-high interest rates if we are unfortunate enough to miss a credit card payment after getting sacked from our job. Bank-created debt-money is structural usury and a major factor, if not *the* major factor, in the obscene level of inequality in our country.

In *The Lost Science of Money*, Zarlenga argues that monetary control of societies has been achieved by confusing people through obscure theories about the nature of money. His one-sentence summary states, "That by mis-defining the nature of money, special interests have often been able to assume the control of society's monetary system, and in turn, the society itself."[13]

After reading *The Lost Science of Money* and attending my first Monetary Reform Conference in 2013, I made two discoveries: *The Lost Science of Money* is a must-read for anyone interested in a just society, and monetary reform is for the people. While the community of monetary reformers certainly opens its arms to invite academic economists to join the movement for publicly created money, most of us involved in this movement are just regular people from all walks of life who want us to have a money system that allows us to realize the American Dream at home and lead the way to helping all our neighbors across the globe put in place their own national systems of publicly created money. Our goal has been set—a just system of publicly created money instead of a private system of bank-created debt-money.

A Word about Cryptocurrencies

Being saddled for so long with the structurally flawed, inequality-producing, bank-created debt-money system has led many people to accept the first shiny new alternative that comes along—cryptocurrencies. They mistakenly think that there must be something inherently wrong with our present money system because it comes from the government. They believe that because our government has done so many god-awful things over the years, government is bad and should be replaced by the private sector. There is much truth to the first part of that statement that our government has often done the wrong thing, but our job as citizens is to change our government when it is misbehaving. Not to give up control of society's lifeblood, money, to the private sector.

As an anti-war and social justice activist, I have a twenty-year history of speaking out against a wide range of the most serious of crimes committed by our government such as war, torture, the exploitation of people in the developing world, and the war on the poor and working class at home. I have taken these stands not because I want to destroy our government, but rather because I want our government to live up to the promise upon which it was created—liberty, equality and democracy. Anyone thinking that completely destroying our present government will lead to an increase in liberty, equality and democracy is residing in a pipe-dream fantasy world. Yes, there is plenty wrong with the actions of our government over the last 230 years. But our job is to fix our government, not destroy it.

Money is a function of government. It is the responsibility of government to create a supply of money to facilitate the functioning of society. It is beyond appalling that our government gave up the responsibility to create our money a century ago with the creation of the Federal Reserve System and this will be covered in detail in Book Two: *History of Money 101*. But the solution cannot be to allow random others to create private systems of alleged "money" completely outside the control of the people and our government.

Former Secretary of Labor in the Clinton Administration Robert Reich and filmmaker Jacob Kornbluth started the nonprofit digital media company Inequality Media in 2015. They make short entertaining videos with Reich doing the voice-over explaining topics that relate to inequality in our society. "How Crypto Could Take Your Savings" is a short 5 minute video that should properly scare you enough to keep you from losing your savings on an "investment" in what Reich describes as the "crypto Ponzi scheme."[14]

Ponzi schemes are investment frauds that use funds collected from new investors to make huge payments to those that started the scheme in the first place. They promise huge returns to new investors, although there is no legitimate business going on that could generate any real income. They derive their name from a 1920s postage stamp speculation scheme concocted by Charles Ponzi.[15]

Super PACs (political action committees) with ties to the cryptocurrency industry have spent at least $31.2 million in 2022 Congressional primary races by June 21, 2022.[16] The crypto donations are spread out to politicians of both parties, indicating that this Ponzi scheme is quite serious about taking the American people for a ride. If that is not frightening enough, perhaps the cryptocurrency industry hiring of three former chairs of the Securities and Exchange Commission—Jay Claton, Paul Atkins and Arthur Levitt; three former chairs of the Commodity Futures Trading Commission—Jim Newsome, Christopher Giancarlo and Mark Wetjen; three former U.S. Senators—Bill Bradley, Blanche Lincoln and Max Baucus; and former U.S. Secretary of

Treasury Larry Summers as lobbyists to assist our Congress in taking a favorable look at their Ponzi scheme will properly get out collective attention.[17]

Once you get past the bells and whistles, cryptocurrencies are nothing more than a gambling scheme. The purchase of cryptocurrencies is the same as taking your mad money to a casino. There is a reason that criminals use cryptocurrencies to launder and disguise their criminal financial activities, but you do not have to join them. What happens to you if the whole thing goes poof in the air and disintegrates before your eyes? Who is going to make good to you for your crypto folly? The answer—no one.

The above was originally written in 2020, and then added to in August 2022, as Bitcoin was tumbling from a high price of $68,991 in November 2021 to $18,000 in December 2022.[18] On March 20, 2023 Bitcoin was at $27,705 after briefly topping $28,000 a day or two earlier. This is a Ponzi-style gambling scheme. If you want to participate, please only do so with money you are comfortable losing. Cryptocurrencies represent no store of value of any sort. For those that get in on the ground floor and make a killing, they do so at the expense of everyone else who comes in later.

As I update this on March, 20, 2023, the above was also written before the meltdown of crypto trading company FTX that occurred in November 2022. The company was founded by 27 year old Sam Bankman-Fried in 2019. FTX lawyers claimed the company's value was $40 billion in January 2022.[19] FTX went poof in the night and there is great doubt that there is anything left for those swindled investors who had listened to the siren song of celebrities hawking the latest Ponzi scheme on television and social media. Seinfeld creator Larry David, football superstar Tom Brady, basketball superstars Shaquille O'Neal and Stephen Curry, and tennis star Naomi Osaka were included in the civil lawsuit against FTX for their role promoting the Ponzi scheme.[20]

I have no reason to believe that these celebrities were nothing other than hapless dupes, glad to take another big corporate endorsement.

On December 13, 2022, FTX founder Sam Bankman-Fried was indicted by the U.S. Department of Justice for the following crimes:

Conspiracy to commit wire fraud, wire fraud, conspiracy to commit commodities fraud, conspiracy to commit securities fraud, conspiracy to commit money laundering, and conspiracy to defraud the Federal Election Commission and commit campaign finance violations.[21]

CHAPTER 7

PUBLICLY CREATED MONEY IN ACTION—THE NEED ACT

After Stephen Zarlenga researched and wrote *The Lost Science of Money* and founded the American Monetary Institute (AMI), he turned his attention to writing the American Monetary Act with fellow monetary reformers Robert Poteat and Jamie Walton—a citizen-written initiative outlining a system of U.S. publicly created money. Their work began with revisiting the *Chicago Plan*, a Depression-era call for publicly created money.

CHICAGO PLAN IGNORED

From the depths of the Great Depression in the 1930s, a plan had been proposed to change our nation's money from the bank-created debt-money system to a system of publicly created money as called for in the Constitution. The *Chicago Plan* began:

The great task confronting us today is that of making our American system, which we call 'democracy,' work. No one can doubt that it is threatened. However, the danger lies less in the propaganda of autocratic governments from abroad than in the existence, here in America, of ten millions of unemployed workers, sharecroppers living barely at subsistence level, and hundreds of thousands of idle machines. On such a soil, fascist and communist propaganda can thrive. With full employment, such propaganda would be futile.[1]

Originally proposed in 1933, the *Chicago Plan* was ignored by our federal government. The plan was put forward again in July 1939 by economists Paul H. Douglas of the University of Chicago, Irving Fisher of Yale University, Frank D. Graham of Princeton University, Earl J. Hamilton of Duke University, Willford I. King of New York University and Charles R. Whittlesey of Princeton University officially titled, "A Program for Monetary Reform." They sent this *Chicago Plan* to the list of American Economic Association university economists and 318 responded; 235 (74%) gave their general approval and another 40 (12.5%) gave their approval with some reservations. Thus, 86.5% of the nation's university economists surveyed approved of the *Chicago Plan*. Only 40 (13.5%) expressed disapproval.[2]

Even with 86.5% support from the university economics community, the Federal Reserve failed to acknowledge that the *Chicago Plan* even existed, let alone to either agree or take issue with its proposed reforms. President Franklin Delano Roosevelt and Congress also ignored it. Instead, they chose to apply a generous amount of lipstick to the pig (bank-created debt-money system) by way of the Glass-Steagall Act.

The Great Depression began with the stock market crash of 1929. Franklin Delano Roosevelt (FDR) was elected president to rescue us from the Depression in 1932. FDR took office on March 4, 1933, and two days later, on March 6, declared a bank holiday, shutting down the banks that were in the midst of a month-long run of people withdrawing their money. The reason that bank runs threatened the solvency of banks was because of the fractional reserve banking system. When a large number of people are fearful that they will not be able to withdraw their money, it precipitates what is called a bank run. My father had told me about his experience in high school in the 1930s. His economics teacher explained how the Bank Calumet Building in Hammond, Indiana, was constructed so grandly: eight stories, a limestone exterior of arches and columns with ornate cornices, and a stately two-story vaulted lobby, so as to show the people the solid financial foundation of the bank.[3] Shortly after this explanation was given to my dad's high school class, Roosevelt declared the bank holiday, and all the banks were closed. So much for the soundness of the bank-created debt-money system.

Roosevelt and Congress did what they had to do to continue the debt-money system. Congress passed and FDR signed into law what I have referred to as "the lipstick on the pig," the Emergency Banking Act on March 9, 1933. This allowed the banks to reopen on March 13 following FDR's first fireside chat on the radio the night before. In the chat, FDR assured the people that the banks would be safe with the new legislation. The Federal Reserve relates, "The Bank Holiday and the Emergency Banking Act of 1933 reestablished the integrity of the U.S. payments system and demonstrated the power of credible regime-shifting policies."[4]

The Banking Act of 1933 is commonly referred to as the Glass-Steagall Act after its two main sponsors, Senator Carter Glass and Representative Henry Steagall. There were two main components of the legislation. The first reform was the beginning of the Federal Deposit Insurance Corporation (FDIC), which insured our bank deposits with a pool of funds collected from the banks. The original amount of FDIC insurance was $2,500 in 1933 and today it is $250,000 per depositor per account.[5] FDIC insurance was absolutely necessary to shore up the crisis-prone bank-created debt-money system. The American Monetary Act became the NEED Act when it was put into Congress in 2011. If and when it is enacted, it will definitely continue FDIC insurance, although the need for it should not be anywhere near as great under the NEED Act as it is under bank-created debt money.

The second major reform of the Banking Act of 1933 was to separate commercial banks, such as we use for our personal and business use, from investment banks. This separation of the two classes of banks is what has been usually referred to as the Glass-Steagall Act within the overall Banking Act of 1933.[6] While the separation of the two classes of banks, commercial and investment, was an improvement to the flawed debt-money system, a far better solution would have been ending the debt-money system and beginning a publicly created money system such as the Chicago Plan proposed first in 1933 and again in 1939. Although the Banking Act of 1933 provided some reform, it continued the structurally flawed bank-created debt-money system and the nation remained in the Great Depression. It was followed by the Gold Reserve Act of 1934 that stopped people in the U.S. from converting their bank-created debt-money Federal Reserve Notes to gold.[7] This was necessary because the banks did not have gold to back up the notes. In 1971 President Nixon completely stopped the pretense that our money was backed by gold when he ended the international convertibility of our money to gold.[8]

Eventually, it was only the massive public spending beginning in December 1941 on the World War II war effort that finally pulled us out of the Great Depression. The *Chicago Plan* of publicly created money, proposed in 1933 and again in 1939, supported by the vast majority of university economists surveyed, was ignored and forgotten.

If we had only followed the advice of 86.5% of the nation's university economists surveyed, we could have ended the bank-created debt-money system in the 1930s. Instead, we got regulation (Glass-Steagall Act) that was ultimately abandoned by President Clinton, Congress and the too smart for our own good Wall Street lobby, in the form of the Graham-Leach-Bliley Act of 1999. The Graham-Leach-Bliley Act gave commercial and investment banks permission to work together fleecing the public again. Ultimately, this led to the 2008 Great Recession/Global Financial Crisis (GR/GFC) that devastated poor and working families across the country and the globe. The level of financial chicanery that led up to the Great Recession was considerable and will be covered in greater detail in Chapter 8.

The *Chicago Plan* formed the basis for the American Monetary Act written by the American Monetary Institute under Stephen Zarlenga's leadership. Stephen Zarlenga, Robert Poteat, and Jamie Walton fortuitously found a U.S. Congress member with both the vision to see the societal benefit of publicly created money and the intestinal fortitude to take on the bank-created debt-money system—Congressman Dennis Kucinich of Ohio. Kucinich and Congressman John Conyers of Michigan worked with the nonpartisan House Legislative Counsel on Money and Banking to transform the American Monetary Act into the National Emergency Employment Defense Act (NEED Act)[9] that was put into Congress on September 21, 2011, during the Great Recession/Global Financial Crisis. And yet again in 2011, as in 1933 and 1939, this legislative call for action was ignored by Congress without even being given the opportunity to debate its reforms.

The fact that the NEED Act was basically ignored by both sides of the aisle in Congress is in no way a statement on the soundness of the publicly created money system it would have created. It was written to conform to the Constitution and all other legislation at the time it was passed. It is ready-to-go legislation that easily can be updated by the Congressional Legislative Counsel's office, if necessary, to conform to legislation that has become law after 2011. We are now in 2023, confronted with additional crises whose funding solutions could be found in a new updated version of the NEED Act.

UNDERSTANDING THE NEED ACT

We began our discussion of our money system by saying that most of us think that:

1. Our federal government creates our money.
2. Banks loan us money that has already been created by our federal government.
3. The Federal Reserve Banks are part of our government.

Then we discovered that none of the above is true, although it all should be true. The NEED Act would make what we think should be true, true. It makes our money system resemble what we intuitively and mistakenly think it is now:

1. Our federal government will create all of our money. It will not be created as debt as is done now by bank money creation. Our money will be publicly created by the people's representative federal government—debt-free and spent into existence, as US Money, for the needs of the nation as determined by our Congress. The seigniorage or profit from the creation of our money will go to our federal government, benefitting our people and planet.
2. The present system of bank creation of our money as debt, referred to as fractional reserve lending, credit creation, or the money multiplier, will be decisively stopped. Banks will only be allowed to loan us money that already exists.

3. The entire Federal Reserve System will be streamlined. It will no longer be involved in supporting the bank creation of money as debt. The remaining parts of the Federal Reserve will be put into the Treasury Department as the Bureau of the Federal Reserve. It will become a part of the federal government.

The publicly created money system of the NEED Act will decisively end our present debt slavery to a system of private bank-created debt-money. This will then give us the public funds necessary for our society to live in harmony with our planet, committed to ensuring that none of our citizens are left behind hungry, jobless, homeless and unable to provide for their families. Of course, we as a people will have to do the work to bring these things about, but publicly created money gives us the ability to do so. Or we can continue to borrow our money from banks who create it out of thin air and other countries that pay their workers less than we do, putting our country deeper and deeper in debt, all the while accomplishing little in respect to the existential threats facing our people and planet.

There is plenty of work that needs to be done in our country. The American Society of Civil Engineers (ASCE) 2017 Infrastructure Report Card gave our 16 categories of infrastructure an overall grade of D+. Twelve categories representing 75% of our infrastructure: aviation, dams, drinking water, energy, hazardous waste, inland waterways, levees, public parks, roads, schools, transit and wastewater received a grade in the D range, indicating they are in "poor" condition and "at risk." Bridges, ports and solid waste received a grade in the C range, indicating "mediocre" condition that "requires attention." Only one category, rail, received a B grade, indicating that it is in "good" condition and "adequate for now." The ASCE estimated that bringing all categories of infrastructure up to a B grade would take $4.6 trillion over a 10-year span, with $2.1 trillion completely unfunded.[10]

While *The People, Planet & the Power of Money Project* was in the rewriting/editing phase, the ASCE released its updated 2021 Infrastructure Report Card.[11] America's infrastructure received an upgraded score of C–. With 11 of the categories remaining in the D range and spending having been very much neglected in the last four years, it does seem that the ASCE's score for this report card was what was termed in a different era a "Gentleman's C." Two new categories of infrastructure were added, broadband and stormwater, bringing the number of categories included to 18. Stormwater infrastructure was specifically added because of the "impacts from climate change" necessitating its inclusion. It was given a D rating. Broadband, for some unexplained reason, was not given a letter grade. But it was noted that 65% of America's counties do not have what the FCC defines as broadband, possessing only average internet speed connections. Also, 20% of U.S. children were not able to access a high-speed internet connection that would allow remote learning, especially important during COVID-19. Perhaps the ASCE could not find a letter grade low enough for a broadband system that excludes 65% of its counties and 20% of its children.

Keeping our planet in mind, it is also important to note that beginning in 2018 our nation's civil engineers officially embraced a policy of sustainable development:

The American Society of Civil Engineers defines sustainability as a set of economic, environmental and social conditions (aka "The Triple Bottom Line") in which all of society has the capacity and opportunity to maintain and improve its quality of life indefinitely without degrading the quantity, quality or the availability of economic, environmental and social resources. Sustainable development is the application of these resources to enhance the safety, welfare, and quality of life for all of society.[12]

When legislation was put into Congress in 2011 for publicly created money, the American Monetary Institute used data from the American Society of Civil Engineers, U.S. Conference of Mayors Water Council, Association of General Contractors of America, Federal Highway Administration and the American Public Transportation Association to conclude that the NEED Act would create 7.2 million new, good-paying, full-time jobs. Dividing 7.2 million by 435 Congressional Districts would give us more than 16,500 new, good-paying, full-time jobs for each U.S. Congressional District.[13]

These good-paying union jobs would have a tremendous effect on the rest of our local economies. Imagine if the leading industry in your area closed down. What would the cascading effect be on the other jobs in the entire community? You probably think that it would be devastating. Have no fear, publicly created money does not take jobs away, it adds them. Now imagine 10 new industries coming into your Congressional District, each one employing 1,650 people at good-paying jobs with union benefits spread across your district. Also, that publicly created money will rebuild the 18 different categories of crumbling infrastructure in your Congressional District. Is this something your community might be interested in? That is what publicly created money can accomplish.

What the NEED Act Can Do for Gary, Indiana, and Your Town Too

Gary, Indiana, has a population of 74,000 people. In 2019 *Business Insider* called it the "most miserable city" in the country.[14] As a lifelong resident of Lake County, Indiana, it breaks my heart to see Gary in its current condition. I remember when some of the Iraq War vets in the area held a community meeting in Gary against our ongoing wars in Iraq and Afghanistan. They brought in a fellow Iraq War vet as a speaker who had never been to Gary before. He began his talk remarking that the drive to the Genesis Center in downtown Gary gave him flashbacks of the Iraq war zone.

Based on an even distribution of new jobs throughout our Congressional District, Gary would get about 1,600 new good-paying jobs with a system of publicly created money. I'm pulling for Gary to get those jobs, along with every other town, city and village in our country. But we will all get more than jobs; we will get a rebuilt modern infrastructure system that will facilitate the growth of private businesses. These are but two of the benefits we will all derive from publicly created money. And let's not forget that our nation's engineers at the ASCE have taken the pledge to rebuild and develop sustainably in harmony with our Mother Earth.

If the NEED Act had been enacted by Congress in 2011, it would have squarely put the Money Creation Power back into our government as called for by the Constitution in Article I, Section 8. It would have established a nonpartisan Monetary Commission to determine how much U.S. Money needs to be created, in noninflationary/deflationary amounts, to accomplish the goals of full employment, public investment in our nation's infrastructure, retiring the public debt, stabilizing Social Security, and any other purposes as determined by Congress. All bank creation of money as debt would have been decisively stopped. The Federal Reserve System would have been streamlined, putting the retained parts into the Treasury Department.

With the NEED Act, The American Society of Civil Engineers Infrastructure Report Card would have been implemented putting 7.2 million Americans to work at good-paying jobs. Our federal debt would be repaid as it comes due with newly created U.S. Money, an absolute impossibility under the debt-money system. As of June 6, 2021, federal debt was at $28.4 trillion and on March 20, 2023 it is $31.6 trillion. Under the debt-money system, this can only be repaid by replacing the old debt with new debt.

The NEED Act would have provided interest-free loans to local communities for capital improvement projects such as roads, schools, libraries, sewers, and parks. Health care, education and the mortgage crisis were mentioned as items to be addressed for which money could be created, without specific programs in the bill. Climate change and other environmental concerns along with the cancellation of student loans would be topics to consider specifically when we move forward with a renewed version of the NEED Act. Just as the *Chicago Plan* was not given serious consideration by our politicians during the Great Depression, despite 74% of the nation's university economists generally supporting it and 86.5% of the nation's university economists surveyed supporting it either generally or with some reservations,[15] the NEED Act was also ignored in 2011 by our politicians, Federal Reserve and university economics departments. The result: our government and people continue to be saddled with huge debt and the all-important crises of our day remain unfunded or underfunded under the current bank-created debt-money system.

The entire NEED Act is available online for your examination.[16] The NEED Act was put into Congress in 2011 and the findings address that crisis stage in our monetary history. Those findings would normally be the first part of the bill and are available online. Since the economic conditions are vastly different today than in 2011 they will definitely need to be updated and rewritten to address our present and evolving crises.

THE NEED ACT: A BILL

"To create a full employment economy as a matter of national economic defense; to provide for public investment in capital infrastructure; to provide for reducing the cost of public investment; to retire public debt; to stabilize the Social Security retirement system; to restore the authority of Congress to create and regulate money, modernize and provide stability for the monetary system of the United States; and for other public purposes."[17]

---

* Findings are available online. [18]

"(b) Purposes – The purposes of this Act are as follows:
(1) To create a Monetary Authority which shall pursue a monetary policy based on the governing principle that the supply of money in circulation should not become inflationary nor deflationary in and of itself, but will be sufficient to allow goods and services to move freely in trade in a balanced manner. The Monetary Authority shall maintain long run growth of the monetary and credit aggregates commensurate with the economy's long run potential to increase production, so as to promote effectively the goals of maximum employment, stable prices, and moderate long-term interest rates.

(2) To create a full employment economy as a matter of national economic defense; to provide for public investment in capital infrastructure; to provide for reducing the cost of public investment; to retire public debt; to stabilize the Social Security retirement system; to restore the authority of Congress to create and regulate money, to modernize and provide stability for the monetary system of the United States, and for other public purposes.

(3) To abolish the creation of money, or purchasing power, by private persons through lending against deposits, by means of fractional reserve banking, or by any other means.

(4) To enable the Federal Government to invest or lend new money into circulation as authorized by Congress and to provide means for public investment in capital infrastructure.

(5) To incorporate the Federal Reserve System into the Executive Branch under the United States Treasury, and to make other provisions for reorganization of the Federal Reserve System.

(6) To provide for an orderly transition.

(7) To make other provisions necessary to accomplish the purposes of this Act."[19]

HIGHLIGHTS OF THE NEED ACT:

For ease of understanding, I use my own words to describe the following text, with the exception of what is within quotation marks. The text within brackets represents my explanation or opinion, as it does throughout the *People, Planet & the Power of Money Project*.

SEC. 101. EXERCISE OF CONSTITUTIONAL AUTHORITY TO CREATE MONEY

(b) The sovereign power of the sovereign people of the sovereign nation—the money is us. [Publicly created money represents the people, just as two previous forms of publicly created money in our history enabled us to win our independence and later keep our country intact. The Continental Currency represented the

American people's revolution against the British king, and the Greenbacks represented the American people's revolution against slavery and the secession of slave states. The story of the Continentals and Greenbacks will be told in Book Two: *History of Money 101*.]

SEC. 102. UNLAWFUL FOR PERSONS TO CREATE MONEY

Banks will no longer be allowed to create money as debt. The penalty for doing so under Title 18, United States Code, will be a fine and imprisonment for up to five years.[20]

SEC. 103. PRODUCTION OF UNITED STATES MONEY &

SEC. 104. LEGAL TENDER

New US Money will be created to replace Federal Reserve notes. Federal Reserve notes will continue to be honored until they are all taken out of circulation.[21]

SEC. 106. ORIGINATION IN LIEU OF BORROWING

In general, US Money will be created and spent into existence to fund government expenses as needed, above the amount of tax revenue in the Treasury.

"(c) Rule of Construction – No provision of this Act shall be construed as preventing the Congress from exercising its constitutional authority to borrow money on the full faith and credit of the United States."[22] In other words, Congress retains the constitutional power to borrow money, although it will not be necessary to do so. This is merely an affirmation of the constitutional power of Congress to borrow money that already exists and a requirement of government lawyers to ensure that the NEED Act conforms to the Constitution. Yes, the NEED Act is constitutional.

SEC. 107. RETIREMENT OF INSTRUMENTS OF INDEBTEDNESS

The Secretary of Treasury will repay our federal debt in full, as it comes due. As U.S. bonds and other instruments of indebtedness come due, they will be repaid with US Money.[23] [This is an absolute impossibility under the present bank-created debt-money system, in which we can only repay current debt by taking out new debt.]

TITLE III – RECONSTRUCTION OF THE FEDERAL RESERVE SYSTEM

SEC. 301. RECONSTITUTION OF THE FEDERAL RESERVE

The Secretary of Treasury shall purchase all net assets of the Federal Reserve System, including Federal Reserve Banks, from the member banks. Any reserve funds in the individual bank reserve accounts will be repaid to the banks in US Money.[24] [Not only does the NEED Act not appropriate any money from banks, but it also fully repays the banks for their Federal Reserve stock and present funds within the Federal Reserve. On the other hand any funds of this sort that were created by the Federal Reserve and deposited into individual private banks accounts should not be repaid to the private banks.]

SEC. 302. ESTABLISHMENT OF THE UNITED STATES MONETARY AUTHORITY

U.S. Monetary Authority will be established within the Treasury Department, "under the general oversight of the Secretary of Treasury," but independent of the Secretary. The Monetary Authority will consist of 9 public members, appointed by the president with the advice and consent of the Senate, serving staggered 6-year terms. No more than 4 members of the Monetary Authority may belong to any one political party.

The Monetary Authority will determine how much US. Money is to be created. The Congress will continue to specify with legislation what the US Money is spent on:

"(5) GOVERNING PRINCIPLE OF MONETARY POLICY – The Monetary Authority shall pursue a monetary policy based on the governing principle that the supply of money in circulation should not become inflationary nor deflationary in and of itself, but will be sufficient to allow goods and services to move freely in trade in a balanced manner. The Monetary Authority shall maintain long run growth of the monetary and credit aggregates commensurate with the economy's long run potential to increase production, so as to promote effectively the goals of maximum employment, stable prices, and moderate long term interest rates."[25]

SEC. 314. BUREAU OF THE FEDERAL RESERVE

The Bureau of the Federal Reserve is established within the Treasury Department, with a Commissioner and Deputy Commissioner appointed by the president with advice and consent of the Senate to staggered 7-year terms.

Two jobs for the new Bureau of the Federal Reserve.

1. Administer the creation of new US Money and its entry into circulation, subject to the Monetary Authority's determination of the amount to be created.
2. Administer the lending of US Money from the "Revolving Fund" (Sec. 403) to banks. Ensure that the creation of the money is the function of our government and fractional reserve lending ceases.

The Board of Governors of the Federal Reserve System will be dissolved and the Bureau of the Federal Reserve will take over those functions that have been transferred to the Bureau.[26]

SEC. 304. FORECASTING OF DISBURSEMENT REQUIREMENTS

The Secretary of Treasury shall provide daily, monthly, and annual disbursement requirements to the Congress and the public. They will "report to the Congress and the public regularly on the economic impact of disbursements of United States Money and the status of the monetary supply."[27] The people will be consistently informed of what is going on with our money supply.

SEC. 305. LENDER OF LAST RESORT; EMERGENCY PROCEDURES

The third undesignated paragraph of Section 13 of the Federal Reserve Act[28] deals with emergency procedures in the event of a member bank's or banks' insolvency, popularly known as "bailouts." Because banks will not be allowed to use depositors' funds, any use of depositors' funds would be a criminal act. While it should not happen under a publicly created money system, there is a provision in the event a bank breaks the law and it becomes necessary. Any sort of federal bailout shall only be done if the president has declared a National Emergency at the direction of 2/3 of the House of Representatives and 2/3 of the Senate.

SEC. 402. REPLACING FRACTIONAL RESERVE BANKING WITH THE LENDING OF UNITED STATES MONEY

All deposits at banks and savings and loan establishments (cash or electronic) will immediately become US Money when the NEED Act takes effect. No interest may be paid or accrued on US Money in a transaction account (checking, savings accounts, etc.). US

Money on deposit in transaction accounts (checking, savings) shall be treated as a "bailment" [the act of placing property in the custody and control of another, usually by agreement in which the holder (bailee) is responsible for the safekeeping and return of the property], and not an asset of the depository institution or a source of credit. Long-term saving and fixed-term saving Certificates of Deposit, that are currently exceptions to FDIC Insurance, will continue to be exceptions and not subject to FDIC Insurance, nor do the restrictions on paying interest apply to them.[29]

(2) OUTSTANDING CREDIT

(3) DEPOSIT IN REVOLVING FUND

(5) RETENTION OF INTEREST PAYMENTS

As loans made before the NEED Act goes into effect are repaid, the principal amount of the loan has already been converted from being a liability of the bank into becoming US Money and is owed by the bank to the U.S. Treasury. As such, when principal amounts of loans are repaid to banks, these principal amounts will immediately, when received, be transferred from the bank to a Revolving Fund created at the Treasury Department. The banks are allowed to keep all interest paid to them.[30]

(1) FRACTIONAL RESERVE BANKING ENDED

Banks will have a fiduciary responsibility for the money of depositors. "Fiduciary" means that the bank has a legal and ethical responsibility to act in the best interest of its depositors. Depositors' money may not be used to fund loans or investments. Banks may charge a reasonable fee for providing their deposit services.[31]

(e) United States Money as Source of Loans – After the effective date of the NEED Act, all lending by banks may be done only by lending of actual United States Money that is:

(1) "owned by the depository institution from earnings and or capital contributions by investors;

(2) borrowed at interest from the Federal Government;

(3) or borrowed at interest through the issuance of bonds or other interest-bearing securities by the lending bank, to the extent that such bonds or securities are structured in a manner consistent with the purposes of this Act."[32]

(f) Encouragement of Private, Profit-Making Money Lending Activity—The banks are encouraged to participate in "private, profit-making lending activity," but are prohibited from "the creation of private money through the establishment of lending credit against depository receipts, sometimes referred to as "fractional reserve banking."[33]

SEC. 403. ESTABLISHMENT OF FEDERAL REVOLVING FUND

A Revolving Loan Fund will be established in the Treasury Department, administered by the Bureau of the Federal Reserve, "for relending to banking institutions and for other purposes."[34] We have already learned that as the present debt-money loans are repaid to the banks, the banks will then immediately forward this paid principal amount of the loans to the revolving fund in Treasury and replenish the fund.

SEC. 501. DIRECT FUNDING OF INFRASTRUCTURE IMPROVEMENTS

"Before the effective date, the Secretary, after consultation with the heads of Executive branch departments, agencies and independent establishments shall report to the Congress on opportunities to utilize direct funding by the United States Government to modernize, improve and upgrade the physical economy of the United States in such

areas as transportation, agriculture, water usage and availability, sewage systems, medical care, education, and other
infrastructure systems, to promote the general welfare,
and to stabilize the Social Security retirement system."[35]

The American Society of Civil Engineers Infrastructure Report
Card[36] can be entirely implemented and funded as needed using
the NEED Act. The Monetary Authority will determine that
infrastructure monies are equitably disbursed to all states based
on population. The Social Security retirement system can be
stabilized.

SEC. 502. INTEREST RATE CEILINGS

The total amount of interest, fees and service charges on any loan,
with the exception of mortgages, shall not exceed the amount of
the loan. The maximum interest rate allowed is 8%.[37] [The average
30-year fixed-rate mortgage was 6.34% in 2007 and 4.45% in
2011[38] when the American Monetary Act and then the NEED
Act were written. It is possible that we might want to consider
reducing this maximum rate of 8% even more as we move
forward.]

SEC. 503. AUTHORITY OF FDIC

With the exception that already exists in the present system and is
made in Sec. 402 3(b) for long-term saving and fixed-term saving
Certificates of Deposit, "No provision of this Act shall be
construed as altering or affecting any authority or function of the
Federal Deposit Insurance Corporation."[39] After one year of
operation, the Chairperson of the Board of Directors of the
Federal Deposit Insurance Corporation will study FDIC Insurance and make recommendations to Congress as to whether it
needs to be strengthened or changed in any way.

SEC. 504. MONETARY GRANTS TO STATES

Each state will receive monetary grants from the Monetary Authority based on the state's population, representing 25% of the US. Money created in the previous year. In the first year, the amount will be 25% of the US Money anticipated to be created in that year. "The States may use such funds in broadly designated areas of public infrastructure, education, health care and rehabilitation, pensions, and paying for unfunded Federal mandates."[40]

SEC. 505. EDUCATION FUNDING PROGRAM

Within 6 months of enactment of the NEED Act, the Treasury Secretary in consultation with the Secretary of Education will make recommendations to Congress for a program to fund our education system on a par with other highly developed countries, "to sufficiently provide for universal pre-kindergarten, fully funded State programs for elementary and secondary education and universal college at every 2- and 4-year public institution of higher learning and create a learning environment so that every child has an opportunity to reach their full educational potential."[41]

[Cancellation of student debt could also be easily addressed here. All student debt that has been created with bank-created debt-money could simply be extinguished, based on the fact that the money lent to the student was created out of thin air. Student loans that were made with actual, existing money could be repaid by the federal government. Since we are trying to move forward with programs for universal public education, why not alleviate the significant hardship many of our younger people are experiencing with student debt, accrued before that funding was available for them?

For those who object because they paid their own way through school or they did not go to college, they will have the comfort in knowing that their children and grandchildren will be able to benefit from this program. If all that does not seem satisfactory to the majority of American people, we could also consider limiting the amount of Citizen Dividends (discussed below) to those receiving a substantial write-off of student debt.]

SEC. 506. SOCIAL SECURITY TRUST FUNDS

The NEED Act will cover any future deficits in Social Security and Disability Insurance Trust Funds.[42]

SEC. 507. INITIAL MONETARY DIVIDEND TO CITIZENS

Upon passage of the NEED Act, as it will take time to get infrastructure projects up and running, an infusion of cash into the economy may very well be needed. Coupled with the fact that the debt-money system has been oppressive to "the bottom half of Americans combined [who] have a negative net worth,"[43] payment of a Citizens Dividend should be established. Amounts of $10,000–$15,000 per person were considered by those involved with the NEED Act, but no specific amount is in the bill.[44] While a one-time Citizens Dividend should be considered, in Book Three: *Spaceship Earth 101* we discuss and consider Universal Basic Income as a form of Citizens Dividend.

SEC. 508. UNIVERSAL HEALTH CARE FUNDING

The NEED Act is available for any unfunded portion of a national health care plan.[45] Expanded Medicare for All can be a reality with the NEED Act.

SEC. 509. RESOLVING THE MORTGAGE CRISIS

Funding is available through the NEED Act for resolving aspects of the mortgage crisis.[46] That was 2011 and now it is 2023. It would be justice for there to be some sort of assistance given to the millions of American families that lost everything, in both the 2008 and 2020 crises, through foreclosures that were in many cases not their fault.

SEC. 510. INTEREST-FREE LENDING TO LOCAL GOVERNMENTAL BODIES

Interest-free funding will be made available for capital improvements to local and state governments. US Money will be made available in an equitable manner based on population. Mentioned are school districts and emergency fire services, but also included should be libraries, sewers, water departments, parks, roads, bridges, broadband, etc.

[End of NEED Act]

HOW THE NEED ACT GIVES AN IMMEDIATE, SEAMLESS AND NON-DISRUPTIVE OVERNIGHT TRANSITION FROM A CRISIS-PRONE BANK DEBT SYSTEM TO A STABLE GOVERNMENT MONEY SYSTEM

Jamie Walton[47] is a civil engineer in New Zealand. He has previously served as the acting director of the American Monetary Institute and is also an ardent supporter of publicly created money. Over the years he has made many trips to the U.S. and other countries in the quest for a just system of money. In 2011 Walton, working with Congressman Kucinich's staff, played a huge role in getting the NEED Act written and put into Congress.

Mr. Walton's paper explains the nuts and bolts of how the NEED Act would be seamlessly implemented overnight with no disruption to our financial and banking system.[48] The bank-created debt-money that currently exists would be instantly transformed into US Money. The deposits that were created through lending [outstanding bank-created debt-money] would no longer be considered a liability of the banks, thus dramatically reducing the risk exposure of banks. As the current bank loans are repaid by borrowers instead of the banks extinguishing the deposits that represent the loans as they presently do, the banks will send this repaid US Money to the Treasury Department, where it will be put into the Revolving Account created at Treasury by the NEED Act. Funds from the Revolving Account will then be available to be used to lend to banks for future loans.

Private investors, like you or I, will also be able to invest our money with banks to be used in making loans—if we so desire. This will have a degree of risk and our participation will be entirely voluntary. But money we deposit into bank checking and savings accounts will be put into safekeeping accounts, not to be used for issuing loans. Future lending will no longer create our money. We will no longer be held hostage to a system of money in which we are forced into debt for there to be money in existence for society to function. The following chapter will clearly illustrate how precarious our claim is to our present bank savings and checking accounts. Bank safekeeping accounts under the NEED Act would be infinitely safer.

PUBLIC EDUCATION DESPERATELY NEEDED ON MONEY

Monetary reform or publicly created money is not an attack on banks. It is rather an end to banks creating our money. Money creation is a duty and responsibility of the sovereign people through their government, not the private banking industry. Book Three: *Spaceship Earth 101* will discuss revising the NEED Act to deal with today's crises.

A year or two passed and I continued to work with Stephen Zarlenga. I attended monetary reform talks he gave in Chicago. He and I met with my then Congressman Pete Visclosky and discussed the NEED Act. We and other monetary reformers have reached out to all manner of people we thought were influential and could help the cause of monetary reform, such as Congress members and Senators, private sector officials, union officials, and social justice and anti-war activists. We have had very little luck. It seemed the more influential the individual, the less likely that person would be to get involved in supporting something outside the mainstream. "What does the Federal Reserve think about this?" was the first rejoinder I was usually given by those in high places. I could not even tell them truthfully that the Federal Reserve was against it, because the Federal Reserve has chosen to ignore monetary reform and the concept of publicly created money that is the NEED Act, instead of scholarly critiquing it.

The fact that we were not successful in amassing support for the NEED Act does not mean that it should be abandoned. People and activists have a whole host of issues that they are very passionate about, all of which relate in some way to our economy. My experience has been that decision makers, both political and organizational, have not been willing to step outside the box to challenge our money system. They all have so much on their plates now, that they are not interested in taking up a new cause unless we absolutely force them to do so. The only way to get moving on reforming our monetary system is to put pressure on them to do so. The only way to pressure them is for groups of citizens to create public pressure as they advocate for publicly created money. To mobilize, we need to educate our fellow citizens. Education of the public is absolutely necessary to move forward on monetary reform. *The People, Planet & the Power of Money Project* is an outreach to the public to get people involved in supporting publicly created money. We absolutely need the Money Power to be in the hands of the people to save our planet and ourselves.

Throughout *The People, Planet & Power of Money Project* we refer to an updated version of the NEED Act as *The NEED Act Revisited*. Colleagues at The Alliance For Just Money have drafted an updated revision of the 2011 NEED Act—the American Monetary Reform Act of 2022.[49] In Book Three: *Spaceship Earth 101* we discuss bringing the NEED Act up to date.

CHAPTER 8

FINANCIAL SHENANIGANS & THE CULTURAL HEGEMONY OF DEBT-MONEY

The NEED Act would convert our crisis-prone bank debt-money system into a reliable system of US Money in fully secure accounts. Most of us assume that when we put our money in a bank savings or checking account, that money continues to belong to us. Not true—the money belongs to the bank, and we only have a claim against the bank for it. Yes, there is Federal Deposit Insurance Corporation (FDIC) insurance of $250,000 per person, per account.[1] While that is certainly a good thing, there is a limit as to how much total money is in the FDIC account to fund a large-scale bank failure.

The FDIC Insurance Fund is charged with insuring the total of all savings and checking accounts in U.S. banks. At the close of 2020, the FDIC Deposit Insurance Fund was $117.9 billion.[2] On April 27, 2020, the Federal Reserve Economic Data website stopped publishing Total Savings Deposits. At that date, Total Savings Deposits were $10.9 trillion. It is not clear if Total Savings Deposits includes the deposits banks create when they create money that we have no access to.

The U.S. population is 330 million people, and the average household size is 2.53 people. This computes to 130,434,783 U.S.

households. Consumer financial services company Bankrate analyzed data from the most recent published 2019 Federal Reserve Survey of Consumer Finances (SCF).[3] The average or mean amount of U.S. savings account balances per U.S. household was given as $41,600 or $8,400.[4] Unable to find clarification at the Fed's Survey of Consumer Finances, it seems entirely possible that the higher figure includes the bank-created debt money and the smaller figure the actual money a household can actually access in their account. If we multiply the number of U.S. households by the smaller $8,400 average in savings, we arrive at $1.1 trillion in savings accounts for U.S. households. Whether or not money in checking accounts is included in this figure is not clear. Dividing $1.1 trillion in savings by the FDIC Insurance Fund amount of $117.9 billion gives us the sad news that only 9.3% of our insured savings is actually covered by money to repay us. This is a best-case scenario because if checking accounts are not contained in the above calculations then the 9.3% will be lower. If the $41,600 figure cited above is the correct figure for the average household bank accounts, then only 2% of our money is guaranteed. If the Federal Reserve's figure of $10.9 trillion for total U.S. savings deposits represents actual money in our accounts that we have deposited and not bank-created debt-money that we have no access to, then only a tiny 1% of our FDIC-insured bank accounts have actual money backing it.

Failure by any of the huge U.S. megabanks would certainly trigger failure by other banks down the line. The FDIC would very quickly run out of insurance money to repay depositors for their losses, whether they have FDIC funds to back up 1%, 2% or 9.3% of our money insured. But the bad news doesn't stop there. Actually the situation gets much worse than our Federal Deposit Insurance having only a tiny fraction of the funds necessary to cover all the deposits it insures:

In addition to the FDIC encouraging big banks to seize deposits during bankruptcy to maintain the stability of the banking system as it protects the FDIC Insurance Fund from being totally depleted by over-sized bank failures, depositors in the U.S. face an additional risk of loss under U.S. bankruptcy law among all sizes of banks that invest in derivatives. During bankruptcy, derivative counterparties receive 'super-priority' status *above all other creditors, including depositors.* This means that derivative holders will get *all* of the bank's assets before *any* other creditors, including depositors, are paid.[5]

— STEVE SEUSER, DC PUBLIC BANKING

Derivatives are financial securities whose value is derived from underlying assets or groups of underlying assets. The derivative is a contract between two or more parties, with the derivative getting or deriving its price from fluctuations in the underlying asset.[6]

I tried to get my head around derivatives when the Global Financial Crisis/Great Recession came on the scene in 2008. Their "super-priority" status in bankruptcy puts them ahead of all other creditors and depositors. What I discovered scared the heck out of me then, and still does. More recently, I have taken a look at Harvard Law School Professor Mark J. Roe's paper "The Derivatives Market's Payment Priorities as Financial Crisis Accelerator" published in the 2011 Stanford Law Review. Professor Roe's conclusion is particularly frightening: the super-priority status given to derivatives within the Bankruptcy Code encourages derivatives to accelerate financial crises rather than slow them down.[7] Unless I've misunderstood, derivatives were allegedly created to even out a crisis-prone system and Professor Roe tells us that the Bankruptcy Code actually encourages derivatives to speed up a crisis.

How many derivatives are there? Some estimate the total derivative exposure to be a quadrillion dollars ($1,000 trillion). The Bank of International Settlements had the "notional value" pegged at $640 trillion.[8] Notional value is the total underlying value of the position. For example, if you are buying 100 gold futures at $1,900/ounce, the notional value of the contract would be 100 x $1,900 = $190,000. The market value of the contract is how much it costs you to buy that futures contract. This market value estimate of all derivative contracts is quite a bit less, $11.6 trillion.[9] Quite a bit less, but still significant. The U.S. GDP or our total yearly economic output is $19.5 trillion at the close of the 2nd quarter, 2020.[10] The market value of all derivatives thus represents 59.5% of U.S. GDP, and the "notional value" is an incomprehensible 3,282% of U.S. GDP.

The $640 trillion notional value estimated by the Bank for International Settlements does not include certain non-cleared derivatives. Their inclusion would push the total notional value up to $1 quadrillion notional value of derivates. One quadrillion dollars equals $1,000 trillion, a number that's nearly impossible to grasp. The International Swaps and Derivative Association cites an International Monetary Fund paper that estimates "25% of the interest rate derivatives market, 33% of the credit default swaps market, and significant percentages of other types of OTC derivatives will remain non-cleared."[11]

What does all this mean? Under present bank accounting, our money in bank savings and checking accounts does not belong to us, but we have a claim on the bank for it. If our bank goes bankrupt and our bank owns derivative contracts, these derivative contracts will have first priority, or "super-priority" status *above*

all other creditors, including depositors."[12] We do have FDIC insurance on our bank savings and checking accounts, but the FDIC
Insurance Fund holds, at best-case scenario, 9.3% and at worst
case, 1 or 2% of the total money it insures.

While I was unable to find a total derivative figure for U.S. banks,
I did find a listing of exposure of individual categories of
derivative types by U.S. banks. I needed to bust out my calculator
again. The financial reporting institution iBanknet lists exposure
for the following derivative categories: interest rate, foreign
exchange, equity derivative, and commodity & other. I totaled the
big five banks' derivative exposure: JP Morgan Chase & Co.,
$50.5 trillion; Goldman Sachs Group Inc., $41.2 trillion; Citi-
Group Inc., $40.4 trillion; Bank of America Corporation, $35.1
trillion; and Morgan Stanley, $30.5 trillion.[13] Thus, total
derivative exposure of the big five U.S. banks is $197.7 trillion.[14]
We can assume that this $197.7 trillion is the higher notional
value and not market value. Worldwide, the market value is $11.6
trillion and the notional is $640 trillion (low end), making the
market value 1.8% of the notional. Applying 1.8% to the big five
banks, $197.7 trillion notional value would give the big five U.S.
banks direct exposure of $3.6 trillion in market value derivative
holdings. This direct exposure for the five biggest U.S. derivative
holding banks of at least $3.6 trillion indicates that if and when
these banks were to fail, the first $3.6 trillion of the banks' assets
would go to the holders of these derivative contracts.

Although derivatives are represented as a hedge for investors, they
are ultimately just exotic financial gambling instruments. They
represent nothing other than a bet that something somewhere
will go up or down in value at some future time. This is all fine for
financial gamblers and investors until something bad happens and
they are forced to come to the American taxpayer, hat-in-hand,
asking to be bailed out yet again. Even if we all agree to put up
with the occasional bailout for these huge banks, what happens

when bank bankruptcies push our savings and checking accounts to the end of the line? Do we really want $3.6 trillion in derivatives prioritized over our money when the big banks go belly up again? Especially when the FDIC insurance safeguarding our money represents only somewhere between a penny and a dime for every dollar of our money that it insures?

What exactly happened in the Global Financial Crisis/Great Recession?

After reading the preceding section on the super scary derivative mess, you might assume that your author has a thing against banks. Nothing could be further from the truth. My wife and I have bank checking and savings accounts. I want banks to be successful businesses that provide financial services to the people, but I do want the banks to stop creating our money as debt. Money creation should be done by our government. Perhaps a quick story will reveal my previous ignorance of banking, especially big banking.

Our weekly Saturday protest vigils in Northwest Indiana started in 2005 as actions against the Iraq and Afghanistan Wars and continued for 15 years, until we stopped in 2020 in response to the COVID Crisis. In 2008 I was standing on a street corner in front of the Highway of the Flags Veterans Memorial in Highland, Indiana, with a university philosophy professor. While our protests originally began against our country making war on poor people halfway across the globe, they quite naturally began to include the repercussions of these actions on our own poor and working class at home. The Global Financial Crisis and the chicanery of the big Wall Street banks had just been revealed to the public. My professor friend said, "Well, I guess we'll have to nationalize them." After protesting against the Bush Administration's wars for years, I had become much more aware of the war on the poor and working class in our own country in addition to our policy of economic domination of foreign countries. But even though my awareness was expanding as I became cognizant of the suffering that was being caused on so many fronts, I was blissfully unaware of the nuts and bolts of the financial flimflam that was at the root of the problem. At the time the concept of nationalizing banks was not something I really understood, and the concept of banks creating our money as debt was completely alien to me.

In 2008, the American public had just been informed that our entire financial system was collapsing because banks had lent money to poor people who were not financially qualified to buy houses. This was the lie we were told, and poor black people were the first to be blamed. The truth is banks had qualified people of all colors as being able to afford the homes they were buying. But the U.S. Department of Housing and Urban Development assessed that "borrowers in upper-income black neighborhoods were twice as likely as homeowners in low-income white neighborhoods to refinance with a sub-prime loan."[15] This would seem to indicate that black people were targeted with sub-prime loans. I knew nothing about bank money creation at the time. It was right at the start of the crisis, and I could not understand how a relatively few people going into foreclosure was anything more than a terrible tragedy to their families. I had been a real estate broker in the 1980s and '90s, and knew how difficult it could be for families to qualify for a home mortgage—so how could so many people be put in home mortgages that they could not afford?

Of course, people should not have bought homes that they could not afford in the first place, but these people were told they could afford the homes. Evidently, those annoying bothersome regulations, in which home buyers previously had to prove that they had the income and that their monthly expenses were within the loan parameters required to qualify for a home mortgage, were no longer in play. While there is certainly a degree of blame on the part of home buyers for allowing themselves to be conned, there is doubtless a much greater level of culpability on the part of the mortgage industry that engineered and oversaw the process. The crash of the entire system happened because the loans had been bundled together and could not be separated. That blame falls squarely on the mortgage and banking industry.

The problem began with the geniuses on Wall Street offering adjustable-rate mortgages to families with poor credit ratings, some of whom required interest-only payment at the beginning of their mortgages. When the mortgage rates went up, these families couldn't afford to pay the mortgage, and so defaulted. The same Wall Street geniuses also concocted schemes to bundle large groups of these mortgages together in what was termed a mortgage-backed security (MBS), also called a collateralized debt obligation (CDO), which they would sell on the secondary market to investors. This allowed those who concocted the scheme to then wipe their hands clean of the whole mess if something bad happened. Well, something bad did happen; mortgage rates went up and many of these families could no longer pay their mortgage. They went into default and the Wall Street geniuses who had concocted the bundling of the loans found that the loans in default could not be separated from the rest of the batch. One bad loan thus spoiled a batch of hundreds of good loans. What a tangled mess they had created, especially for the bank, institution or investors left holding the toxic batch when the music stopped and there was no chair in which to sit and unload the noxious asset to anyone else. Banks and investors sold mortgage-backed securities back and forth. Both banks and investors had purchased derivatives that supposedly hedged or protected their investments if the interest rates went up or down and if the mortgage-backed securities increased or decreased in value.

Regulations are those pesky little things that free market capitalists just hate. Their dogma is that the invisible hand of the free market will guide us. That is the mantra of capitalism. Years ago, I spent several years as a real estate broker. Individual deeds and mortgages by law must be recorded in the county recorder's office. Recording these documents requires the witnessed owner's signature verifying that he/she is the owner. Whenever a deed changes from one owner to another, it must be recorded so that there is a legal paper trail on file with the county of who owns the property. Mortgages put a lien on the property: "A claim or legal right against assets that are typically used as collateral to satisfy a debt."[16] Mortgages must also be recorded because they put a legal claim on the property. The bundling and creation of these derivative MBS/CDOs made all of this annoying recording of deeds and mortgages impossible, as they were sold back and forth between Wall Street investors and speculators. The deeds and mortgages were not recorded properly, putting ownership into question. The foreclosed properties could not be separated from the healthy ones. It was the wild west with no regulations. How our government allowed it to happen is beyond my comprehension.

When the Mortgage-Backed Securities/Collateralized Debt Obligation excrement hit the fan in 2008, the U.S. Congress passed a $700 billion bailout for the banks that set up a Troubled Asset Relief Program (TARP) to purchase failing bank assets.[17] But that $700 billion was hardly the extent of the big bank bailout. We also found out long after the fact that the Federal Reserve had given the big banks an additional $7.77 trillion in zero-to-low interest loans, and that the big banks had picked up an additional $13 billion profit just by taking advantage of these below market rates.[18] The $7.7 trillion given to the banks in low interest loans allowed them to blow the bubble back up. At the same time, these same big banks denied the vast majority of families in foreclosure the modifications to their mortgages that would have allowed them to stay in their homes.

But all of that is just the icing on the cake of the bank-bailout depravity. The Office of Inspector General (OIG) is the federal government office that independently audits, evaluates and reviews the Government Accountability Office (GAO) programs and operations. The Office of Inspector General then makes recommendations to promote the efficiency and effectiveness of the GAO programs and operations being reviewed. The OIG also investigates allegations of GAO employees committing fraud, waste, mismanagement and violations of rules and laws.[19]

Created by the Inspector General Act of 1978, inspectors general were put into different government departments to look out for the people's interests. If the ship of state is sailing along smoothly, we are essentially unaware of their existence. On the other hand, if the said ship of state is experiencing the rough waters of fraud, waste, mismanagement and violations of rules and laws, then we become much more aware of the existence of inspectors general than we would like to be.

The expert witness we are calling in here to testify was the inspector general assigned to the Economic Stabilization Act of 2008 that created the Troubled Asset Relief Program known as TARP. He presided over the bank bailout. The very day his job finished overseeing the bank bailout, Inspector General Neil Barofsky went public in the *New York Times* with a scathing indictment of the entire process.

EXPERT WITNESS: NEIL M. BAROFSKY

INSPECTOR GENERAL TROUBLED ASSET RELIEF PROGRAM

New York Times Op-Ed

"Where the Bailout Went Wrong"[20]

March 29, 2011

Highlights of Inspector General Barofsky's severe assessment of the Obama-administered Troubled Asset Relief Program (TARP):

Inspector General (IG) Barofsky begins by saying, "The government has declared its mission accomplished," calling the program remarkably effective "by any objective measure." But the inspector general strongly disagreed with the government's opinion, stating, "The bank bailout...failed to meet some of its most important goals." Yes, the big banks that were on the "brink of collapse" and had been given "billions of dollars in taxpayer money" not only survived but flourished, enjoying "record profits and the seemingly permanent competitive advantage that accompanies being deemed "too big to fail."

While avoiding a financial meltdown was all well and good, "The Emergency Economic Stabilization Act had far broader goals, including protecting home values and preserving homeownerships." IG Barofsky states that the Treasury Department changed horses midstream, by suggesting that the Main Street goals of protecting home values and preserving homeownership were but mere window dressing that had only to be taken into account when they were in fact a central component of "the compromise with reluctant members of Congress to cast a vote that in many cases proved to be political suicide."

The act would not have passed Congress without promising the preservation of homeownership. This "emphasis on preserving homeownership" became "particularly vital to passage." Congress had voted $700 billion for the TARP program with the understanding that it would be used to purchase troubled mortgage assets and that "Treasury promised that it would modify those mortgages to assist struggling homeowners. Indeed, the act expressly directs the department to do just that."

Almost immediately, Treasury shifted from a plan to purchase mortgages to the "infusion of hundreds of billions of dollars into the nation's largest financial institutions, a shift that came with the express promise that it would restore lending." Treasury went from helping struggling homeowners stay in their homes to assisting the banks in restoring lending.

[Why was it more important for Treasury to restore lending than to help people stay in their homes? Because under the bank-created debt-money system, if there is no lending there is no money. Treasury and every other governmental department did whatever was necessary to save the bank-created debt-money system. That is where our money, our country's lifeblood, comes from in this perverted system. When we stop using our credit cards, stop buying cars, stop taking out student loans and stop buying houses, money ceases to be created. While Inspector General Barofsky did not make this connection in his op-ed, that is exactly why all efforts were redirected to getting bank lending going while millions of American families lost their homes.]

The Treasury Department made the loans to the big banks with no policy to compel the banks to extend credit. There were no strings attached, no requirement or incentive to increase lending to home buyers. Even against the recommendation of the Inspector General's Office, Treasury did not even make a request that banks report how the TARP funds were used until after the TARP funds had been loaned to the banks and repaid. They then found out that lending decreased instead of increasing. Even well into the recovery, lending continued to decline. Mr. Barofsky even apologized for his inability to make necessary changes. In his words, he "could only make recommendations to the Treasury Department."

No help was given to struggling homeowners until the Home Affordable Modification Program was announced in February of

2009, promising to help 4 million families with modifications. IG Barofsky calls the program a "colossal failure" with only 540,000 successful permanent modifications and 800,000 unsuccessful families that tried and failed to get modifications through the program. As the one program to help homeowners floundered, 8 to 13 million additional foreclosure filings were forecast over the life of the program.

Treasury Department officials continued to maintain the program was a success, instead of trying to fix it. They could not publicly admit that their Main Street promise to the American people that homeownership and home values would be maintained would in fact be broken. Barofsky then quotes Treasury Secretary Timothy Geithner when he does admit the program "won't come close" to fulfilling original expectations, that it was not "powerful enough" in its incentives and that those servicing the mortgages were "still doing a terribly inadequate job." [21]

We, the people, were assured that the threat to our country posed by the huge banks would be addressed properly, yet no matter how reckless their behavior has been, they operate with impunity and have increased their assets by 20% during the crisis.

"In the final analysis, it has been Treasury's broken promises that have turned TARP—which was instrumental in saving the financial system at a relatively modest cost to taxpayers—into a program commonly viewed as little more than a giveaway to Wall Street executives. It wasn't meant to be that. Indeed, Treasury's mismanagement of TARP and its disregard for TARP's Main Street goals—whether born of incompetence, timidity in the face of a crisis or a mindset too closely aligned with the banks it was supposed to rein in—may have so damaged the credibility of the government as a whole that future policy makers may be politically unable to take the necessary steps to save the system the next time a crisis arises. This avoidable political reality might just be TARP's most lasting, and unfortunate, legacy."[22]

— NEIL M. BAROFSKY, INSPECTOR GENERAL
TARP

DISCUSSING FINANCIAL SHENANIGANS ON THE STREET CORNER

The geniuses on Wall Street had concocted this scheme to sell adjustable-rate mortgages to families who were qualified for the mortgages only if the interest rate did not go up. But adjustable-rate mortgages are just that—adjustable, and volatile. They bundled these "sub-prime mortgages" with the regular or prime mortgages, into these financial instruments called mortgage-backed securities (MBS) or collateralized debt obligations (CDOs), and then sold them to investors or other banks. It was a win-win for everyone involved on Wall Street. Unfortunately for the rest of us, they had failed to take into account what would happen if a few of these bundled mortgages went into foreclosure. Would it spoil the whole batch? Evidently, yes. The result was the Global Financial Crisis/Great Recession of 2008. It began in 2007 as things started to fall apart while the rest of us were kept blissfully in the dark until September of 2008.

There I was, on the street corner with the philosophy professor and our anti-war signs. He said, "Well, I guess we'll have to nationalize them." He was talking about nationalizing the big banks that were responsible for the crisis. That meant the government would take over the big banks and operate them, using whatever government money was necessary to keep them from failing. Because we are a capitalist country, presumably once the big banks were on solid financial footing, they would then be sold back to whoever wanted to buy them in the private sector. My knowledge of high finance at that point in my life was rather limited.

My professor friend was more of a socialist, and the standard socialist response to the crisis would be to nationalize the big banks. As I now look back at the crisis of 13 years ago, having the benefit of my friendship with Stephen Zarlenga and my own deep dive into monetary history, this broader look at the problem would now yield a different solution from me. "Nationalize money creation, not banks." That was Stephen Zarlenga's solution then, and mine now.

Yes, it is as simple as that: nationalizing money creation by publicly creating our money is the solution. That would give us a stable and adequate supply of money. It would also allow us to tell big banks that if they care to engage in risky behavior in the future, they should do so knowing that they can potentially sink or swim in the free market should something go terribly wrong. Under a system of publicly created money, we can survive their potential wreckage. We would have our own system of publicly created money, entirely separate from their financial shenanigans. We would not be held hostage to the bank-created debt-money system in time of crisis as we were in the Great Depression, the Great Financial Crisis in 2008 and continue to be now in 2022.

Money creation was not nationalized for the simple reason that the Money Power (those who create the money) and their apologists at the Federal Reserve have kept the system of bank-created debt-money secret from us. The banks weren't nationalized in 2008 because we are a capitalist country, and our immediate knee-jerk reaction is to keep our present system intact. So, instead of even considering nationalization, we just directly bailed them out, while most of us sitting on the sidelines did not understand what was happening.

The collateral damage in this fiasco: 10 million[23] American families consisting of 25 million Americans in total who lost their homes. These 25 million Americans would have remained in their own homes if we had a system of publicly created money in place in 2008. Now, in 2021, with the aftermath of COVID-19, we may very well see an even greater level of hardship fall on our people. Trillions of dollars have already been advanced by Congress and many more trillions of dollars will be needed to avert disaster. Some small businesses have received aid, but many have closed and will never reopen. The trillions of dollars being spent now are borrowed, and our government will pay interest on the loans. Under this debt-money system, this new debt, along with all our old debt, cannot be repaid. If we had a system of publicly created money, we could create and spend, debt-free, into existence whatever money is necessary to adequately handle the crisis.

Hegemony, Cultural Hegemony, Gramsci & Our Money System

Years earlier when I became involved in the anti-war movement, I began to see more and more of a word I was not familiar with—

hegemony: "Preponderant influence or authority over others: DOMINATION."[24] The Merriam-Webster online dictionary uses all caps for the word domination, much like the former 45th U.S. president was wont to do with his tweets. The all caps used by Merriam-Webster are meant to emphasize that the domination is complete within a hegemonic system.

Antonio Gramsci was an Italian intellectual and a founder of the Italian Communist Party that opposed dictator Benito Mussolini's fascist government between the First and Second World Wars. Mussolini had Gramsci arrested while he was a member of the Italian Parliament, in violation of Gramsci's parliamentary immunity.[25]

From his prison cell, Gramsci wrote and smuggled out his famous *Prison Notebooks*, 30 notebooks with a total of 3,000 pages. This was his analysis of history. Gramsci's theory of cultural hegemony was that the state and ruling capitalist class use cultural institutions to maintain power. The state prefers to use ideology instead of violence, economic force or coercion, although all will be used as necessary. Exhibit #1 for the use of force is Gramsci's own arrest and imprisonment for opposing the dictator. After 8 years in prison of a 20-year sentence, Gramsci, in rapidly deteriorating health, was released from prison to be hospitalized, soon to die at the age of 46.[26]

Regardless of these violent exceptions as needed, cultural hegemony propagates its own values and norms so that they become the automatic or default value of all and maintain the status quo of capitalism. Cultural hegemony is the realization of automatic default consent to the capitalist order, although the iron fist of violence is always available if needed. An example of that automatic default was the 2008 bailout of the big banks. There was absolutely no push of any kind to go outside the default parameters and question the capitalist system, or to even consider nationalizing the big banks.

Another example of Gramsci's theory of cultural hegemony was the attack on Medicare before it was enacted in 1965. It was attacked because the American Medical Association and none other than future President Ronald Reagan labeled it socialistic. Similar attacks had kept President Franklin Delano Roosevelt in 1938[27] and his successor Harry Truman in 1945[28] from passing national health and disability insurance to protect workers. Fortunately for this senior citizen and my 44 million co-beneficiaries of the Medicare system,[29] the cultural hegemony against change to the capitalist system was not strong enough to offset the absolute necessity of national health care for senior Americans. Hopefully, the day will soon come when we are able to include *all* Americans into the program that now covers only seniors. The passage of the Medicare legislation is examined further in Book Three: *Spaceship Earth 101*.

Once we are able to grasp the concept of hegemony, we can begin to understand that both capitalism and the bank-created debt-money system are hegemonic systems. Capitalism's hegemony is demonstrated by the absolute derision any mention of socialism is met with in our national discourse. Both capitalism and the bank-created debt-money system achieved hegemony by not allowing competition to exist. Of course, using persuasion first to eliminate competition is always preferable, but violence or the threat of violence has always been used as needed to maintain cultural hegemony. Our foreign policy is rife with examples of using economic pressure and force as needed to ensure hegemony across the globe. The simple fact that almost none of us understand how our money is created is the best example of the hegemonic nature of the bank-created debt-money system.

Full disclosure: My father, who was a wonderful father, surgeon and member of the American Medical Association (AMA), accepted and agreed with the AMA-sponsored position on the proposed Medicare legislation: that it was socialistic and bad for our country. Fortunately, both the AMA and Reagan were wrong, and my father and mother were able to enjoy long lives with most of their health care expenses as they aged paid for by Medicare. As I matured, I became convinced that all members of our society should have the benefit of the same all-inclusive socialized medicine that my brothers Mike, Alex, John and I received while serving our country in the military.

Although my father and I argued the subject of socialized medicine over the years, he was hardly an uncaring person. He simply provided his own form of socialized medicine to his patients. While I was in grade school, he had his medical office in a separate building behind our house and over our garage. Patients were always dropping off vegetables that they had grown in their gardens or delicious dishes that they had cooked. We graciously accepted them, and it was only many years later that I learned that my father did not send bills for his services to those who could not afford to pay for them. They were happy to occasionally reciprocate with stuffed peppers, nut rolls, pies, or veggies from the garden. Our acceptance of these gifts allowed his patients to retain their dignity. Even though my dad and I vigorously disagreed about socialized medicine for all, my father was a great man who provided his own personal version of socialized medicine for his patients.

Sun Tzu's Version of Achieving Cultural Hegemony

Sun Tzu was a Chinese general and military strategist who lived in the 5th and 6th centuries BC. His book *The Art of War* has become a classic on military strategy. His first dictum on strategy is his most famous and has been translated, "For to win one hundred victories in one hundred battles is not the acme of skill. To subdue the enemy without fighting is the acme of skill."[30] In other words, convince the enemy that resistance is useless.

While this strategy completely fits in with the concept of cultural hegemony used to propagate both capitalism and the bank-created debt-money system, it is quite possible that this commonly accepted interpretation or translation is incorrect. John F. Sullivan's analysis of *Sun Tzu's Fighting Words* gives a different interpretation of the difficult-to-translate ancient Chinese text: "Achieving victory in every [pitched] battle is not the height of excellence. Routing the enemy's soldiers [before they have an opportunity to form orderly ranks] is the height of excellence."[31] In other words, excellence is the annihilation of the opposition before they are ready to fight. Both translations fit the tactics of capitalism and the Money Power in maintaining their cultural hegemony.

Your author has been referred to as a socialist on more than one occasion, as well as a communist. These are terms of perceived vindictiveness hurled at those of us who make the effort to critique the capitalist system in any way, shape or form. I have certainly never considered myself a communist. As far as socialism I am open to the concept, but I have never considered myself a socialist. As an anti war activist and critic of capitalism I did write many letters to the editor of my local newspaper pointing out the shortcomings in the capitalist system and asking readers to consider adding a little socialism to the mix. I consider myself more of a pragmatist who understands that neither a pure capitalist nor a pure socialist America will ever exist. Capitalism is voracious and eats itself; regulations and a little socialism are absolutely necessary to protect it from itself and to make life at least somewhat bearable for the people who live under it.

Neither capitalism nor socialism can be truly successful within an overall system of private bank-created debt-money. We need a blended compromise economic system: we can have markets, but they must be tightly regulated; a social safety net for all, including our planet; and finally, a publicly created money system. We can live with that, can't we? Perhaps better phrased, we can't live without a blended social-economic system and a system of publicly created money. Maybe then we will be able to stop calling each other names. We have much work to do in saving both our people and our planet. Book Three: *Spaceship Earth 101* examines capitalism and socialism in much greater detail.

CHAPTER 9

IN DEFENSE OF PUBLICLY CREATED MONEY

As we have already related, both during the Great Depression of the 1930s and the Great Recession of 2008, our public federal government and private Federal Reserve System chose to completely ignore proposed systems of publicly created money. By ignoring proposals for publicly created money, both our government and the Federal Reserve System have clearly demonstrated that continuing the bank-created debt-money system is of much greater importance to them than considering what type of money system might actually be best for our country.

Studies on the efficacy of a publicly created money system were undertaken before and after the NEED Act was put into Congress. Conducted by respected economists, the studies showed that publicly created money would pay off our federal debt, create millions of new, good-paying jobs rebuilding our infrastructure, create a full-employment economy, reduce private debt, and keep our economy on an even keel, helping to avoid disruptive harmful recessions and depressions. The following two studies were written by economists for the benefit of other economists. You and I do not have to be able to understand all of their technical language to understand their conclusions.

NICK EGNATZ

THE YAMAGUCHI STUDY: MONEY OUT OF NOTHING

The System Dynamics Method was developed by a pioneer in engineering and computer design Jay W. Forrester in the late 1950s. Using simulation modeling based on feedback systems theory, it is an analytical approach that complements systems thinking.[1] Japanese economist Kaoru Yamaguchi is a member of the System Dynamics Society and has used this type of computer modeling to examine our money system with an emphasis on sustainability, both in relationship to our natural environment and our modern economy.[2]

Dr. Yamaguchi received his doctorate in economics from the University of California, Berkeley. He was with the prestigious Doshisha University, Kyoto, Japan, when he began to research and write on publicly created money. In 2013, he was terminated from his faculty position at Doshisha.[3]

Dr. Yamaguchi's termination from his university position included the termination of the classes he was teaching using the System Dynamics Method of analysis. Doshisha simply did away with all the courses he was teaching. It was not until 2018, five years after being fired by Doshisha University, that this internationally distinguished economist was again given a full professorship, this time at Ankara University, Turkey.[4]

Doshisha terminated Dr. Yamaguchi by canceling his System Dynamics classes, but it appears doubtful that all of a sudden Doshisha University had a problem with the System Dynamics method of computer modeling. It seems much more likely that Doshisha's problem was that the results obtained using System Dynamics offered compelling evidence that a publicly created system of money was far superior to the present crisis-prone, bank-created debt-money system. We don't know the answer, but further evidence will be presented in the following chapter showing that economists do risk career suicide whenever they

154

choose to speak out against the bank-created debt-money system.

Many letters were written by distinguished academics across the globe beseeching Doshisha University to reinstate Dr. Yamaguchi. This is how Congressman Dennis Kucinich, who put a system of publicly created money (NEED Act) into the U.S. Congress, closed his entreaty to Doshisha University to reinstate Dr. Yamaguchi:

> Herein is the relevance of Dr. Yamaguchi's work and his vision: It is only by being able to unchain ourselves from the wheel of endless debt that society can aspire to higher levels of social evolution. Professor Yamaguchi may someday win the Nobel Prize for economics, given his extraordinary insight into system dynamics. It would be a tragedy as he strives to continue to make worldwide contributions to monetary science if his own university would turn its back on him and his work. Let Doshisha University be known as a world-renowned sanctuary of academic freedom for a visionary man, not a graveyard where great ideas have come to die. Thank you for your careful consideration of my humble plea on behalf of a great man.[5]

I have had the honor of meeting Dr. Yamaguchi on two occasions and listening to his presentations at the American Monetary Institute's Annual Conferences on Monetary Reform. His entire life is devoted to sustainability achieved with a System Dynamics approach that in turn gives us a system of publicly created money. He lives in an ecologically designed log house on Awaji Island, Japan. His approach begins with the observation that our democracies are doomed to failure if we do not take into account the interests of three very important parties—children, the natural world and future generations. Instead of ignoring children, the natural world and future generations in his calculations, Dr. Yamaguchi's entire body of work puts them front and center.

Before the NEED Act was put into Congress in 2011, it was called the American Monetary Act. Dr. Yamaguchi's 2011 paper, *Workings of A Public Money System of Open Macroeconomies – Modeling the American Monetary Act Completed*, put both the present debt-money system and the reforms of what would later be named the NEED Act into his System Dynamics Computer Model of the economy. Dr. Yamaguchi describes our present bank-created debt-money system as follows:

> Commercial banks then create credits under a fractional reserve banking system by making loans to producers and consumers. These credits constitute a great portion of the money supply. In this way, money and credits are only created when commercial banks and government as well as producers and consumers come to borrow at interest. Under such circumstances, if all debts are repaid, money ceases to exist. This is an essence of a debt money system. The process of creating money is known as money out of nothing.[6]

In his analysis, Yamaguchi concluded:

1. The 2008 Great Recession/Global Financial Crisis was the result of a "systemic failure of the current *debt-money system*."
2. Within the debt-money system, repayment or liquidation of debts "triggers recessions, unemployment and foreign economic recessions contagiously."

3. Repayment or liquidation of debts under an alternative public money system "can be put into effect without causing recessions, unemployment and inflation as well as foreign recessions."

4. Finally, public money policies are "much simpler and more effective than the complicated Keynesian policies" [used to lessen the disastrous results of the privately created debt-money system]. Public money policies "incorporate balancing feedback loops such as anti-recession and anti-inflation" thus "curbing GDP gap and inflation."[7]

JOHN MAYNARD KEYNES MERELY REARRANGES THE DECK CHAIRS ON THE TITANIC

British economist John Maynard Keynes was and still is largely considered by many economists as a sort of god of modern economics. Keynes published his masterwork *The General Theory of Employment, Interest and Money* in 1936. The book basically renounced his prior allegiance to classical economics. His general theory, in a nutshell, is that an inverse relationship exists between unemployment and inflation and that governments should manipulate fiscal policy [interest rates] to ensure a balance between the two.[8]

Dr. Keynes was certainly correct that within the bank-created debt-money system government needed to step up to the plate and spend money when the private sector was unable to keep people employed. Unfortunately, Dr. Keynes was never able to think outside the box of the bank-created debt-money system. Much like those who rearranged the deck chairs on the steamship *Titanic* as it began to sink, Dr. Keynes and the professional economics community during both the Great Depression and the Great Recession, have never considered changing from a private bank-created system of debt-money to a just system of sovereign, publicly created money.

It is May 9, 2022, as I go over editing and the number one economic crisis for poor and working class Americans today is inflation and the uncertainty it brings. Those on the political right are doing their best to try and score points by blaming President Joe Biden's $1.9 trillion COVID relief bill, the American Rescue Plan[9] for the inflation. At the same time these same alleged experts are complaining that the recent rate hikes by the Federal Reserve are the reason for the inflation, although within the bank-created debt-money system, as Dr. Keynes has told us, this is the main tool the Federal Reserve has to fight inflation. As referenced in Chapter 4, Richard Werner and Kang-Soek Lee in their paper *Reconsidering Monetary Policy: An Empirical Examination of the Relationship Between Interest Rates and Nominal GDP Growth in the U.S., U.K., Germany and Japan*[10] demonstrate that fighting inflation by raising interests rates is what I would call a fool's errand. Simply put, the bank-created debt-money system is poorly equipped to either fight inflation or to pay for fighting pandemics or crises of any kind. The NEED Act would give us what we need to pay for both relieving crises and controlling inflation—publicly created money.

DR. YAMAGUCHI COMPARES A PUBLIC MONEY SYSTEM WITH THE DEBT-MONEY SYSTEM:

- A public money system gives society a stable money supply and stable prices, while the debt-money system gives society bubbles, credit crunches, inflation and deflation.
- A public money system gives society financial stability and a stable banking system, while the debt-money system gives society booms and busts in the business cycle.

- A public money system gives society full employment, while the debt-money system gives the people involuntary unemployment.
- A public money system would repay the current government debt without incurring any new government debt. The debt-money system has a built-in feature of debt accumulation leading to recession and unemployment.
- While there is a built-in level of inequality between workers and capitalists within both a capitalist public money system and a capitalist debt-money system, the capitalist debt-money system adds on the major layer of inequality that exists between financiers and the rest of us.
- Under a public money system sustainability is possible, while under the debt-money system we have a future of accumulated debt leading to forced growth and environmental destruction.[11]

THE CHICAGO PLAN REVISITED

Deputy Chief of Modeling at the International Monetary Fund, Michael Kumhof, and colleague Jaromir Benes put the monetary reforms that were in both the *Chicago Plan* and the NEED Act into the same computer modeling system used by Federal Reserve economists when they make their predictions (dynamic stochastic general equilibrium—DSGE models).[12] They discovered that under the publicly created money system of the *Chicago Plan* that the NEED Act was based on, we would experience:

1. Much better control of a major source of business cycle fluctuations than the sudden increases and contractions of bank credit and money supply [under the bank-created debt-money system].
2. Complete elimination of bank runs.

3. Dramatic reduction of the (net) public debt.
4. Dramatic reduction of private debt, as money creation no longer requires simultaneous debt creation.[13]

They also found that publicly created money would do all of the above with zero inflation. Publicly created money would better control the recessions, depressions, financial crises and panics that the debt-money system visits upon us with great regularity. There would be no bank runs, and both public and private debt would be dramatically reduced.

Kumhof and Benes assure us that credit will continue to exist: "Credit, especially socially useful credit that supports real physical investment activity, would continue to exist. What would cease to exist however is the proliferation of credit created, at the almost exclusive initiative of private institutions, for the sole purpose of creating an adequate money supply that can easily be created debt-free."[14] Dr. Kumhof left the International Monetary Fund several years ago for his new job at the Bank of England as Senior Research Advisor in the Research Hub.[15]

While Dr. Kumhof, Dr. Yamaguchi, Dr. Werner and other economists who have made presentations at the AMI Annual Conferences are all wonderful gentlemen, much of their presentations and papers soon turn to the much more technical language of economists. It can be very difficult to follow them when they get going. I relate this so that you will not get discouraged if and when you decide to read their papers. At a certain point, they are no longer talking to us; instead, they are talking to the economics community in the language that only this community understands.

Kumhof/Benes Examine Government versus Private Control over Money Issuance

Why do we have private control of our money? How did the first money originate? Was it issued privately or publicly? The bible of modern economics, Adam Smith's *The Wealth of Nations*, tells a story of private money creation that began as barter and as a matter of convenience turned into exchanging money for goods instead of goods for goods. Kumhof/Benes in *The Chicago Plan Revisited* provide an academic counter to Mr. Smith's commonly accepted, but inaccurate narrative.

In 1776, Adam Smith's *The Wealth of Nations* explained how money originated as an outgrowth of ancient barter economies. A butcher would trade his meat for a baker's bread or a tailor's clothes and the baker, tailor and other tradespeople would do likewise. He described it as a cumbersome, unwieldy process that was replaced when someone came up with the idea of money to be used to expedite the transfer of goods and services within a society.[16] Carl Menger, founder of the Austrian School of Economics, echoed Smith's claim of money being the outgrowth of barter economies.[17] The problem with this story of money originating as a refinement or replacement of ancient barter economies is that it has no basis in fact. It was simply conjured from the imagination of Mr. Smith and has become a staple of what passes for modern economic thought.

American anthropologist David Graeber's *Debt – The First 5,000 Years* (2011) found there are no anthropological or historical examples of ancient barter economies. The first transactions were based on intricate credit systems typically represented in agricultural commodities such as cattle and grain and, in some societies, tools.[18] These elaborate credit systems represented the needs of the state as described by William Ridgeway, *The Origin of Metallic Currency and Weight Standards* in 1892;[19] Stephen Zarlenga, *The Lost Science of Money*, in 2002;[20] Paul Einzig, *Prim-*

itive Money, in 1966;[21] Bernhard Laum, *Heiliges Geld*, in 1924;[22] and A. Hingston Quiggin, *A Survey of Primitive Money*, in 1949.[23] While Mr. Smith in 1776, along with much of today's economics profession, makes the unsubstantiated assertion that private trading relationships, instead of these documented early versions of public money, were the first forms of money and thus justifies the bank-created debt-money system we have now. This is the basis for mainstream economic thought, despite the complete lack of evidence supporting early barter economies and the substantial evidence above that the earliest forms of money were a creation of the state.

While all of the above books documenting the first money systems as creations of the state were written after Mr. Smith wrote *The Wealth of Nations*, he did have many of the same historical sources used by those that later countered his imagined tale of barter as the first form of money. But modern economists who continue to follow Mr. Smith's inaccurate depiction of the first money systems as barter have no excuse for their muddled scholarship.

In 1895, American monetary historian Alexander Del Mar called out this ignorance of the past: "As a rule political economists do not take the trouble to study the history of money; it is much easier to imagine it and to deduce the principles of this imaginary knowledge."[24] Kumhof /Benes and Zarlenga tell us that studying the origins of money is important because it leads to a consideration of what is the nature of money.[25] This takes us to the crucial question of who should control the issuance of money—the people through their government, or private banking interests?

Ever since Smith published *The Wealth of Nations* in 1776, the story of barter being the origin of money has been embraced by the economics profession as a justification for the private issuance of money, all without a shred of evidence to its veracity. This has resulted in monetary systems of money as a commodity, such as gold or silver. And even though the government controlled the issue of the money as coins, the gold and silver tended to end up in the hands of the wealthy. The wealthy then lent the money out at interest, which led to the creation of the fractional reserve system of banking and money creation in Europe. According to Kumhof and Benes, "The historically and anthropologically correct state/institutional story for the origins of money is one of the arguments supporting the government issuance and control of money under the rule of law."[26] A question we must ask ourselves is, why has there been no response from Federal Reserve economists on these and other important studies supporting publicly created money?

CHAPTER 10

A PLEA TO THE ECONOMICS PROFESSION

We have talked about how money is necessary for survival in the modern world. No one can doubt this. In fact, money is the most necessary thing for our survival in modern society. While clean air and water may be naturally provided by our Mother Earth, there is little doubt that the very existence of clean air and water is under assault by humanity. As such society collectively uses money to counter the assault on clean air and water. Certainly in a capitalist society we are largely on our own to provide the needed food, shelter and clothing and we use money for this purpose. If simple existence can't be accomplished without money, then existence above a subsistence level must certainly also require money. If the present bank-created debt-money system is unable to achieve good results for at least half of our people, should we not consider an alternative system of publicly created money? A system that has been vetted by top economists, Yamaguchi and Kumhof & Benes, as documented in the preceding chapter. A system that has proven its mettle in both the ancient world and our own country's past, as will be documented in Book Two: *History of Money 101*.

American sociologist Barrington Moore warned us in his 1966 book *Social Origins in the Making of Dictatorship and Democracy: Lord and Peasant in the Making of the Modern World* of what we can now expect from the dominant monetary establishment as we begin to examine the bank-created debt-money system:

> In any society, the dominant groups are the ones with the most to hide about the way society works. Very often therefore truthful analyses are bound to have a critical ring, to seem like exposures rather than objective statements…. For all students of human society sympathy with the victims of historical processes and skepticism about the victors' claims provide essential safeguards against being taken in by the dominant mythology. A scholar who tries to be objective needs these feelings as part of his working equipment.[1]

Proceeding is not for the faint of heart but proceed we must. Hopefully, more members of the economics profession will make the choice to get on the right side of history and join the movement for publicly created money. Consider this as a challenge to the economics profession—begin a critical examination of the debt-money system in America and the rest of the world and support the change to a moral, just system of publicly created money, if it becomes apparent that such a system would better serve both our people and our planet.

Knowledge of our monetary history at both the citizen and economist level has been effectively wiped almost clean from our collective memory bank over the last century. It was just over a century ago that the Federal Reserve System was created in 1913. Before the Fed was created our people had a better understanding of bank money creation than we do now. Henry Macleod's textbook, quoted earlier and originally published in 1856, correctly described the bank creation of the money system. This was available to the people a century and a half ago. He wrote:

> Nothing can be more unfortunate or misleading than the expression...that banking is only the 'Economy of Capital', and that the business of a banker is to borrow money from one set of persons and lend it to another set.... The business of banking is not to lend money, but to create Credit... And all these Credits are in the ordinary language and practice of commerce exactly equal to so much cash or Currency.... These banking Credits are, for all practical purposes, the same as Money.[2]

Richard Werner used Macleod's quote in *A lost century in economics: Three theories of banking and the conclusive evidence* to illustrate that before the creation of the Federal Reserve System in 1913, the political economists of the time had a much better understanding of money creation—as debt or credit by private banks (Credit Creation Theory)—than the modern economics profession does today.

Currently, the Financial Intermediation Theory (banks are financial intermediaries taking in deposits and loaning them out, they do not create money) is predominant within the economics profession. As discussed earlier, Werner goes on to prove that the Credit Creation Theory of banking (bank creation of debt-money) is actually how our money is created.[3]

In his paper *How do banks create money, and why can other firms not do the same? An explanation for the coexistence of lending and deposit-taking*, Werner argues:

> One reason for the neglect of the institutional and operational details of banks in the research literature in the past decades is likely the fact that no law, statute or bank regulation explicitly grants banks the right (usually considered a sovereign prerogative) to create and allocate the money supply.... There is also virtually no scholarly literature on the question of which regulations precisely enable banks to create money.... As a result, many economists, finance researchers, lawyers, accountants, even bankers, let alone the general public, have not been aware of the role of banks as creators and allocators of the money supply.[4]

Let's see if we can understand what Dr. Werner is saying. Economists do not write about the details of banks creating debt-money because no law, statute or bank regulation gives banks the right to create our money supply. Money creation is normally and legally considered a sovereign privilege of the nation's government. There is almost no scholarly literature documenting which laws, statutes or regulations grant banks the power to create our money because no such laws, statutes or regulations exist. As a result, many of those at the top of the academic, government, financial, legal, accounting and banking food chain are as ignorant as the general public on the subject of banks creating and controlling our money.

Of course, the one U.S. law that allows the banks to continue in the practice of banking within the umbrella of the Federal Reserve System and thus create money as debt is the Federal Reserve Act of 1913. That brings us to the U.S. Constitution and the statement which squarely puts the power to create money with Congress: "The Congress shall have Power...To coin [create] Money, regulate the Value thereof" (Art. I, Sec. 8). Since the Power to create (coin) money is vested to the Congress in the

Constitution, it cannot be given away by Congress without a Constitutional amendment. While regulation of banks is certainly within the purview of the Congress, giving away the power to create money to banks is not something that the Constitution empowers Congress to do without specifically amending the Constitution. Book Two: *History of Money*, Chapter 6: *The U.S. Constitution and Money Creation* continues this argument in greater detail.

"The bottom half of Americans combined have a negative net worth."[5] America is the richest nation on Earth and yet, even before the disastrous effects of COVID-19, half of our people have no net worth. This from economist Gabriel Zucman's analysis of Emmanuel Saez and Thomas Piketty's *Wealth Inequality in the United States since 1913*.[6][7] I seriously doubt that any economist worth his or her salt would even try to argue that a monetary system that results in zero net worth for half of the country's people should continue to be used.

For a little more than a century, the Federal Reserve System has overseen the creation and control of our nation's very lifeblood by private banks, and the result of this is that half of our people are worth nothing. How can any economist go to sleep at night if he or she is not actively looking into an alternative money system?

The net product of more than a century of the Federal Reserve's system of bank-created debt-money is that the economics profession has become almost entirely subservient to the Federal Reserve System's culture. That culture is to support and continue the present system of bank-created debt-money, thus leaving no room for vigorous debate, original thought or examination of monetary history for answers to the needs of our people and planet.

American Politicians Are Ignorant of Monetary History and Thus Unable to Challenge the Money Power

In 2010, in the case of *Citizens United vs. Federal Election Commission*, the U.S. Supreme Court, in a 5 to 4 decision, ruled that as a matter of free speech, corporations and labor unions were effectively free to spend unlimited money on "electioneering communications" and to directly advocate for the election or defeat of candidates (although not to contribute directly to candidates or political parties). The ruling allows unlimited election spending by corporations and labor unions leading to the rise of Super PACs (Political Action Committees), which can raise endless funds from individuals, corporations, unions and other groups.[8]

The majority ruling, which overturned two lower court rulings, argued that political spending was free speech and, as such, curtailing it would be a violation of the First Amendment. The net effect has been to allow billionaires, wealthy corporations and even well-funded labor unions to spend massive amounts of money on election campaigns. In federal elections, PACs can file monthly or quarterly financial reports. Filing quarterly allows them to keep donor names secret prior to an election.

All democracies are representative to some degree. We vote to choose, in our case, Congress members and Senators to represent us in Congress and make the laws that we live by. However, when our representatives do not represent the people's interests, we have a problem. When we have huge inequality, with billions of dollars residing in the hands of just a few, and they are able to use this wealth to disproportionately influence our politics and elections, then we have a problem. When we are kept in the dark about our money system of private banks creating our very lifeblood as debt, imprisoning both our government and ourselves in the modern equivalent of a debtor's prison, then we have a major problem.

We have had champions in past Congresses who had the courage to take on the Money Power. Wright Patman, the Chairman of the House of Representatives Committee on Banking and Currency from 1963–1975, was a critic of the Federal Reserve System. In 1938, during the Great Depression, Patman put into Congress H. R. 7230, a Bill Providing for Government Ownership of the Twelve Federal Reserve Banks,[9] which was co-sponsored by 160 Democratic members of the House. Patman stated in a Congressional hearing that many other Congress members had already told him that they would vote for the bill if it was put on the floor for a vote.[10] During the Congressional hearing on the bill, he said that the handling of money was a function of banks, and that the issuance [creation] of money was a function of the nation.[11] He further stated in a back and forth discussion with other Congress members that there were certain things that the federal government should do, such as national defense and the building of and operation of battleships. He argued that government at some level, local, state, or federal, should be responsible for building our nation's highways and bridges. "I am in favor of the Government staying out of business so that local individuals or others may engage in it, but when it is in the Government's interest and in the interest of the people to do something that the Constitution provides the Government shall do, that is a different matter."[12] The creation and issuance of money is that thing that is both in the interest of the people and government, and that the Constitution provides the government shall do.

Henry Gonzalez, Chairman of the House of Representatives Financial Services Committee from 1989–1995, regularly introduced legislation to repeal the Federal Reserve Act.[13] While the proposed NEED Act, put into Congress 16 years after Gonzalez left Congress, would negate the Federal Reserve Act, it would retain certain portions of the Federal Reserve to administer the "origination and entry into circulation of United States Money,... the lending of United States Money to authorized depository institutions,... to insure that money creation is solely a function of the United States Government, and... fractional reserve lending is ended." [14]

Dennis Kucinich and John Conyers put the NEED Act into Congress in 2011. Today, there is not a single member of Congress or the Senate advocating for a publicly created money system such as the NEED Act. Why is this so? When monetary reform is presented to our representatives by their constituents, the first question your Congressperson will likely ask is: "Who at the Federal Reserve supports this legislation that would change us from bank-created debt-money to publicly created money?" This is important because Congress is in charge of telling the Fed what to do. It has this power in the Federal Reserve Act created by Congress: "The right to amend, alter, or repeal this Act is hereby expressly reserved."[15] But when our Congress members themselves do not understand the money system, they certainly are in no position to demand or even meekly ask for change.

Meanwhile, we have no one to turn to at the Federal Reserve. I visited the Federal Reserve's websites for the 12 Federal Reserve Banks and the Board of Governors, and I counted an estimated 348 macroeconomists employed by the Federal Reserve. Macro-economics is the study of a national or regional economy's behavior as a whole.[16] The study of our nation's money system would be under macroeconomics. The 348 number is an esti-mate because some of the Federal Reserve Banks don't individu-ally list their macroeconomists. But I took the Fed banks that did and used like numbers for the ones that didn't list them and came up with 348 estimated macroeconomists. Their job is to, among other things, write papers about economic thought. I am sure that these 348 highly trained intellects are just that, highly trained intellects. I am also wondering why there is no vigorous debate among these highly trained intellects about a system of publicly created money that was put into our Congress in 2011.

EXPERT WITNESS: MILTON FRIEDMAN, NOBEL LAUREATE IN ECONOMICS:

"500 economists is extremely unhealthy" [17]

I am in strong disagreement with the late Milton Friedman's Chicago School policies, often referred to as the Washington Consensus (globalization, privatization of everything public, no tariffs, deregulation, tax cuts, float currency value in financial markets and make the world a single, laissez-faire, free market).[18] [19] Author Naomi Klein compares the implementation of the Washington Consensus policies in the '70s, '80s and '90s, which brought stubborn nations into the US-led Western capitalist economic empire, to the use of electroshock therapy that has been previously used on the mentally ill. After an economic crisis, a natural disaster or a military coup occurred, the US-led West would ride to the rescue of the shocked victims with the Chicago School policies of privatization of their economies and austerity for their people. When people are in a state of shock, big changes are often easy to implement. *The Shock Doctrine – The Rise of Disaster Capitalism* by Naomi Klein is the definitive work on the subject.[20]

Milton Friedman had been an influential economics professor at the University of Chicago and was an unabashed supporter of free market capitalism. The Washington Consensus policies were nothing more than the free market capitalism on steroids, touted by Professor Friedman. The Chicago School policies of Professor Friedman were embraced by President Ronald Reagan and British Prime Minister Margaret Thatcher, both of whom he advised.

Please take note that the Chicago School economic policies, which became known as the Washington Consensus as championed by Milton Friedman in the 1970s, '80s and '90s, is in no way related to the *Chicago Plan* that began in the same institution, the University of Chicago, and was put forward in the 1930s by the nation's leading academic economists that called for publicly created money. While not exactly opposite in thought, they have nothing in common. The *Chicago Plan* is about instituting a system of publicly created money. The Chicago School economic policies are about bringing the entire world into an unchecked capitalist economic system.

The *Chicago Plan* would have freed us from debt slavery in the U.S. and would have been a great example for the rest of the world to follow, while the Chicago School policies guaranteed the indebtedness of the Third World to the private banks of the First World.[21] Under the *Chicago Plan*, the U.S. would have changed from the present bank-created debt-money system to a system of publicly created money. If and when we do change to publicly created money in the future, there is little doubt that the rest of the world's nations will quickly join us in the switch. Those nations making the transition to public money will then join us in being able to provide for our people and planet, while also repaying their debts.

Even though I disagree with many of Nobel Laureate Friedman's theories and policies, he was arguably the most influential economist of the latter half of the last century. He was an elite member of the economics profession's intelligentsia. Therefore, his opinion as an expert witness on the employment of monetary economists by the Federal Reserve is worth including.

Dr. Friedman believed that the Federal Reserve's employment of 500 economists was unhealthy and not conducive to independent, objective research. In a 1993 letter to former Fed Economist Robert D. Auerbach, Friedman wrote:

I cannot disagree with you that having something like 500 economists [at the Federal Reserve] is extremely unhealthy. As you say, it is not conducive to independent, objective research. You and I know there has been censorship of the material published. Equally important, the location of the economists in the Federal Reserve has had a significant influence on the kind of research they do, biasing that research toward noncontroversial technical papers on method as opposed to substantive papers on policy and results.[22]

Dr. Friedman expanded on this position in a 1993 interview with Reuters, stating that the relatively enhanced reputation of the Fed with the public was aided "by the fact that the Fed has always paid a great deal of attention to soothing the people in the media and buying up its most likely critics" and acknowledging that the Fed employs "probably half of the monetary economists in the U.S. and has visiting appointments for two-thirds of the rest." Friedman saw precious few in academia who were in a position to critique the Fed's policies.[23]

While Dr. Freidman referenced 500 economists at the Fed in 1993, I estimated 348 macroeconomists at the Federal Reserve in 2019. I am quite sure that the Fed has many more than 500 economists today; my estimate was only for those designated as macroeconomists. Alan Greenspan, Chairman of the Federal Reserve 1987–2006, wrote a letter in 1993 to the House Banking Committee that listed 360 economists at the Fed. When including economists who were statisticians, support staff and officers, the total jumped to 730.[24]

EXPERT WITNESS: RYAN GRIM, PULITZER PRIZE-WINNING JOURNALIST:

PRICELESS: HOW THE FEDERAL RESERVE BOUGHT THE ECONOMICS PROFESSION

American journalist Ryan Grim is currently *The Intercept*'s Washington, D.C. Bureau Chief. Previously he was with the *Huffington Post*, where he twice led teams that were finalists for the Pulitzer Prize, winning once.[25] In 2009, Grim wrote a revealing article on the relationship of the Federal Reserve to the economics profession. It was updated in 2013.[26]

> The Federal Reserve, through its extensive network of consultants, visiting scholars, alumni and staff economists, so thoroughly dominates the field of economics that real criticism of the central bank has become a career liability for members of the profession, an investigation by the Huffington Post has found.[27]

In the aftermath of the 2008 economic crash, Mr. Grim called out the Fed for failing to see the Great Recession coming, largely due to its stranglehold on the economics profession. Past, current and future Fed economists almost completely control the editorial boards of the major economics journals. "A HuffPost review of seven top journals found that 84 of the 190 editorial board members were affiliated with the Federal Reserve in one way or another."[28]

Grim quotes American economist James Galbraith: "Try to publish an article critical of the Fed with an editor who works for the Fed."[29] Publishing in these journals determines who gets tenure, who doesn't, who is considered a respectable economist, and who isn't. Those economists who choose independence and publish articles critical of the Fed, do so with the very real risk of committing career suicide. And, of course, they would not be considered serious articles because they would only appear in less prominent venues and not in the Fed-controlled must-publish journals. The Fed also keeps many former employees and other prominent economists outside the Fed circle on their payroll by asking them to review occasional submissions or articles about the Fed. All this has the chilling effect of silencing diverging views and opposition to the Fed.[30]

Earlier we related that world-renowned economist Dr. Kaoru Yamaguchi was terminated from his position at Doshisha University after using System Dynamics modeling to show that a system of publicly created money was superior to the crisis-prone, bank-created debt-money system in place today. What sort of message does this send to the future economics profession now studying at universities?

"THE TYRANNY OF THE TOP FIVE JOURNALS"

University of Chicago Economist James Heckman and Predoctoral Fellow Sidharth Moktan wrote in the *Institute for New Economic Thinking* that young economists understand that publishing in the top five (T5) economic journals is a "powerful determinant of tenure and promotion in academic economics..."[31] The top five consists of the *American Economic Review* (AER), *Econometrica* (ECMA), the *Journal of Political Economy* (JPE), the *Quarterly Journal of Economics* (QJE) and the *Review of Economic Studies* (ReStud).

This finding of strong T5 influence is corroborated by results from a survey of current assistant and associate professors hired by the top 50 U.S. economics departments. On average, junior faculty rank T5 publications as having the greatest influence on their tenure and promotion outcomes, outranking seven different areas of research and teaching performance.[32]

Relying on rankings rather than reading to promote and reward young economists subverts the essential process of assessing and rewarding original research. Using the T5 to screen the next generation of economists incentivizes professional incest and creates clientele effects whereby career-oriented authors appeal to the tastes of editors and biases of journals. It diverts their attention away from basic research toward blatant strategizing about lines of research and favored topics of journal editors with long tenures. It raises entry costs for new ideas and persons outside the orbits of the journals and their editors. An overemphasis on T5 publications perversely incentivizes scholars to pursue follow-up and replication work at the expense of creative pioneering research since follow-up work is easy to judge, is more likely to result in clean publishable results, and hence is more likely to be published.[33]

— AMERICAN ECONOMIC ASSOCIATION 2017
ROUNDTABLE DISCUSSION

This behavior is consistent with basic common sense: you get what you incentivize.[34] And who do we find on the editorial boards of the Top Five? None other than past, present and future Federal Reserve economists. Within this Fed-dominated system, any criticism of Fed policies is very measured at best, while consideration of an alternative monetary system is unthinkable.

Think about it... how many up-and-coming young economists are likely to stake their entire professional careers jousting with the Federal Reserve's bank-created debt-money system? Knowing that if they do so it will be extremely difficult to get a paper published, not just in a Top Five journal, but in any respected economics journal that has past, present and future Federal Reserve economists on their editorial boards. Knowing that it will probably be impossible to ever get employment at the Federal Reserve. And knowing that none other than Nobel Laureate Milton Friedman has said that the Fed employs "probably half of the monetary economists in the U.S. and has visiting appointments for two-thirds of the rest."

I was unable to find the average student debt of a newly minted economics PhD, but in 2018 the average debt for a doctorate degree (that was not in the fields of education, medicine, other health fields or law) was $132,200.[35] We can assume that the average economics PhD candidate and graduate is very well aware of their own particular debt level and quite cognizant of the possible financial repercussions of taking on the Federal Reserve-led economics system. It is naive to assume that this has anything but an absolutely chilling effect upon independent economic thinking and research by our recent PhD graduates.

This is not a healthy democratic system of probing academic thought. Quite the contrary; it is a rigid system of closed thought that has evolved over the last century to support the fraudulent, dysfunctional system of bank-created debt-money. It is also the same system that has created a country in which one half of our people have no net worth [36] [37] and the needs of the planet are ignored because of a lack of money.

ACADEMIC EXCLUSION: THE CASE OF ALEXANDER DEL MAR

Alexander Del Mar's prescient and profound contributions to monetary economics have been basically disregarded for the duration of a century. The contemporary arbiters and judges of intellectual merit were aware of Del Mar's writings, but Del Mar was excluded from contemporary reference and recognition. His exclusion had led to his having been denied his rightful place in the history of economic thought. One explanation for the silencing of Del Mar is that his intellectual position placed him in opposition to the views of the leaders of the profession. Del Mar was also forthright in his criticisms of his contemporaries' views and was open in his writings in commenting on prior anti-Semitism. We present evidence suggesting that prejudice and bigotry in high places in academia were involved in Del Mar's exclusion from the consolidating profession of academic economists in the late 19th century.[38]

— AMERICAN ECONOMISTS JOSEPH
ASCHHEIM & GEORGE TAVLAS

Alexander Del Mar wrote eight books on monetary history, including the *History of Money in America* (1900). In Book Two: *History of Money 101*, we quote Mr. Del Mar's statement that that the American colonists' act of publicly creating the Continental Currency, which allowed the colonists to effectively fight and win the Revolution, was the essence of the American Revolution.[39] Little wonder that the modern economics profession ignores his scholarship and rejects him as a pariah. How is it possible that arguably America's greatest monetary historian has been almost completely scrubbed from history? Much credit to Drs. Aschheim and Tavlas for putting this travesty on record. I remember American Monetary Institute Director Stephen Zarlenga praising Alexander del Mar's work many times. It was only after doing research and actually reading Del Mar that I began to fully appreciate his work and insight. The absence of reference to Del Mar from both his contemporaries and economists today brings into question the credibility of the entire economics profession.

While Alexander Del Mar is long gone from the Earth, his comment on political economists [today's economics profession] is even more valid today than when he wrote it in 1895: "As a rule political economists do not take the trouble to study the history of money; it is much easier to imagine it and to deduce the principles of this imaginary knowledge."[40]

WHAT IS ABSENT AND UNACCOUNTED FOR IN AN ECONOMICS EDUCATION?

Money. PhD economists at our nation's top three economics schools don't study monetary history. Monetary history or history of money was not in any way listed as a course amongst the 489 courses offered in 2019 by the top 3 *US News and World Report* rated economics programs, Harvard, MIT and Stanford.[41] [42]

While I am sure that other courses in the economics programs of these prestigious universities cover some aspects of monetary history, it would seem that actual courses about the history of money would be extremely beneficial to the education of their students. Because of COVID-19, I was unable to find and search the Harvard, MIT and Stanford economics programs offered during the pandemic to see if they continue to omit courses that are specific to monetary history. Beta Reader Mishel G. Salazar, who read the first draft of this book, found a course at Rutgers

University, *Financial and Monetary History of the United States*,[43] taught by Professor Eugene N. White. Kudos to Professor White and Rutgers University for teaching monetary history, and to Ms. Salazar for discovering it. While we can celebrate finding the occasional course on monetary history, we should also be asking why is monetary history not being taught at every university?

Updating: A search in August 2022 found Harvard University listed 167 courses within their economics undergraduate and graduate programs. None of these courses mention the history of money or monetary history in their titles.[44] Stanford University lists 194 courses within their economics undergraduate and graduate programs, all without mention of history of money or monetary history in their titles.[45] Massachusetts Institute of Technology lists 121 courses in their Economics Department, again all without mention of history of money or monetary history in their titles.[46] A total of 482 courses listed in our country's most prestigious university economics programs, all without a single mention of the history of money. Heaven forbid that the students in these programs would be exposed to the history of the most necessary thing for survival in modern society—money.

How is it possible to formulate proper ideas and theories if the students and the professors have not studied the history of what in the past has worked well as money and what has not? Another way to look at the current consensus of academic thought: If we don't study alternatives to the bank-created debt-money system, we don't have to be concerned with considering an alternative to the bank-created debt-money system. The bank-created debt-money system is a colossal failure. Debt and progressively greater and greater inequality between those at the top and the rest of us are the historical results.

This is a plea to economics professionals at the Federal Reserve, economics journals and universities across the country. Please read about the publicly created money system in the NEED Act.[47]

Read Stephen Zarlenga's *Lost Science of Money*.[48] Read the Bank of England's *Money Creation in Modern Society*.[49] Read Richard Werner's *A lost century in economics: Three theories of banking and the conclusive evidence*.[50] Read Kaoru Yamaguchi's *Workings of A Public Money System of Open Macroeconomies – Modeling the American Monetary Act Completed*.[51] Read Jaromir Benes & Michael Kumhof's *The Chicago Plan Revisited*.[52] Read Joseph Huber's *Split-circuit reserve banking – functioning, dysfunctions and future perspectives*.[53] Critically examine them. Write about them. Technical articles are fine for your educational equals, but the rest of us without that specialized background would greatly appreciate reading some accessible economic thought that ordinary people can all understand.

I am beside myself. Whenever I get into a discussion with an influential person in our society, be it in government, private business or academia, they want to know what the Federal Reserve economists say about publicly created money. The only answer I can give them is—nothing. The Federal Reserve System is complicit in the shunning of open academic discussion of publicly created money. Let me be clear, this silent treatment or shunning is a form of abuse.[54] I beg all economists to ask themselves if they want to be a part of this abuse. The ultimate target of the abuse is not publicly created money, but rather our people and our planet who are denied the system of publicly created money that we desperately need.

ECONOMICS TEXTBOOKS – TRUE OR FALSE?

Do they or do they not accurately explain money creation? Students today pile up huge amounts of debt to get a university education. Do their economics textbooks lie to them? Do the smartest economics students and future economists even realize that their textbooks lied to them?

EXPERT WITNESSES: MICHAEL MCLEAY, AMAR RADIA AND RYLAND THOMAS

BANK OF ENGLAND MONETARY ANALYSIS DIRECTORATE

According to the Bank of England's *Money Creation in the Modern Economy*:

> The reality of how money is created today differs from the description found in some economics textbooks: Rather than banks receiving deposits when households save and then lending them out, bank lending creates deposits [bank-created debt-money].[55]

EXPERT WITNESS: JONATHAN ADAIR TURNER

BRITISH HOUSE OF LORDS

Adair Turner is not just any witness. He is Baron Adair Turner of Ecchinswell, a member of the British House of Lords since 2005. He is a British businessman, an academic, a member of the UK's Financial Policy Committee, and was Chairman of the Financial Services Authority until its abolition in March 2013. He is also the former Chairman of the Pensions Commission and the Committee on Climate Change. He has described himself in a BBC *Hardtalk* interview with Stephen Sackur as a "technocrat." [In other words, he checks off every box as a honcho of the elite financial upper class.]

Credit, Money and Leverage: What Wicksell, Hayek and Fisher Knew and Modern Macroeconomics Forgot is the lecture Turner gave to the prestigious Stockholm School of Economics via video in September 2013. This is what he said 14 minutes into his talk:

I think it is reasonable to say that both in undergraduate textbooks today and in advanced economics and in central bank orthodoxy we have tended to work on a way of thinking about the credit creation process which is simply not true.

Modern textbook assumptions. I think it's fair to say that they make 3 assumptions which are dramatic and wrong over the best simplifications. [The textbooks have lied to us but have done so with a dramatic flair.]

They tend to assume that what banks do is take deposits from household depositors and lend it to borrowers. That misses the insight that banks create credit and money and purchasing power.[56]

Does that not mean, Baron Turner, that the banks do not lend money that already exists as the Financial Intermediation Theory of Banking purports and that they also do not create some multiples of reserve money as the Fractional Reserve Theory of Banking/Money Creation proposes? Do we have it correct, sir? Banks create money? If this is true, Baron Turner, could you please give a thumbs-up to Professor Werner? He has been standing out there, practically all alone, saying this is so for quite some time now, with none of the financial leaders paying any attention to him at all. Also perhaps a thumbs-up for Dr. Yamaguchi, who lost his job over critiquing the debt-money system and demonstrating its structural flaw [that we must always be in debt] and its inferiority to a system of publicly created money. I am quite sure that both Dr. Yamaguchi and Dr. Werner would be very appreciative of a word of support from someone as distinguished as Baron Jonathan Adair Turner.

Again, Baron Turner: "Credit creation [debt-money creation] process which is simply not true....That misses the insight that banks create credit and money..." While we certainly have to appreciate Baron Turner for his candor, why is he not shouting from the rooftops that we need publicly created money? I'm quite sure that the United Kingdom monetary reform group Positive Money would be delighted to help him spread the word.

While we have had a little fun with the British for their manner of breaking the bad news to us, at least they are saying something. Where are the American economists of prominence on the same subject?

Op-Eds for Monetary Reform

Using internet searches, I have been unable to find any articles or papers written by Federal Reserve economists and other members of the economics profession discussing or critiquing the Bank of England's *Money creation in the modern economy*,[57] or Stephen Zarlenga's book *The Lost Science of Money*.[58] This is simply unacceptable. The economics professionals, both within the Federal Reserve and within academia, have a duty to explain how our money is created. They also have a duty to answer legitimate academic criticism of the debt-money system. Their failure to do so suggests that they are unable to logically defend the fraudulent bank-created debt-money system.

Martin Wolf, Chief Economics Commentator of the British *Financial Times,* wrote an April 24, 2014, column titled, "Strip private banks of their power to create money."[59] But we have been unable with internet searches to find any similar American newspaper columns critiquing the bank-created debt-money system.

I'm referring to 500-word op-ed columns typically found on the newspaper's editorial page.

Incredibly, the only op-eds in U.S. newspapers that I could find through internet searches that argue for a change from a debt-money to publicly created money system are the three that I have written myself. You might find an op-ed arguing for a return to the gold standard, upon which the debt-money system is based, or critiques of Federal Reserve monetary policy within the present debt-money system, but no critique of and proposal to end the debt-money system. I have already owned up to my lack of formal economics education and yet my three op-eds are the only critiques of the Federal Reserve–led, bank-created debt-money system that I could find in American newspapers?

These three articles have all appeared in my local newspaper, *The Times*, formerly the *Northwest Indiana Times*, Indiana's third largest newspaper:[60]

- "Fund infrastructure work with NEED Act," *NWI Times*, October 24, 2014.[61]
- "NEED Act erases big steel's call for worker concessions," *NWI Times*, September 3, 2015.[62]
- "Gary could fulfill development needs with the NEED Act," *NWI Times*, May 13, 2016.[63]

The op-eds that I wrote were not pushing some quack idea. No, I advocate for a money system that conforms to the Constitution, in which our government would create and spend our money into existence, debt-free, putting millions to work rebuilding our nation. The complete proposal supported in my op-eds had already been put into Congress by Dennis Kucinich and House Judiciary Committee Chairman John Conyers in 2011 as the NEED Act (National Emergency Employment Defense Act).[64]

It was a well-reasoned proposal that had been vetted by top econo-mists, a proposal that was completely ignored by both political parties, the Federal Reserve, academia and the nation's media. To have a functioning, vibrant democracy, citizens need to be informed. When our nation's major institutions ignore informa-tion that challenges the status quo, democracy suffers. Our nation's citizens need all the knowledge they can get about our nation's very lifeblood. Restricting this knowledge threatens democracy to the very core.

All three guest commentaries were written around the NEED Act's system of publicly created money enabling a specific benefit to society that was in the news of the day. The first dealt with Indiana highway improvements that were to be financed with a gas tax increase while the NEED Act could have used publicly created money for the highways instead of increasing the gas tax. The second dealt with a possible steel strike affecting local workers and the entire local economy, which could be avoided by infrastructure repairs using our U.S. made steel and paid for by the NEED Act. The third dealt with a proposal to build a prison in Gary, Indiana, to create a few jobs while the NEED Act could be used as the lever to rebuild the entire city of Gary.

Author's note: Much of this material was covered in my 2019 paper, "Challenging the Economics Profession" posted on the Alliance For Just Money website.[65]

BREAKING NEWS: UNIVERSITY OF ILLINOIS AT CHICAGO HISTORY PROFESSOR JEFFREY SKLANSKY ADVOCATES FOR PUBLIC DIGITAL DOLLAR TO BOOST AMERICAN DEMOCRACY

As of July 21, 2021, we now have four op-ed/guest commentaries that call for publicly created money. American History professor at UIC Jeffrey Sklansky's "A new public digital dollar could be a big boost to American democracy"[66] was recently published in

The Washington Post. Congratulations to Dr. Sklansky. While Dr. Sklansky is not calling for a complete changeover to publicly created money in this article, at least he is pushing for the addition of some publicly created money to the mix; in this case, it would be Federal Reserve–created digital dollars (CBDC—central bank digital currency). I believe that Dr. Sklansky is in agreement with publicly created money and believes that digital dollars would be a step on the way to achieving it.

There is nothing magical about digital money. Almost the entirety of our present money is digital. It is created by the private banks when they make loans. It exists as credit and only for the life of our loan. "Crypto-currency...is any form of currency that exists digitally or virtually and uses cryptography to secure transactions. Crypto-currencies don't have a central issuing or regulating authority, instead using a decentralized system to record transactions and issue new units."[67] Since there is no regulating authority, your crypto "investment" is nothing more than a gamble that others will also join you and the price will go up instead of down. In addition, just one type of cryptocurrency, Bitcoin, uses more electric energy than 166 individual countries do, ranking behind Sweden and Ukraine and ahead of Argentina and the Netherlands.[68] Crypto uses crazy amounts of energy and is no way to save the planet. As far as cryptocurrencies as an investment, please listen to an old poker player—don't gamble anything you aren't comfortable losing.

While not created electronically in exactly the same manner as is the privately created Bitcoin and other examples of cryptocurrency, almost all of what we use for money is created by private banks and exists electronically on their computers. Yes, digital money created by the Federal Reserve and spent into existence, debt-free, for needs of the nation would certainly be better than what we have right now. But it is no panacea; it is a partial reform. Let's remember for starters that the Federal Reserve is not a part of our government; it has a somewhat ambiguous status. Make the Federal Reserve a part of our government, stop the bank creation of debt-money and then allow the Federal Reserve to create digital currency as a function of our federal government. Now that's a plan that I believe Dr. Sklansky would heartily support. Whenever partial reforms have been tried in the past, the Money Power was always able to keep a good part of their power and ultimately defeat the reforms.

THREE EXAMPLES OF PARTIAL REFORMS NOT WORKING

Examples 1 & 2 are covered in Book Two: *History of Money 101*, while example 3 was covered in Chapter 2 of this book.

Example #1: Publicly creating the Greenbacks, but also leaving the banks with the power to create money. As we will soon discover in Book Two: *History of Money 101*, during the Civil War the federal government publicly created money that was called Greenbacks, because of their green color. They were used to fight the Civil War and they saved the nation as we know it. Although the federal government publicly created the Greenbacks, it neglected to also stop the bank creation of money as debt. By not taking the Money Power away from the private banks, the private banks were able to eventually get the upper hand and get rid of their competition: the publicly created Greenbacks.

Example #2: Ending the role of the private 2nd Bank of the U.S. as our central bank and stopping bank creation of money. Presidents Andrew Jackson and Martin Van Buren had a mighty struggle with the 2nd Bank of the United States, which was the privately owned central bank, or shall we say Federal Reserve of the day. When they were able to keep the 2nd Bank of the U.S. from renewing its charter, lending and money creation came to a virtual standstill. But because both Jackson and Van Buren had no knowledge about publicly created money, the money supply also dried up, causing the terrible Panic of 1837–44. Van Buren had made the fatal error of thinking that money was gold, and therefore the government did not have to create money for society to function. There was not nearly enough gold to act as our nation's money system, most of it belonging to the rich. There was simply a grossly inadequate supply of money for society to function.

Example #3: Nationalizing the Bank of England, but allowing private banks to continue to create money. Founded in 1694, the Bank of England was the privately owned central bank for England and the UK. The British nationalized the Bank of England in 1946 at the urging of the Archbishop of Canterbury William Temple, and thus brought about the third reform of making the Bank of England (their equivalent to our Federal Reserve) a part of their government. Because the Money Power was not taken from the other private banks, the money creation simply morphed over to the other private banks. Things functioned much like before, with the private banks creating almost the entirety of their money as debt when making loans. The one difference between the Federal Reserve and the Bank of England after 1946 was that the creation of the British paper money, their pound notes, was now done by the British government with the nationalization of the Bank of England. In the U.S. our paper money dollars are given to the private Federal Reserve banking system for the cost of printing them, and they become a part of the bank-created debt-money system. The difference is that in the UK, the private sector banks create about 97% of their nation's money supply[69] while in the U.S. it is even more, with only the coins in our pockets and piggy banks that are publicly created.

For these reasons, I refuse to get too excited about publicly created digital currency or CBDC (central bank digital currency), if when doing so we continue to allow the Money Power to continue to create the vast majority of our money as debt through the private banks, and continue to allow the Federal Reserve to be independent of the people and government. Implementing the NEED Act legislation allows us to heal our people and planet with programs funded by publicly created money. It also allows us to create and spend whatever money that our Congress deems necessary for our society. Within the current bank-created debt-money system, CBDC is now primarily a diversion away from a comprehensive system of publicly created money.

CHAPTER 11

STUDENT INITIATIVES IN THE FIGHT FOR MONETARY REFORM

STUDENT RUMBLINGS FOR REFORM

In 2014, 82 different student economics organizations in 30 different countries signed on to an International Student Initiative for Pluralism in Economics:[1]

Theoretical pluralism emphasizes the need to broaden the range of schools of thought represented in the curricula. It is not the particulars of any economic tradition we object to. Pluralism is not about choosing sides, but about encouraging intellectually rich debate and learning to critically contrast ideas. Where other disciplines embrace diversity and teach competing theories even when they are mutually incompatible, economics is often presented as a unified body of knowledge. Admittedly, the dominant tradition has internal variations. Yet, it is only one way of doing economics and of looking at the real world. Such uniformity is unheard of in other fields; nobody would take seriously a degree program in psychology that focuses only on Freudianism, or a politics program that focuses only on state socialism. An inclusive and comprehensive economics education should promote balanced exposure to a variety of theoretical perspectives, from the commonly taught neoclassically based approaches to the largely excluded classical, post-Keynesian, institutional, ecological, feminist, Marxist and Austrian traditions ... Most economics students graduate without ever encountering such diverse perspectives in the classroom.

The students held Global Action Days in May of 2015 and 2016. The United States group, Rethinking Economics, held a three-day conference at three different New York universities: Columbia, The New School, and NYU.[2] Rethinking Economics also held a digital festival in July 2021 debating 5 key aspects of our economic futures:

- Political and Economic Impacts of COVID-19
- Social Economics of Climate Change
- Digital Economy
- Informal, Forgotten & Hidden Economies
- Global South Economics[3]

MAASTRICHT UNIVERSITY ECONOMICS STUDENTS QUESTION HOW MONEY CREATION IS PRESENTED AND TAUGHT IN THEIR TEXTBOOKS

In 2019, economics students at the Maastricht University in the Netherlands posted "An Open Letter to the Dean of SBE and all Economics Professors Maastricht University (UM)." The letter begins:

We are a student-driven initiative at Maastricht University [UM] that is eager to improve the economics curriculum. With this open letter, we want to raise your awareness that what is currently taught in economics at UM on how banks work and how money is created is contrary to existing evidence and does not fit with the high-quality education that UM offers. Professors and textbooks at UM teach the mainstream but faulty view of "loanable funds" and "money multiplier," even though central banks and commercial banks openly admit that those concepts are misleading.

We'd like to present convincing peer-reviewed evidence to demonstrate that both the approaches of "loanable funds" and "money multiplier" are incorrect and unproven, and that teaching these concepts has implications for UM's education in economics.[4]

The letter then goes on to show examples from their textbooks that back up their premise that they are not being taught how money is being created. This was a great initiative on the part of the Maastricht University students, and they should be congratulated for their effort in speaking truth to the Money Power. I believe the letter was written early in 2019. In October 2021, I am unable to discover whether their concerns were addressed or even find a copy of the letter online. Is it possible that the powers that be at Maastricht University were not interested in a public airing of the bank-created debt-money system's dirty laundry? Or did they address the students' concerns and then take the letter down?

EXPERT WITNESS:

LINO ZEDDIES – *WHAT'S WRONG WITH ECONOMICS?*

Lino Zeddies was an earlier expert witness on the correlation between the debt-money system and inequality. Here, we will tap into his experience within the economics profession's education system. Lino has a Master of Economics Degree and has expressed deep frustration with his field of study. He relates that he studied economics because he desired to grasp the big relationships in society. He wanted to learn why we have unemployment and inequality and then use his economics education to fix these problems. What he discovered was that structural economics education is not wired into finding the solutions to unemployment and inequality.

When I reached out to Mr. Zeddies, he told me that he found economics education "extremely one-sided, dogmatic, neoliberal,"[5] while he has found individual members of the economics profession "more diverse and deliberate." Overall, Zeddies did find that "many economics professors have a more balanced view than the stuff that is taught at economics classes or usually put forward in the public as the economic wisdom."[6]

He attributes this problem to "physics envy"; the idea that early economists attempted to follow the lead of physics that explained the physical world in mathematical terms. Economists thought that society's economic behavior could also be condensed into precise, objective, scientific, and oh so beautiful mathematical-theoretical models.

The modern economist's primary tool to explain our complex economic behavior is his mathematical-theoretical model. First, the economist assumes that everyone is the same: sensible, egotistical, unemotional, knows what will happen in the future and constantly trying to maximize her "utility" (consume the most while doing the least work). Second, he assumes that all goods are the same, all markets are in perfect balance, there is equal competition between all businesses, and that all businesses are primarily interested in maximizing profits. Third, she assumes that money, banks and financial markets have no effect on the real economy, so they may be left out of the equation. Voilà, our economist now has the "foundation" to begin his or her analysis. Of course if any of these assumptions are wrong then the analysis will be flawed.

Beginning with this "foundation," our economist is now free to assume anything they please. "The motto is: the more advanced, the more ridiculous the assumptions."[7] But trying to model reality can be a fool's errand at best for the simple reason that endless variables cannot be shoehorned into trite assumptions to simplify the model and make it work. And economic models made by economists require squeezing the real world into a precise mathematical formula so that the economist can conclude with strong certainty all manner of policies harmful to the common good.[8]

In addition to his broad critique of economic modeling, Zeddies proposes that 95% of university economics classes are based on the neoclassical school of economics: the economy is made up of individuals; individuals are selfish and rational; the world is certain with calculable risks; the most important domain of the economy is exchange and consumption; economies change through individual choices; policy recommendations are either free market or interventionism depending on the economist's view on market failures and government failures. This almost completely neglects the Classical, Marxist, Developmentalist, Austrian, Schumpeterian, Keynesian, Institutionalist and Behavioralist schools of economics[9] [to say nothing of publicly created money which has no current status as a school of economics]. Students only hear one side of the story, the neoclassical one. The International Student Initiative for Pluralism in Economics joins Zeddies in calling for economics programs to include other economic disciplines in their programs.

Zeddies is also spot-on in assessing the economics profession's blind allegiance to the lie that banks do not create our money:

> The common view among mainstream economists on banks is that banks collect savings and then lend them on to those people that need credit. The problem with this view is that it is just plain wrong. Private banks actually do create new money every time they extend a credit and if you look at the institutions and bank balance sheets you CAN'T come to a different conclusion. [10]
>
> Zeddies cites the Bank of England's *Money creation in the modern economy* [11] and Richard Werner's *A lost century in economics: Three theories of banking and the conclusive evidence* to substantiate his claims. [12]

EXPERT WITNESS: RETHINKING ECONOMICS

Rethinking Economics is an international network of students, academics and professionals committed to building a better economics in society and the classroom. This growing network of students and teachers, fed up with the dead-end, bank-created debt-money system, numbers 113 student groups in 45 countries, across all continents except Antarctica. [13]

Rethinking Economics posted an Open Letter: Rethinking the Role of Banks in Economics Education. It is signed by 26 student groups, including the same group that authored the previously mentioned letter—Pluralism In Economics (PINE), Maastricht University. It has also been signed by twelve civil society organizations and more than fifty individuals, the majority of whom have PhDs.

Their letter is so important that is reproduced in its entirety:

OPEN LETTER: RETHINKING THE ROLE OF BANKS IN ECONOMICS EDUCATION

Dear Economics Professors and Teaching Staff,

Banks and their role in the creation of money are integral to our modern, financialised economies. Yet, the teaching economics students receive doesn't give them the full picture. As those with the power to influence the next generation of economists, it is essential that you review the teaching of the role of banks in economics courses and bring it in line with up-to-date research. Our economics graduates need to understand how banks function in the real-world, in order to avoid past crises and to create better economies in future.

WHAT IS CURRENTLY TAUGHT?

Economics textbooks across the world, some of them first published in the 1960s, continue to teach students a model of the monetary system in which commercial banks act as intermediaries, that only move existing money around the system, like lubricant in a machine. Many economics courses rely on the models in these textbooks, without recognising the empirical evidence that undermines them. This gives an unbalanced view of the way the monetary system functions and of the role of banks in the economy.

HOW IS MONEY CREATED?

As research from the Bank of England, Bundesbank [German central bank] and numerous academics has shown, banks are not intermediaries channelling pre-existing funds from savers to borrowers. Commercial banks create the vast majority of money in circulation. Unlike other financial institutions, they create money when they extend loans to borrowers. In the process of extending a loan, banks do not move pre-existing funds from any other account but newly 'invent' the money by crediting the borrower's account. Therefore, banks' lending is constrained by borrowers' demand, profitability considerations and financial regulations, not by pre-existing funds (i.e., people's savings) nor by central bank reserves. This reality is in line with the credit creation or endogenous money theory, which is absent from most current economics textbooks and teaching.

Commercial banks also determine where money is directed in the economy. Around 80% of new money created in countries like the US and UK currently goes towards existing property and financial markets, rather than the 'real' or productive economy, leading to soaring house and land prices, and housing crises. In the Global South, 33 major global banks poured $1.9 trillion into fossil fuels since the 2015 Paris Climate Agreement, directly influencing the trajectory of economies that will be hit first and hardest by climate change. The power of banks to create money therefore has enormous implications for the shape and stability of our economy. Yet, in an overwhelming number of cases, economics textbooks and courses do not teach this to the economists of tomorrow.

What are the consequences of this teaching?

These models, taught without balance or regard for existing evidence on the financial sector, lead economics graduates – who often gain influential positions in society – to draw flawed conclusions. One example is the misconception that in order to increase investment in the economy we need to encourage people to save money first. Other misconceptions that arise are that money is a scarce resource and that public investment always 'crowds out' the private sector.

Furthermore, a main driver of the 2008 global financial crisis was the build-up of debt and credit by the private sector, as banks lent unprecedented amounts to property and financial markets. The crash was unanticipated by the majority of academic economists. This was in no small way influenced by blind spots regarding the power of banks to create money and influence the wider economy.

The same theories that led to these blind spots are still being uncritically presented to economics students 11 years on. When real-world evidence demonstrates that banks function a certain way, why is this not taught to students? Any decisions these students take in their future careers – from financial regulation, to approaching issues like asset price bubbles or unproductive lending – will be influenced by their education at university.

WHAT ARE WE CALLING FOR?

Around the globe, economics students from Rethinking Economics are calling on their lecturers to address this gap in their education. They are calling for an education of banking which draws on empirical evidence and not on outdated models in many textbooks, which are useful only for contrasting past beliefs with modern realities. Most importantly, they are calling for balance in the way they are taught about the role of the financial sector, which allows space for simplified models but also includes alternative perspectives. They are submitting this letter to universities in Europe, the Americas, Asia and Africa to push for improvements to the education they receive.

We strongly support the students in their calls. We encourage economics professors and teaching staff to engage with the students' demands and review how a more complete understanding of the role of banks in the monetary system and the modern economy can be better integrated into economics education. Today's economics students will become the policy-makers, economic influencers, politicians, financiers and business leaders of the future. To create stable and productive economies globally, they must have a real-world understanding of banks and money creation.

To achieve this, we ask economics professors and teaching staff to:

* Provide a justification for why the current teaching doesn't include the credit creation theory, as put forward by central banks and numerous academics.

* Include credit creation theory and empirical studies of the function of banks in the economy in their lectures, teaching material and classes. In particular, this includes more diverse textbooks on reading lists that give students the tools to critically assess the role of banks;

* Teach their students that an understanding of what the

financial sector actually does is vital to an understanding of capitalism.

Rethinking Economics is an international student-led movement seeking to improve economics education. In publishing this letter, with the support of the signatories, we are extending an invitation to develop an economics education that is grounded in the real-world and gives students of economics the tools to address the challenges of the twenty-first century economy.

[This open letter from economics student groups, professors and others is a complete affirmation of the basic premise of *The People, Planet & the Power of Money Project*. I had been so engrossed in research and writing that I was unaware of its existence until I came across it while searching for a copy of the Maastricht open letter that seems to have been taken off the web. This happened as I was going over the text with my copy editor and proofreader. As such I made the decision to give the Rethinking Economics open letter, the Maastricht students' open letter and thoughts of former economics student Lino Zeddies their own space and chapter.]

CHAPTER 12

PRESIDENT BIDEN, PUBLICLY CREATED MONEY, AND THE DEBT-CEILING CRISIS

In March 2023, President Joe Biden's wife, Dr. Jill Biden, gave a talk at Ivy Tech, a local community college in Valparaiso, Indiana. Dr. Biden, who herself teaches at a community college, is a huge supporter of community colleges. Since our daughter and her husband both graduated from Ivy Tech Community College's registered nursing program, our family will always have a soft spot in our hearts for the school. Like most citizens, I have no direct access to President Biden. *Money Creation 101* was not yet published when Dr. Biden gave her talk, so I couldn't try to somehow get a copy to her to give to her husband. I'm hoping that someone who has access to the president will give him a copy once it is in print.

Assuming he does eventually read the book, here is the message. Dear President Biden, thank you so much for reading *Money Creation 101*. I hope that you began reading at the beginning and are not just reading the last chapter because it specifically addresses you. If you skipped the first eleven chapters, here is just a little of what you missed.

Money is the one thing each and every one of us needs to exist in today's modern society. Its importance to our people cannot be overstated. Yet, when I went to college in the 1960s, our Econ 101 class was told that we were not smart enough to understand how our money was created under the Federal Reserve System, so we skipped the entire chapter on it. I cannot relate this story to a group of people today, without members of the group saying that similar things happened in their own education.

We began the discussion by stating three facts that are a given in how most of us understand our money system works:

1. Our federal government creates our money.
2. Banks loan us money that has already been created by our federal government.
3. The Federal Reserve Banks are a part of our government.

We then went on to show that although most of us believe the above three statements are true, none of them are true. But they all definitely should be true!

Almost the entirety of what we use for money in the U.S. is created out of thin air by private banks when they make loans and charge us interest for their privilege. This can only be done because all the banks are doing this together and the Federal Reserve Banks, owned entirely by the private banks in their respective districts, move reserve funds around to keep the books balanced. But of course these two caveats exist, so that is our present money system in a nutshell.

This money or credit exists only as debt and is extinguished by the banks as the loans are repaid to them. Money is only created by the bank for the principal amount of the loan. Nothing is created for the considerable interest we must pay over the life of the loan. Immediately that sets in motion a system in which the supply of money in existence is smaller than the overall amount of money we owe to the banks. Our society needs a sufficient supply of money in existence for businesses to employ people, commerce to flourish, and our society to collectively have the monetary ability to tackle existential threats such as climate change, pandemics, and rampant inequality, demonstrated by the fact that almost half of our people combined have no net worth.[1] Our present bank-created debt-money system is structurally flawed because it is unable to respond to any of these crises without increasing debt. Within this dead-end, bank-created debt-money system our society must remain in debt and the level of debt must progressively increase over time.

President Biden, you are a great champion of liberty, equality, and democracy. *Money Creation 101* is but the first book of three that make up the *People, Planet & the Power of Money Project*, with *History of Money 101* and *Spaceship Earth 101* to soon follow. We make the point throughout the entire project that our level of liberty, equality, and democracy is dependent on the type of money system we have. How can we have liberty, equality, and democracy if every action we take is in some way dependent upon the American people being in a state of ever-increasing debt to the private banking system? Our system of private bank-created debt-money is counter-intuitive to liberty, equality, and democracy.

Conversely a just, sovereign system of publicly created money is conducive to all three. We present the NEED Act, a system of publicly created money that was put into Congress in 2011 by Congressmen Dennis Kucinich and John Conyers.[2] It would provide a seamless overnight transition to a system of publicly created money. Throughout the *People, Planet & Power of Money Project* we discuss updating the NEED Act for today and offer the American Monetary Reform Act of 2022, which has done just that.[3] It was drafted by colleagues at the Alliance for Just Money.

We propose that widespread knowledge of who creates our money and how they create it is absolutely necessary for liberty, equality, and democracy to exist and flourish. How can we make the oversight decisions for the one thing we all need—money—if we don't even know who creates it and how they create it? We present evidence of a Federal Reserve economist who agreed that the knowledge of who creates our money and how it is created is very important, but he did not feel comfortable telling me who it is. Instead he referred me to the Federal Reserve Public Relations Department for an answer that four years later has still not yet come.

But it gets ever worse. I sent out inquiries to economics professors at our nation's leading university economics programs. Of the two professors who were gracious enough to respond, one was not sure how our money is created and could only give his best guess (fractional reserve lending), while the other was dismissive and indicated that it was all created by the Federal Reserve without actually stating it. This despite the considerable evidence we provided to the contrary. Economics students across the globe are now banding together to seriously question their university economics programs for providing the wrong information on how our money is created. Added to this is the fact that our own top American university economics programs provide no courses on the history of money or monetary history. The one thing we all need to simply live at an existence level in modern society is money and money's very history is ignored by our leading universities? Little wonder that economics students feel betrayed by their universities. Hopefully, both *Money Creation 101* and *History of Money 101*, scheduled for publication this summer, will be helpful to these students in their search for truth.

We have tremendous inequality and environmental crises that confront our society. Only publicly created money can provide the money necessary to adequately address them and do so without raising taxes or debt. Book Three in our project, *Spaceship Earth 101*, takes its name from American economist Kenneth Boulding's 1960s concept of Earth's perilous voyage through space with only our atmosphere, which is now under siege by climate change, to protect us. It examines these issues along with the type of political and economic system that can best give us the sustainable lifestyle we need to safely continue our journey.

President Biden, here are a few thoughts on the debt ceiling crisis that looms in the immediate future. Please forgive me for going into detail to explain the craziness of the debt ceiling crisis. I am quite aware that you understand this. Since *Money Creation 101* was primarily written for a much wider audience within an overall mission of public education, I have tried to explain this insanity as clearly as I can.

DEBT CEILING LUNACY

As we prepare to publish *Money Creation 101,* the U.S. hit its debt limit on January 19, 2023. The debt limit is administered by the Department of Treasury and is codified into law by Title 31 of the U.S. code.[4]

The debt ceiling refers to the total amount of money that our federal government is authorized by Congress to borrow to pay for expenditures that Congress has already authorized by voting for the legislation that became law to incur this debt in the first place.[5] Such items would include Social Security checks and Medicare payments, paychecks for all federal government employees, food assistance, income tax refunds and interest on the national debt. This includes paychecks for Congress members and their staffs. When Congress votes to raise the debt ceiling, it is voting to pay for all manner of expenses that Congress has already authorized.

The debt limit applies to all federal debt, both that held by the public in the form of bonds and the funds owed by one federal government department to another federal government department. No new spending commitments are created by raising the debt ceiling or debt limit. It simply allows the government to pay for existing obligations already established by Congress.[6] Or, to put it in simpler terms, to pay for goods and services that it has already contracted for, received, and agreed to pay for.

Prior to 1917, Congress authorized each debt issue separately. To finance our involvement in World War I, Congress passed the Second Liberty Bond Act of 1917, which established a limit on the total amount of bonds that the government could issue. During the Great Depression and the outset of the World War II, Congress broadened this limit to apply to all federal debt with the 1939 and 1941 Public Debt Acts. This allowed the Department of Treasury to issue debt necessary to fund government operations authorized by the federal budget, as long as the total debt remained below a debt ceiling that was determined by Congress. Since 1960, Congress has acted to raise this debt ceiling 78 times. Surprise, it has been necessary to raise it 49 times under the fiscally conservative Republican presidents and only 29 times under spendthrift Democratic presidents.[7]

Since the debt ceiling was not raised by Congress on January 19, 2023, Treasury Secretary Janet Yellen must now use accounting gymnastics to avoid default. But these accounting maneuvers can only last a few months at best. If Congress refuses to raise the debt ceiling before this default day comes, our government will have to stop paying our bills and interest payments. This default of our financial obligations will make us a deadbeat nation, raise our interest rates exponentially, and create an economic catastrophe that is impossible to exactly predict.

"The validity of the public debt of the United States, authorized by law...shall not be questioned,"[8] states the U.S. Constitution in the 14th Amendment. Yet it is an absolute impossibility to repay our federal debt within the debt-money system. The way the federal debt is handled now, old debt is repaid by taking out new debt. This is not really a repayment of debt but more of a transfer of debt from one creditor to another. The 14th Amendment statement does not give Congress a choice on whether or not to raise the debt ceiling, but an order to either raise the debt ceiling or do away with the debt ceiling entirely since it serves no practical function.[9] The Republican House Members, who refuse to either raise the debt ceiling or do away with the debt ceiling, have all taken an oath of office to support the U.S. Constitution that requires them to do so.[10]

The law is unclear about who gets paid when there is not enough to pay everyone.[11] When our laws were written, voted on by the House of Representatives and Senate, and signed into law by our U.S. presidents, there was no concern on anyone's part that we would have a future House of Representatives that would refuse to pay the bills which we had already agreed to pay. Republican Houses have previously held us hostage with their debt ceiling antics, but they have only done so when Democratic presidents are in office. These Republican Houses have made numerous proposals over the years on which programs should be funded and which could simply go unpaid. None of these proposals have ever become law or been anything more than a rejected proposal.

Secretary of Treasury Timothy Geithner in 2011, Secretary of Treasury Jacob Lew in 2013, and Assistant Secretary of Treasury Alistair Fitzpayne in 2014 have all stated that attempting to prioritize who gets paid and who doesn't is an impossibility.[12] Funds as taxes come into our Treasury at uncertain times that are unpredictable. If Congress allows us to default, checks could only be written when there was money in the Treasury, so even if something was prioritized it is quite possible that there would not be any money in the Treasury when it came due and it could not be paid. Think of the 70 million plus people who receive Social Security checks each month. If the Treasury would run out of funds before all were paid, as is quite likely, some of them might get paid under prioritization and others wouldn't. Who should be paid first, you or I? Should we go alphabetically or should we have a lottery to determine who might get paid and who might not? And Social Security is only one program. I am unable to find how many federal programs exist. I did find that there are at least 2,300 federal programs that provide assistance to the American people.[13] This does not include programs that pay our military and civilian employees. Do some of them get paid and some not? Perhaps, the Republican House of Representatives will take a vote to only pay those military and civilian employees who voted Republican and not pay those who voted Democratic. Debt ceiling default would be the most convoluted financial catastrophe imaginable.

In 2022, 41 million people received food assistance through the federal Supplemental Nutrition Assistance Program (SNAP).[14] Since the COVID pandemic is no longer considered an emergency the individual states in January, February, and March 2023 have stopped issuing emergency allotments to those in the SNAP program. These emergency allotments amounted to about $90 per person each month. They kept 4.2 million people above the poverty line, reducing poverty by 10% and child poverty by 14%[15] and now they are all gone. The average SNAP benefit in 2023 is now estimated to be $6.10. If the Republican House fails to raise the debt ceiling, those who now receive $6.10 per day in food assistance are in real danger of receiving nothing at all per day for food assistance.

Who currently receives the Supplemental Nutrition Assistance Program? The U.S. Department of Agriculture, which operates SNAP, estimates that 80% of SNAP beneficiaries are working families, people with disabilities, or elderly people and that two-thirds of SNAP households include children.[16] Does the Republican House really want to starve working families, the disabled, the elderly, and our children?

More than 70 million Americans receive Social Security or Supplemental Security checks each month. They include retirees over the age of 65, early retirees between 62 and 65, people with disabilities, and dependents.[17] They include your author and his spouse. If readers are not currently receiving Social Security, chances are that you will be when you retire. If the Republican Congress refuses to increase the debt ceiling, these monthly checks that we all depend upon for our monthly expenses are in danger of stopping.

All government salaries, including the military, are in danger of stopping. Think of a government program, any program, and it is in danger of being reduced or completely stopped. Failure to raise the debt ceiling will trigger a financial calamity ranging from a "catastrophic impact on the economy and federal programs"[18] to an "unmitigated disaster."[19]

EXPERT WITNESSES:

DR. WENDY EDELBERG

DR. LOUISE SHEINER

Dr. Wendy Edelberg is former Chief Economist for the Congressional Budget Office and current Director of the Hamilton Project, dedicated to creating a growing economy that benefits more Americans, at the prestigious Brookings Institution think tank.[20] Dr. Louise Sheiner is a former economist with the Board of Governors of the Federal Reserve System and is currently Policy Director at the Hutchins Center on Fiscal and Monetary Policy at Harvard University.[21] To say that both Dr. Edelberg and Dr. Sheiner are accomplished economists who have a tremendous grasp on public policy and governmental affairs would be a gross understatement. Their conclusion in their article, "How worried should we be if the debt ceiling isn't lifted?" is as follows:

While greatly uncertain, the effects of allowing the debt limit to bind [economist-speak for take effect] could be quite severe, even assuming that principal and interest payments continue to be made. If instead the Treasury fails to fully make all principal and interest payments—because of political or legal constraints, unexpected cash shortfalls, or a failed auction of new Treasury securities—the consequences would be even more dire.

The workarounds that have been proposed—the platinum coin, borrowing anyway, prioritizing payments—either bring significant legal uncertainty or are not sustainable solutions. These unlikely workarounds do not avoid the chaos that is inherent to the debt ceiling binding. The only effective solution is for Congress to increase the debt ceiling or, better yet, abolish it.[22]

Drs. Edelberg and Sheiner predict dire consequences even if the Treasury is able to prioritize and stay current on all principal and interest payments. I agree with them that the proposed workarounds of simply ignoring the debt ceiling and continuing to borrow, prioritizing payments and the platinum coin (discussed below) are hardly ideal. They believe that the only true solution is to either increase the debt ceiling or abolish it, with the preference being to abolish it.

PUBLICLY CREATED MONEY SYSTEM WOULD BE IMMUNE TO DEBT CEILING DEFAULT

Why are we in danger of seeing this potential financial Armageddon? Because we have a system of bank-created debt-money, it allows our aggrieved Republican-controlled House of Representatives to hold our entire society hostage to their demands and they have not even bothered to tell us what said demands are. Why? Because they have no specific demands. A just system of publicly created money would not be subject to such childish shenanigans. Why? Because our bills and debt would be paid on time with publicly created money and we would not have to go into debt to do so and put our entire society in harm's way with a Republican Party hell-bent on sticking it to a Democratic president, for the sole reason that they believe it will help them win the next election.

Since Republican Congresses routinely used the debt ceiling fight during the Democratic Obama and Biden administrations, talk surfaced about minting trillion-dollar platinum coins and depositing them with the Federal Reserve to cover the deficit. *31 U.S. Code § 5112 - Denominations, specifications, and design of coins*—Section (k) would seem to give the Secretary of Treasury the power to mint platinum coins and determine their value:

(k) The Secretary may mint and issue platinum bullion coins and proof platinum coins in accordance with such specifications, designs, varieties, quantities, denominations, and inscriptions as the Secretary, in the Secretary's discretion, may prescribe from time to time.[23]

Treasury Secretary Janet Yellen expressed disapproval of this idea when first proposed during the Obama administration and continues to oppose it in 2023. In the last showdown with Congress in 2021 Secretary Yellen said,

I'm opposed to it, and I don't believe we should consider it seriously.... It's really a gimmick, and what's necessary is for Congress to show the world can count on America paying its debts.[24]

In addition to not being an economist, I am certainly not a lawyer. I do agree that we should not use what Secretary Yellen refers to as a "gimmick" to do the country's business of paying our lawful debts. But if the "gimmick" she refers to is in fact a valid option within U.S. law and it alone can keep food assistance going out to the hungry, Social Security payments to more than 70 million seniors and, dependent and disabled people, and paychecks to millions of federal government employees, military employees and their dependents, then please do mint the platinum coins. Save our country from defaulting on its debts and plunging our civilization into a financial calamity the likes of which we have never seen before.

Both the power to create money and the power to borrow money reside with Congress in the Constitution. Article 1, Section 8 of the U.S. Constitution gives Congress, "the Power...To coin [create] Money, regulate the Value thereof." It also gives Congress, "the Power...To borrow Money on the credit of the United States."[25] I have reservations about the legality of Congress giving up its delegated power in 1913 to coin/create money away to the privately owned Federal Reserve (discussed in Chapter 10 of *History of Money 101*). I also have reservations about whether or not Congress can delegate its power to coin/create money to the Secretary of Treasury. But in the 110 years of the Federal Reserve System, to my knowledge its power to coin/create money has never been challenged in court. If we can use the unconstitutional bank-created debt-money system for the past 110 years, then we can certainly use a system of publicly created, fiat platinum coins today to avoid an unmitigated, catastrophic disaster.

If Congress refuses to raise the debt ceiling, I believe that President Biden should tell Secretary Yellen to mint trillion-dollar coins and use them to repay the federal debt. Early publicly created Spartan and Roman money was made of iron and bronze. This easily showed that they were a fiat, legal creation of the state as compared to other early forms of money in which its value was represented in the commodity value of the gold and silver used to make the coins. Book Two: *History of Money 101* will cover these money systems in detail. While I personally would like to see the new trillion-dollar fiat coins issued to be made of iron and bronze, as a show of respect to their historic Roman and Spartan fiat nature, my reading of the above law unfortunately does not allow for this. Iron and bronze coins are out and if necessary fiat platinum coins should be used to save us from Republican Party debt-ceiling default extremism.

Our nation is in desperate need of a system of publicly created money. Only with such a system of publicly created money will we not have to worry about any future Congress holding our society hostage to score political points by refusing to raise the debt ceiling. The debt ceiling only exists because Congress in 1913 unconstitutionally gave away its power and responsibility to create our money to the Federal Reserve System and the private banks that now presently create our money as debt. Reclaiming the ancient lost power of publicly created money by passing an updated version of the NEED Act (presented in Chapter 7) would make the entire debt ceiling controversy, which today threatens our entire economy and way of life to the core, null and void.

President Biden, minting the trillion-dollar platinum coins in themselves is merely a stopgap on the way to reclaiming the ancient lost power of publicly created money. I urge you to invite former Congressman Dennis Kucinich and his wife, Elizabeth, over for dinner and a conversation about the publicly created money in the NEED Act that was put into Congress in 2011 by Congressmen Kucinich and John Conyers. Please feel free to include representatives from the Alliance for Just Money and the American Monetary Institute, along with Treasury Department and Federal Reserve officials.

Most of us who advocate for monetary reform are just regular people from all walks of life and we might need a little help, not in presenting our case for just, sovereign, publicly created money to you, but in being able to understand the objections the economics establishment will in all probability present. So far the said economics establishment has been quite successful in completely ignoring the concept of publicly created money. Shunning is the word I have used throughout the *People, Planet & the Power of Money Project* and I stand by what I have said. Shunning is a form of abuse and those in the economics profession responsible need to take a long hard look at their abusive passive-aggressive behavior. Perhaps, we could include a handful of economists who could help us all get a better understanding of who creates our money and how they create it. I believe economists Joseph Huber, Michael Kumhof, Richard Werner, and Kaoru Yamaguchi should be able to help us in this regard.

President Biden, I don't need to tell you that we have both an inequality and environmental crises confronting us that need huge investments. We can continue to let the banks create our money and then try and get a recalcitrant Congress to go further into debt as we borrow the money to alleviate these crises, paying interest on this borrowed bank-created debt-money. Or we can publicly create the money and attack the crises with the entire resources of our society, allowing much of this publicly created money to stay within the economy, helping all our people to build wealth and security, instead of just those at the top of the heap.

President Biden, thank you for allowing me to vent. I have spent the last two decades advocating for peace and social/environmental justice. Publicly creating our money is the way forward to achieving all of these. Thanks for reading and don't forget to also read *History of Money 101* and *Spaceship Earth 101*. My author's website NickEgnatz.com will inform you when they will be available.

Author's note: On June 3, 2023, just days before Money Creation 101 was sent to publication, President Joe Biden signed into law the Fiscal Responsibility Act of 2023, a bipartisan bill that avoided the debt default two days before it would have occurred. Biden said, "I just signed into law a bipartisan budget agreement that prevents a first-ever default while reducing the deficit, safeguarding Social Security, Medicare, and Medicaid, and fulfilling our scared obligation to our veterans. Now, we continue the work of building the strongest economy in the world."[26]

President Biden chose to take the same bipartisan route he has taken throughout his career. He did so just days before my book and advice could have ever reached his ears. By not using platinum coins or simply invoking the 14th Amendment and ignoring the debt ceiling, confrontations over the debt ceiling loom in our country's future. I have every reason to believe that President Biden chose this route because he believes that working together in a bipartisan manner is the only way to avoid our country splitting apart, with a third of the country completely abandoning the imperfect system we have had for 230 some years, for the charm of a confidence man from New York, now residing in Florida, who has convinced his followers that he himself is their messiah reincarnated.

I believe that President Biden's course is worth trying. If it holds us together in a lawful manner, then we have a chance to make more perfect, our imperfect union. As I bid adieu until a *History of Money 101* is published, I leave readers with a determination I reached while writing it. I do so to illustrate the potential consequences of our present precarious fractured national discourse today.

Years ago before I became an activist and lived a more normal life, I did a somewhat deep dive into the history of the Civil War. But it was only while writing Book Two: *History of Money 101* that I came to what I consider is a remarkable conclusion: If the South had been allowed to peacefully secede or had been militarily successful in defeating the massive effort by the North to keep the Union intact, there is absolutely no reason to believe that the South would not continue to be a slaveholding society today.

Afterword

I thank you for having the intellectual curiosity to take a look at who creates our money by reading *Money Creation 101*. The best first action you can take to help get us to a system of publicly created money is to let others know what you discovered by providing a short review on Amazon. com.

If we are to take our economics professionals' pronouncements on the subject of money creation seriously, you now have a much better grasp on the money creation question than Professors A and B of Chapter 4 demonstrated in their email exchanges with me. These two gentlemen are both highly respected economists at top-level American university economics programs, yet in their limited dialogue with your author they were unable to correctly answer who creates our money and how they create it. You have been exposed to a frank discussion of money creation. This is exactly what current economics students are asking their universities to provide to them. I encourage you to read Book Two: *History of Money 101* and Book Three: *Spaceship Earth 101* to further your knowledge base on the most necessary thing in modern society—money.

Book Two: *History of Money 101* reveals the rich history of publicly created money which has been largely ignored in our nation's leading university economics programs. It takes you to the beginnings of modern civilization in the Fertile Crescent and the first money as intricate, publicly created systems of credit based on agricultural commodities or in some cases tools. The *History of Money*'s next stop is in ancient Greece and Rome, where early forms of publicly created money provided the support for the societies that then built much of our civilization's democratic and legal traditions. It brings to life the vital history that publicly created money had in building the struggling American colonies, fighting the Revolution and then saving the Union fourscore and seven years later. *History of Money 101* is exactly the type of information that economics students across the globe are now pleading with their university programs to include in their own education.

Spaceship Earth 101 is your author's attempt to propose publicly created money as the funding mechanism for the things we are told that we simply cannot afford within the present bank-created debt-money system—real action on climate change to achieve drawdown of the carbon in our atmosphere, clean oceans and freshwater, a reasonable policy of stopping the endless creation of unrecyclable plastic that presently litters our planet, and the extreme inequality in our society that will certainly continue to increase as artificial intelligence robots begin to take more of our jobs. It frankly discusses socialism and capitalism as theoretical concepts which are then used to divide us and keep us from democratically working out the solutions that will heal both our planet and ourselves.

A complete bibliography of sources is available on the author's website (NickEgnatz.com).

Book 2: *History of Money 101* and Book 3: *Spaceship Earth 101* should both be available later in 2023 or early 2024. My author's website (NickEgnatz.com) will have information on dates as we get closer to them.

The Alliance For Just Money (monetaryalliance.org) and the American Monetary Institute (monetary.org) are both at your service to help you further your education about what kind of money system we should have. Readers outside the U.S. should be able to also find local organizations at the International Movement for Monetary Reform (internationalmoneyreform.org).

NOTES

PREFACE

1. Boulding, Kenneth E., "The Economics of the Coming Spaceship Earth," Sixth Resources for the Future Forum on Environmental Quality in a Growing Economy in Washington, D.C. on March 8,1966, http://www.ub.edu/prometheus21/articulos/obsprometheus/BOULDING.pdf

PROLOGUE: YOU'RE NO DUMMY

1. Picchi, Aimee, "70% of Americans say they are struggling financially," CBS News, Nov 14, 2019, https://www.cbsnews.com/news/70-americans-are-struggling-financially/
2. Financial Health Network, "U.S. Financial Health Pulse: 2019 Trends Report," Nov 13, 2019, https://finhealthnetwork.org/research/u-s-financial-health-pulse-2019-trends-report/

1. INTRODUCTION: MODERN MONEY AS EASY AS 1, 2, 3

1. Brown, Ellen Hodgson J.D., *The Web of Debt*, Third Millennium Press, Baton Rouge, 2010.
2. National Emergency Employment Defense Act (NEED Act), 112th Congress, Sept. 21, 2011, https://www.congress.gov/bill/112th-congress/house-bill/2990/text
3. McLeay, Michael; Radia, Amar; Thomas, Ryland of the Bank's Monetary Analysis Directorate, Bank of England, Quarterly Bulletin 2014 Q1, "Money creation in the modern economy," p. 14, https://www.bankofengland.co.uk/-/media/boe/files/quarterly-bulletin/2014/money-creation-in-the-modern-economy
4. International Movement for Monetary Reform, https://international-moneyreform.org/
5. Alliance For Just Money, https://www.monetaryalliance.org/
6. American Monetary Institute, https://monetary.org/
7. McLeay, Michael, Radia, Amar, Thomas, Ryland of the Bank's Monetary Analysis Directorate, Bank of England, Quarterly Bulletin 2014 Q1, "Money creation in the modern economy," p. 14.
8. Wolf, Martin, Financial Times, April 24, 2014, "Strip private banks of their power to create money," https://www.ft.com/content/7f000b18-ca44-11e3-

bb92-00144feabdc0

9. Proctor, Robert N. & Londa Schiebinger, Editors, *Agnotology – The Making & Unmaking of Ignorance*, Stanford University Press, Stanford, CA, 2008.

2. THE FEDERAL RESERVE SYSTEM

1. "Modern Money Mechanics," Federal Reserve Bank of Chicago, 1994, copied and reprinted by Wikipedia, https://upload.wikimedia.org/wikipedia/commons/4/4a/Modern_Money_Mechanics.pdf

2. Zarlenga. Stephen, *The Lost Science of Money,* American Monetary Institute, 2002, Valatie, N.Y., Chapter 11, https://www.monetary.org/buy-the-book

3. Smith, Adam, *The Wealth of Nations,* 1776, Great Books Collection, p.138.

4. Zarlenga, *The Lost Science of Money,* Chapter 11, p. 286.

5. Zarlenga, Stephen, *Lost Science of Money,* American Monetary Institute, 2002, Valatie, New York, pp. 570-571.

6. Positive Money, "How Banks Create Money," https://positivemoney.org/how-money-%20works/how-banks-%20create-money/

7. Board of Governors of the Federal Reserve System, FAQs, "How much does it cost to produce currency and coin," https://www.federalreserve.gov/faqs/currency_12771.htm

8. Board of Governors of the Federal Reserve System, FAQs "What does it mean that the Federal Reserve is 'independent within the government'?" https://www.federalreserve.gov/faqs/about_12799.htm

9. Zarlenga, *The Lost Science of Money,* pp. 523-527.

10. Zarlenga, *The Lost Science of Money,* pp. 526-27, Jan.3, 1924 Letter from Benjamin Strong to J. Hollander, quoted by Lester V. Chandler, *Benjamin Strong, Central Banker,* Brookings, Washington, 1958, p. 17.

11. McLeay, Michael, Radia, Amar, Thomas, Ryland of the Bank's Monetary Analysis Directorate, Bank of England, Quarterly Bulletin 2014 Q1, "Money creation in the modern economy," p. 14.

12. McLeay et al, "Money Creation in the Modern Economy," p. 15.

13. Skousen, Mark, "The Perseverance of Paul Samuelson's *Economics,*" Journal of Economic Perspectives, Vol. 11, Number 2, Spring 1997, pp. 137-152, https://www.aeaweb.org/articles?id=10.1257/jep.11.2.137

14. Samuelson, Paul, *Economics,* McGraw-Hill, New York, 1948, p. 324.

15. Huber, Joseph, "Split-circuit reserve banking – functioning, dysfunctions and future perspectives," Real-World Economic Review, #80, 2017, http://www.paecon.net/PAEReview/issue80/Huber80.pdf

16. Huber, Joseph, *Sovereign Money. Beyond Reserve Banking,* Palgrave Macmillan, 2017, p. 39.

17. Zarlenga, *The Lost Science of Money,* Chapters 11,19.

18. Zarlenga, *Lost Science of Money,* pp. 280-281.

19. Coletta, Paola E., "William Jennings Bryan and Currency and Banking Reform," Nebraska History 45, 1964, p. 52, https://history.nebraska.gov/sites/history.nebraska.gov/files/doc/publications/NH1964BryanBanking.pdf

20. Federal Reserve History, "Gold Reserve Act of 1934," January 30, 1934, https://www.federalreservehistory.org/essays/gold-reserve-act#:~:text=Roosevelt%20in%20January%201934%2C%20the,from%20redeeming%20dollars%20for%20gold.
21. Federal Reserve History, "Nixon Ends Convertibility of U.S. Dollars to Gold and Announces Wage/Price Controls," August 1971, https://www.federalreservehistory.org/essays/gold-convertibility-ends
22. Board of Governors of the Federal Reserve System, "What does it mean that the Federal Reserve is 'independent within the government?'" http://www.federalreserve.gov/faqs/about_12799.htm
23. Board of Governors of the Federal Reserve System, "Federal Open Market Committee," http://www.federalreserve.gov/monetarypolicy/fomc.htm
24. Friedman, Milton & Schwartz, *A Monetary History of the United States 1867-1960,* Princeton University Press, 1971, p.193.
25. JUSTIA US Law, "John L. Lewis, Plaintiff/appellant, v. United States of America," Defendant/appellee, 680 F.2d 1239 (9th Cir. 1982), http://law.justia.com/cases/federal/appellate-courts/F2/680/1239/200393/
26. Board of Governors of the Federal Reserve System, "What does it mean that the Federal Reserve is 'independent within the government?'"
27. Federal Reserve Bank of Chicago, *Modern Money Mechanics,* p.3, https://upload.wikimedia.org/wikipedia/commons/4/4a/Modern_Money_Mechanics.pdf
28. Merriam-Webster, "Fraud," https://www.merriam-webster.com/dictionary/fraud
29. McLeay, Michael, Radia, Amar, Thomas, Ryland of the Bank's Monetary Analysis Directorate, Bank of England, Quarterly Bulletin 2014 Q1, "Money creation in the modern economy," p. 14.
30. McLeay et al, "Money creation in the modern economy," p. 16.
31. Board of Governors of the Federal Reserve System, FAQs, "How much does it cost to produce currency and coin?" https://www.federalreserve.gov/faqs/currency_12771.htm
32. Federal Reserve Bank of Cleveland, "Why Does the Fed Care about Inflation?" https://www.clevelandfed.org/en/our-research/center-for-inflation-research/inflation-101/why-does-the-fed-care-get-started.aspx
33. Werner, Richard & Lee, Kang-Soek, "Reconsidering Monetary Policy: An Empirical Examination of the Relationship Between Interest Rates and Nominal GDP Growth in the U.S., U.K., Germany and Japan," Ecological Economics, Volume 146, April 2018, pp. 26-34, https://www.sciencedirect.com/science/article/pii/S0921800916307510
34. Werner, Richard, "Professor Richard Werner, interest rates do not drive the economy," YouTube, https://www.youtube.com/watch?v=1lFpLbT8IGI
35. US Wealth Management, "How do supply chain issues contribute to inflation?" U.S. Bank & U.S. Bancorp Investments, Jan 25, 2023, https://www.usbank.com/investing/financial-perspectives/market-news/supply-chain-issues-contribution-to-inflation.html#:~:text=Supply%20chain%20shortfalls%20were%20a,and%20demand%2C%20forcing%20prices%20higher.

36. Bankova, Dea; Dutta, Prasanta Kumar & Ovaska, Michael, "The war in Ukraine is fueling a global food crisis," Reuters, May 30, 2022, https://www.reuters.com/graphics/UKRAINE-CRISIS/FOOD/zjvqkgomjvx/

37. Reich, Robert, "Corporate greed, not wages, is behind inflation. It's time for price controls." Guardian, Sept 25, 2022, https://www.theguardian.com/commentisfree/2022/sep/25/inflation-price-controls-robert-reich

3. THE NITTY-GRITTY ON DEBT-MONEY CREATION

1. London Speaker Bureau, "Richard A Werner," https://us.londonspeakerbureau.com/speaker-profile/richard-a-werner/

2. Werner, Richard A, "A lost century in economics: Three theories of banking and the conclusive evidence," International Review of Financial Analysis, Sept 8, 2015, https://www.sciencedirect.com/science/article/pii/S1057521915001477

3. Federal Reserve Bank of San Francisco, Education, "What is the economic function of a bank?" July 2001, https://www.frbsf.org/education/publications/doctor-econ/2001/july/bank-economic-function/

4. McLeay, Michael, Radia, Amar a, Thomas, Ryland of the Bank's Monetary Analysis Directorate, Bank of England, Quarterly Bulletin 2014 Q1, "Money creation in the modern economy," p. 14.

5. US National Debt, USDebtClock.org, https://www.usdebtclock.org/

6. Federal Reserve Bank of San Francisco, Education, "What is the economic function of a bank?" July 2001, https://www.frbsf.org/education/publications/doctor-econ/2001/july/bank-economic-function/

7. Werner, "A lost century in economics...."

8. Amazon.com, *Economics* 19th edition, Paul Samuelson, https://www.amazon.com/Economics-Paul-Samuelson/dp/0073511293

9. Weinstein, Michael M, "Paul A. Samuelson, Economist, Dies at 94," New York Times, Dec 13, 2009, https://www.nytimes.com/2009/12/14/business/economy/14samuelson.html

10. The Nobel Prize, "Paul A. Samuelson The Sveriges Riksbank Prize in Economic Sciences in Memory of Alfred Nobel 1970," https://www.nobelprize.org/prizes/economic-sciences/1970/samuelson/facts/

11. Samuelson, Paul, *Economics*, McGraw-Hill, New York, 1948, p.324.

12. Samuelson, *Economics*, 1948, p. 325.

13. Samuelson, *Economics*, 1948, p. 325.

14. Samuelson, *Economics*, 1948, p. 326.

15. Samuelson, *Economics*, 1948, p. 326.

16. Samuelson, *Economics*, 1948, p. 324.

17. Samuelson, *Economics*, 1948, p. 326.

18. Samuelson, *Economics*, 1948, p. 329.

19. Samuelson, *Economics*, 1948, p. 329.

20. Samuelson, Paul & Nordhaus, William., *Economics,* McGraw-Hill, New York, 1995.

21. Samuelson, Paul & Nordhaus ,William., *Economics,* McGraw-Hill, New York, 1995, p. 490.
22. Huber, Joseph, "Split-circuit reserve banking – functioning, dysfunctions and future perspectives," Real-World Economic Review, #80, 2017, http://www.-paecon.net/PAEReview/issue80/Huber80.pdf
23. Werner, "A lost century in economics...." p. 366.
24. Werner, "A lost Century in Economics...." pp. 365-366.
25. U.S. Constitution, Article I, Section 8.
26. Kumhof, Michael, & Benes, Jaromir, *The Chicago Plan Revisited,* International Monetary Fund, Working Paper, p. 10-11, https://www.im-f.org/external/pubs/ft/wp/2012/wp12202.pdf
27. Kydland, Finn E. & Prescott, Edward C. (1990), "Business Cycles: Real Facts and a Monetary Myth," Federal Reserve Bank of Minneapolis Quarterly Review, 14(2), 3-18, https://www.minneapolisfed.org/research/quarterly-review/business-cycles-real-facts-and-a-monetary-myth
28. Kumhof, Michael, & Benes, Jaromir, *The Chicago Plan Revisited,* International Monetary Fund, Working Paper, p. 11.
29. Egnatz, Nick, Alpeus.org, Dec 25, 2014, "Linking Social Justice to Monetary Reform," http://www.alpheus.org/linking-social-justice-to-monetary-reform/
30. Egnatz, Nick, Alpheus.org, Dec 25, 2014, "Linking Social Justice to Monetary Reform."
31. NEED Act, National Emergency Employment Defense Act, https://www.congress.gov/bill/112th-congress/house-bill/2990/text

4. Economics Professors on How Our Money Is Created

1. Kumhof, Michael, & Benes, Jaromir, *The Chicago Plan Revisited,* International Monetary Fund, Working Paper, p. 10-11, https://www.im-f.org/external/pubs/ft/wp/2012/wp12202.pdf
2. Clarke, David, "Poll Shows 85% of MPs Don't Know Where Money Comes from," Positive Money, 2017, https://positivemoney.org/2017/10/mp-poll/
3. NEED Act, National Emergency Employment Defense Act, https://www.con-gress.gov/bill/112th-congress/house-bill/2990/text
4. McLeay, Michael, Radia, Amar, Thomas, Ryland of the Bank's Monetary Analysis Directorate, Bank of England, Quarterly Bulletin 2014 Q1, "Money creation in the modern economy," p. 14, https://www.bankofengland.co.uk/-/media/boe/files/quarterly-bulletin/2014/money-creation-in-the-modern-economy
5. Zarlenga, Stephen, *The Lost Science of Money,* American Monetary Institute, Valatie, New York, 2002.
6. Werner, Richard A, "A lost century in economics: Three theories of banking and the conclusive evidence," International Review of Financial Analysis, Sept 8, 2015, https://www.sciencedirect.com/science/article/pii/S1057521915001477
7. Huber, Joseph, *Split-circuit reserve banking – functioning, dysfunctions and future perspectives,* Real-

World Economics Review, Issue #80, 2017, http://www.pae-con.net/PAEReview/issue80/Huber80.pdf

8. Yamaguchi, Kaoru, *Workings of A Public Money System of Open Macro-economies – Modeling the American Monetary Act Completed – (A Revised Version)*, 2011, Doshisha University, http://www.muratopia.org/Yam-aguchi/doc/DesignOpenMacro.pdf

9. Luther, William J., "How the Federal Reserve Literally Makes Money," June 10, 2020, CATO Institute, bit.ly/3NU0J5w

10. Luther, William J., "How the Federal Reserve Literally Makes Money."

11. McLeay, Michael, Radia, Amar, Thomas, Ryland of the Bank's Monetary Analysis Directorate, Bank of England, "Money creation in the modern economy."

12. Y Charts, "US M2 Money Supply," https://ycharts.com/indicators/us_m2_-money_supply

5. The Cost of the Debt-Money System

1. Campbell, Peter Scott, Greenbag.org, "DEMOCRACY V. CONCEN-TRATED WEALTH IN SEARCH OF A LOUIS D. BRANDEIS QUOTE," http://greenbag.org/v16n3/v16n3_articles_campbell.pdf

2. Dilliard, Irving, Editor, *Mr. Justice Brandeis, Great American* (1941), Modern View Press, St. Louis, 1941, As quoted by Raymond Lonergan p. 42. Raymond Lonergan was a pseudonym used by Brandeis's good friend and former Congressman Edward Keating.

3. Kumhof, Michael, & Benes, Jaromir, *The Chicago Plan Revisited*, International Monetary Fund, Working Paper, pp 10-11, https://www.im-f.org/external/pubs/ft/wp/2012/wp12202.pdf

4. Macleod, Henry D, *The Theory and Practice of Banking*, London, Longman Greens & Co., 1906, Vol. 2, pp. 311, 408.

5. Zeddies, Lino, "Money Creation and Inequality – An Underexposed Topic for Monetary Reformers," International Movement for Monetary Reform, Jan 6, 2018, https://internationalmoneyreform.org/news/2018/01/money-creation-inequality-underexposed-topic-monetary-reformers/

6. Peter G. Peterson Foundation, "The Federal Reserve Holds More Treasury Notes and Bonds than Ever Before," April 29, 2021, https://www.pgpf.org/blog/2021/04/the-federal-reserve-holds-more-treasury-notes-and-bonds-than-ever-before

7. Zeddies, Lino, "Money Creation and Inequality – An Underexposed Topic for Monetary Reformers," International Movement for Monetary Reform, Jan 6, 2018.

8. Board of Governors of the Federal Reserve System, "Financial Accounts of the U.S., Flow of Funds, Balance Sheets, and Integrated Macroeconomic Accounts, Household Net Worth and Growth of Nonfinancial Debt," https://www.federalreserve.gov/releases/z1/20180920/z1.pdf

9. Board of Governors of the Federal Reserve System, "Financial Accounts of the U.S. 2019 Front Matter, Household Net Worth and Growth of Nonfinancial

Debt," https://www.federalreserve.gov/releases/z1/20190920/html/introductory_text.htm

10. Steverman, Ben, "The Wealth Detective Who Finds the Hidden Money of the Super Rich," Bloomberg Businessweek, May 23, 2019, Referencing economist Gabriel Zucman's work, https://www.bloomberg.com/news/features/2019-05-23/the-wealth-detective-who-finds-the-hidden-money-of-the-super-rich?srnd=premium

11. Piketty, Thomas & Saez, Emmanuel, *Income Inequality in the United States, 1913–1998*, The Quarterly Journal of Economics, February 2003, https://eml.berkeley.edu/~saez/pikettyqje.pdf

12. Rotten Tomatoes, *The Treasure of the Sierra Madre*, https://www.rottentomatoes.com/m/treasure_of_the_sierra_madre.

13. Rotten Tomatoes, *The Treasure of the Sierra Madre*.

14. Board of Governors of the Federal System, "Report on the Economic Well-Being of U.S. Households in 2013," July 2014, https://www.federalreserve.gov/econresdata/2013-report-economic-well-being-us-households-201407.pdf

15. Board of Governors of the Federal Reserve System, "Report on the Economic Well-Being of U.S. Households in 2014," May 15, 2015, https://www.federalreserve.gov/econresdata/2014-report-economic-well-being-us-households-201505.pdf

16. Board of Governors of the Federal Reserve System, "Report on the Economic Well-Being of U.S. Households in 2015," May 15, 2016, , https://www.federalreserve.gov/2015-report-economic-well-being-us-households-201605.pdf

17. Board of Governors of the Federal Reserve System, "Report on the Economic Well-Being of U.S. Households in 2016," May 15, 2017, https://www.federalreserve.gov/publications/files/2016-report-economic-well-being-us-households-201705.pdf

18. Board of Governors of the Federal Reserve System, "Report on the Economic Well-Being of U.S. Households in 2017," May 2018, https://www.federalreserve.gov/publications/files/2017-report-economic-well-being-us-households-201805.pdf

19. Board of Governors of the Federal Reserve System, "Report on the Economic Well-Being of U.S. Households in 2018," May 2019, https://www.federalreserve.gov/publications/files/2018-report-economic-well-being-us-households-201905.pdf

20. Board of Governors of the Federal Reserve System, "Report on the Economic Well-Being of U.S. Households in 2019, Featuring Supplemental Data from April 2020," May 2020, https://www.federalreserve.gov/publications/files/2019-report-economic-well-being-us-households-202005.pdf

21. Tirado, Linda, *Hand to Mouth – Living in Bootstrap America*, Putnam, New York, 2014, Introduction, p. 23.

22. Tirado, Linda, *Hand to Mouth...*, Introduction, p. 28

23. Levinson, Eric, "Former officer knelt on George Floyd for 9 minutes 29 seconds—not the infamous 8:46," CNN, March 30, 2021, https://www.cnn.com/2021/03/29/us/george-floyd-timing-929-846/index.html

24. Linda Tirado @KillerMartinis, May 30, 2020.

25. Davis, Charles, "After being shot in the face while covering a protest, a freelance journalist and her attorney alleged a conspiracy. A judge just ruled to let

the case move forward." Business Insider, Feb 26, 2021, https://www.businessinsider.com/linda-tiradoblinded-in-one-eye-after-shot-by-police-2021-2

26. Werner, Richard A, "A lost century in economics: Three theories of banking and the conclusive evidence," International Review of Financial Analysis, Sept 8, 2015, https://www.sciencedirect.com/science/article/pii/S1057521915001477

27. US Constitution, 14th Amendment, Sec. 4.

28. FRED—Federal Reserve Economic Data, "Nonfinancial Corporate Business; Debt Securities and Loans; Liability, Level," Updated June 10, 2021, Federal Reserve Bank of St. Louis, https://fred.stlouisfed.org/series/BCNSDODNS

6. DEMANDING CHANGE

1. Zarlenga, Stephen, American Monetary Institute, https://www.monetary.org/

2. Rhoades, Dawn, "175 Chicago protesters arrested after being told to leave Grant Park," Chicago Tribune, Oct 16, 2011, https://www.chicagotribune.com/news/breaking/chi-occupy-chicago-protesters-relocate-to-grant-park-20111015-story.html

3. Nickeas, Peter & Jaworski, Jim, "Police again arrest Occupy Chicago protesters in Grant Park," Chicago Tribune, Oct 23, 2011, https://www.chicagotribune.com/news/breaking/chi-occupy-chicago-aims-to-try-occupying-grant-park-again-tonight-20111022-story.html

4. Wolf, Naomi, "Revealed: how the FBI coordinated the crackdown on Occupy, " The Guardian, Dec 29, 2012, https://www.theguardian.com/commentisfree/2012/dec/29/fbi-coordinated-crackdown-occupy

5. Partnership for Civil Justice Fund, "FBI Documents Reveal Secret Nationwide Occupy Monitoring," http://www.justiceonline.org/fbi_files_ows

6. International Criminal Court, "Situation in Ukraine: ICC judges issue arrest warrants against Vladimir Vladimirovich Putin and Maria Alekseyevna Lvova-Belova," Press Release: March 17, 2023, https://www.icc-cpi.int/news/situation-ukraine-icc-judges-issue-arrest-warrants-against-vladimir-vladimirovich-putin-and

7. Sensini, Paolo, Sowing Chaos – Libya in the Wake of Humanitarian Intervention, Clarity Press, Atlanta, 2016, Foreword by Cynthia McKinney.

8. Adbusters, "8th Anniversary of #Occupy Wall Street," https://www.adbusters.org/campaigns/8th-anniversary-of-occupywallstreet

9. Bakshi, Rashni, "The other economic summit and the New Economics Foundation", Dialogues, Proposals, Stories for Global Citizenship," Sept 2008, http://base.d-p-h.info/en/fiches/dph/fiche-dph-7534.html

10. Zarlenga, Stephen, The Lost Science of Money, p. 177-89

11. Zarlenga, Stephen, The Lost Science of Money, p. 186.

12. Heath, Rachelle, "What are usury laws and maximum interest rates? " Bankrate, Jan 21, 2020, https://www.bankrate.com/finance/credit-cards/does-law-cap-credit-card-interest-rates/

13. Zarlenga, The Lost Science of Money, p. 3

14. Reich, Robert, "How Crypto Could Take Your Savings," YouTube, Aug 16, 2022, https://www.youtube.com/watch?v=TjIFkuPaA20

15. U.S. Securities and Exchange Commission, "Ponzi Scheme," Investor.gov, https://www.investor.gov/protect-your-investments/fraud/types-fraud/ponzi-scheme

16. Reilly, Caitlin, "Crypto-linked super PACs boost spending on primary races," Roll Call, June 21, 2022, https://rollcall.com/2022/06/21/crypto-linked-super-pacs-boost-spending-on-primary-races/

17. Reich, Robert, "How Crypto Could Take Your Savings," YouTube, Aug 16, 2022.

18. Edwards, John, "Bitcoin's Price History," Investopedia, Dec 20, 2022, https://www.investopedia.com/articles/forex/121815/bitcoins-price-history.asp

19. Gura, David, "5 major revelations about the collapse of crypto giant FTX," NPR, WBEZ Chicago, Nov 23, 2022, https://www.n-pr.org/2022/11/23/1138881426/ftx-sam-bankman-fried-bankruptcy-crypto-cryptocurrency-collapse#:~:text=But%20the%20FTX%20lawyers%20-said,at%20a%20whopping%20%2440%20billion.

20. Sweet, Ken, "Tom Brady, Larry David, other celebrities named in FTX suit," AP News, Nov 16, 2022, https://bit.ly/3NKhEFW

21. U.S. Attorney's Office, Southern District of New York, "United States Attorney Announces Charges Against FTX Founder Samuel Bankman-Fried," Department of Justice, Dec 13, 2022, https://www.justice.gov/usao-sdny/pr/united-states-attorney-announces-charges-against-ftx-founder-samuel-bankman-fried

7. Publicly Created Money in Action— The NEED Act

1. Paul H. Douglas, University of Chicago; Irving Fisher, Yale University; Frank D. Graham, Princeton University; Earl J. Hamilton, Duke University; Willford I. King, New York University; Charles R. Whittlesey, Princeton University, "A Program for Monetary Reform", July, 1939, https://faculty.chicagobooth.edu/amir.sufi/research/monetaryreform_1939.pdf

2. Paul H. Douglas, University of Chicago; Irving Fisher, Yale University; Frank D. Graham, Princeton University; Earl J. Hamilton, Duke University; Willford I. King, New York University; Charles R. Whittlesey, Princeton University, "A Program for Monetary Reform", July, 1939.

3. Bank Calumet Building, Emporis, https://www.emporis.com/buildings/123651/bank-calumet-building-hammond-in-usa

4. Silber, William L., "Why Did FDR's Bank Holiday Succeed," Federal Reserve Bank of New York, Economic Policy Review, July 2009, https://www.newyorkfed.org/research/epr/09v15n1/0907silb.html

5. Federal Deposit Insurance Corporation, "Deposit Insurance", Sept 17, 2020, https://www.fdic.gov/resources/deposit-insurance/

6. Federal Reserve History, "Banking Act of 1933 (Glass-Steagall)," June 16, 1933, https://www.federalreservehistory.org/essays/glass-steagall-act

7. Federal Reserve History, "Gold Reserve Act of 1934," January 30, 1934, https://www.federalreservehistory.org/essays/gold-reserve-act#:~:text=Roo-

sevelt%20in%20January%201934%2C%20the,from%20redeeming%20dollars%20for%20gold.

8. Federal Reserve History, "Nixon Ends Convertibility of US Dollars to Gold and Announces Wage/Price Controls," August 1971, https://www.federalreservehistory.org/essays/gold_convertibility_ends

9. National Emergency Employment Defense Act (NEED Act), 112th Congress, Sept. 21, 2011, https://www.congress.gov/bill/112th-congress/house-bill/2990/text

10. American Society of Civil Engineers, "Report Card History," https://www.infrastructurereportcard.org/making-the-grade/report-card-history/

11. American Society of Civil Engineers, "Report Card History, 2021 Report Card for America's Infrastructure, 'America's Infrastructure Scores a C–.'" https://infrastructurereportcard.org/

12. American Society of Civil Engineers, "POLICY STATEMENT 418 - THE ROLE OF THE CIVIL ENGINEER IN SUSTAINABLE DEVELOPMENT," https://www.asce.org/issues-and-advocacy/public-policy/policy-statement-418---the-role-of-the-civil-engineer-in-sustainable-development/

13. American Monetary Institute, "Fact Sheet Infrastructure Job Numbers," https://www.monetary.org/wp-content/uploads/2011/10/revised-Fact-Sheet-plus-Job-Numbers-for-NEED1.pdf

14. ABC Eyewitness News, "Gary, Indiana, named most miserable city in U.S., according to Business Insider," https://abc7chicago.com/society/gary-named-most-miserable-city-in-us/5582601/#:~:text=website%20Business%20Insider.-,GARY%2C%20Ind.,36%20percent%20live%20in%20poverty.

15. Paul H. Douglas, University of Chicago; Irving Fisher, Yale University; Frank D. Graham, Princeton University; Earl J. Hamilton, Duke University; Willford I. King, New York University; Charles R. Whittlesey, Princeton University, "A Program for Monetary Reform", July, 1939.

16. National Emergency Employment Defense Act (NEED Act), 112th Congress, Sept. 21, 2011, https://www.congress.gov/bill/112th-congress/house-bill/2990/text

17. National Emergency Employment Defense Act (NEED Act).

18. National Emergency Employment Defense Act (NEED Act).

19. National Emergency Employment Defense Act (NEED Act), Sec. 2, Findings; Purposes.

20. National Emergency Employment Defense Act (NEED Act), Sec. 102.

21. National Emergency Employment Defense Act (NEED Act), Sec. 103-104.

22. National Emergency Employment Defense Act (NEED Act), Sec. 106.

23. National Emergency Employment Defense Act (NEED Act), Sec. 107.

24. National Emergency Employment Defense Act (NEED Act), Sec. 301.

25. National Emergency Employment Defense Act (NEED Act), Sec. 302.

26. National Emergency Employment Defense Act (NEED Act), Sec. 314.

27. National Emergency Employment Defense Act (NEED Act), Sec. 304.

28. Board of Governors of the Federal Reserve System, Federal Reserve Act, "Section 13. Powers of the Federal Reserve Banks," https://www.federalreserve.gov/aboutthefed/section13.htm

29. National Emergency Employment Defense Act (NEED Act), Sec. 402.

30. National Emergency Employment Defense Act (NEED Act), Sec. 402.

31. National Emergency Employment Defense Act (NEED Act), Sec. 402.
32. National Emergency Employment Defense Act (NEED Act), Sec. 402.
33. National Emergency Employment Defense Act (NEED Act), Sec. 402.
34. National Emergency Employment Defense Act (NEED Act), Sec. 403.
35. National Emergency Employment Defense Act (NEED Act), Sec. 501.
36. American Society of Civil Engineers, "Infrastructure Report Card," https://www.infrastructurereportcard.org/
37. National Emergency Employment Defense Act (NEED Act), Sec. 502.
38. Miller, Peter, "Average 30-year mortgage rates since 1972," The Mortgage Reports by Full Banker Inc., Jan 29, 2021, https://themortgagereports.com/61853/30-year-mortgage-rates-chart
39. National Emergency Employment Defense Act (NEED Act), Sec. 503.
40. National Emergency Employment Defense Act (NEED Act), Sec. 504.
41. National Emergency Employment Defense Act (NEED Act), Sec. 505.
42. National Emergency Employment Defense Act (NEED Act), Sec. 506.
43. Warren, Katie, Business Insider, May 23, 2019, "One brutal sentence captures what a disaster money in America has become," https://bit.ly/41vbApA
44. National Emergency Employment Defense Act (NEED Act), Sec. 507.
45. National Emergency Employment Defense Act (NEED Act), Sec. 508.
46. National Emergency Employment Defense Act (NEED Act), Sec. 509.
47. Walton, Jamie, "How the N.E.E.D. Act gives an Immediate, Seamless and Non-Disruptive Overnight Transition from a Crisis-Prone Bank Debt System to a Stable Government Money System," American Monetary Institute, August 2015, http://www.alpheus.org/wp-content/uploads/2015/10/Walton-Transition.pdf
48. Walton, Jamie, "How the N.E.E.D. Act gives an Immediate, Seamless and Non-Disruptive Overnight Transition from a Crisis-Prone Bank Debt System to a Stable Government Money System," American Monetary Institute, August 2015, http://www.alpheus.org/wp-content/uploads/2015/10/Walton-Transition.pdf
49. Alliance For Just Money, "American Monetary Reform Act of 2022", https://www.monetaryalliance.org/wp-content/uploads/American-Monetary-Reform-Act.pdf

8. Financial Shenanigans & the Cultural Hegemony of Debt-Money

1. FDIC, "Deposit Insurance FAQs," https://www.fdic.gov/deposit/deposits/faq.html#:~:text=The%20standard%20deposit%20insurance%20coverage,held%20at%20the%20same%20bank.
2. FDIC, Federal Deposit Insurance Fund, Press Release: Feb 23, 2021, "The Deposit Insurance Fund's Reserve Ratio Declined from the Previous Quarter to 1.29 Percent," https://www.fdic.gov/news/press-releases/2021/pr21012.html
3. Board of Governors of the Federal Reserve System, "Survey of Consumer Finances, 2019," https://www.federalreserve.gov/econres/scfindex.htm

4. Bennett, Karen, "The Average amount in U.S. savings accounts – how does your cash stack up," Bankrate, Feb 8, 2022, https://www.bankrate.com/personal-finance/savings-account-average-balance/

5. Seuser, Steve, "Legal Framework For Big Banks Puts Depositors At Risk," Aug 25, 2013, DC Public Banking, https://www.dcpublicbanking.org/multimediaarchive/legal-framework-for-big-banks-puts-depositors-at-risk/

6. Fernando, Jason, "Derivative," Investopedia, Feb 3, 2021, https://www.investopedia.com/terms/d/derivative.asp

7. Roe, Mark J., *The Derivatives Market's Payment Priorities as Financial Crisis Accelerator*, Stanford Law Review, Harvard Library, 2011, https://dash.harvard.edu/bitstream/handle/1/30011626/Roe_700.pdf?sequence=1&isAllowed=y

8. Maverick, J.B., "How Big is the Derivatives Market?" Investopedia, April 28, 2020, https://www.investopedia.com/ask/answers/052715/how-big-derivatives-market.asp

9. Desjardins, Jeff, "All of the World's Money and Markets in One Visualization," Visual Capitalist, May 27, 2020, https://www.visualcapitalist.com/all-of-the-worlds-money-and-markets-in-one-visualization-2020/

10. FRED, " Gross Domestic Product," Federal Reserve Bank of St. Louis, https://fred.stlouisfed.org/series/GDP

11. International Swaps and Derivatives Association, Inc., "Non-Cleared OTC Derivatives: Their Importance to the Global Economy," March 2013, https://www.isda.org/a/AeiDE/non-cleared-otc-derivatives-paper.pdf

12. Seuser, Steve, "Legal Framework For Big Banks Puts Depositors At Risk."

13. *i*Banknet, "Derivatives for Leading Domestic Financial/Bank Holding Companies," Quarter ending 2020 06/30, https://www.ibanknet.com/scripts/callreports/fiList.aspx?type=derivatives&sort=foreignexchange

14. *i*Banknet, "Derivatives for Leading Domestic Financial/Bank Holding Companies," Quarter ending 2020 06/30.

15. Thielman, Sam, "Black Americans unfairly targeted by banks before housing crisis, says ACLU," The Guardian, June 23, 2015, https://www.theguardian.com/business/2015/jun/23/black-americans-housing-crisis-sub-prime-loan

16. Investopedia, "Lien," https://www.investopedia.com/terms/l/lien.asp

17. Segal, Troy, "Troubled Asset Relief Program (TARP)," Investopedia, Sept 29, 2020, https://www.investopedia.com/terms/t/troubled-asset-relief-program-tarp.asp#:~:text=The%20Troubled%20Asset%20Relief%20Program%20(TARP)%20was%20an%20initiative%20created,of%20the%202008%20financial%20crisis.

18. Ivry, Bob, Keoun, Bradley &Kuntz, Phil, "Secret Fed Loans Gave Banks $13 Billion Undisclosed to Congress," Bloomberg News, Nov 27, 2011, https://www.bloomberg.com/news/articles/2011-11-28/secret-fed-loans-undisclosed-to-congress-gave-banks-13-billion-in-income

19. U.S. Government Accountability Office, "Office of the Inspector General," https://www.gao.gov/ig/

20. Barofsky, Neil M., "Where the Bailout Went Wrong," Op-Ed New York Times, March 29, 2011, https://www.nytimes.com/2011/03/30/opinion/30barofsky.html?_r=1&ref=opinion

21. Barofsky, Neil M., "Where the Bailout Went Wrong," Op-Ed New York Times, March 29, 2011, https://www.nytimes.com/2011/03/30/opinion/30barof-sky.html?_r=1&ref=opinion

22. Barofsky, Neil M., "Where the Bailout Went Wrong," Op-Ed New York Times, March 29, 2011, https://www.nytimes.com/2011/03/30/opinion/30barof-sky.html?_r=1&ref=opinion

23. Andres, Tommy, "Divided Decade: How the financial crisis changed housing," Marketplace.org, Dec. 17, 2018, https://www.market-place.org/2018/12/17/what-we-learned-housing/

24. Merriam-Webster, "hegemony," https://www.merriam-webster.com/dictio-nary/hegemony

25. European Parliament, "Parliamentary Immunity in Italy," Citizen's Rights and Constitutional Affairs, https://www.europarl.europa.eu/RegDa-ta/etudes/IDAN/2015/536456/IPOL_IDA(2015)536456_EN.pdf

26. Cole, Nicki Lisa, PhD, "Biography of Antonio Gramsci," ThoughtCo, Aug 14, 2019, https://www.thoughtco.com/antonio-gramsci-3026471

27. Cunningham, Paige Winfield, "The Health 202: Trump calls Medicare-for-all 'socialism.' Doctors once said the same about Medicare," Washington Post, Nov 12, 2019, https://www.washingtonpost.com/news/powerpost/palo-ma/the-health-202/2019/11/12/the-health-202-trump-calls-medicare-for-all-socialism-doctors-once-said-the-same-about-medicare/5dc9e04388e0-fa10ffd20d4e/

28. Harry S. Truman Library and Museum, "The Challenge of National Health-care," https://www.trumanlibrary.gov/education/presidential-inquiries/chal-lenge-national-healthcare

29. AARP Public Policy Institute, "The Medicare Beneficiary Population," https://assets.aarp.org/rgcenter/health/fs149_medicare.pdf

30. Sullivan, John F., "Sun Tzu's Fighting Words," The Strategy Bridge, June 15, 2020, https://thestrategybridge.org/the-bridge/2020/6/15/sun-tzus-fighting-words

31. Sullivan, John F., "Sun Tzu's Fighting Words."

9. In Defense of Publicly Created Money

1. System Dynamics Society, "What Is System Dynamics?" https://systemdynam-ics.org/what-is-system-dynamics/

2. Yamaguchi, Kaoru, "About Us," Muatopia.net, October 25, 2018, http://www.muratopia.net/YamaguchiKaoru/Yamaguchi/AboutUs.html

3. Yamaguchi, Kaoru, "About Us."

4. Yamaguchi, Kaoru, "About Us."

5. Muratopia.org, http://www.muratopia.org/Yamaguchi/doc/petition.pdf

6. Yamaguchi, Kaoru, *Workings of A Public Money System of Open Macro-economies – Modeling the American Monetary Act Completed – (A Revised Version)*, p. 17.

7. Yamaguchi, Kaoru, *Workings of A Public Money System of Open Macro-economies – Modeling the American Monetary Act Completed – (A Revised*

Version), 2011, Doshisha University, http://www.muratopia.org/Yamaguchi/doc/DesignOpenMacro.pdf

8. Encyclopedia Britannica, "The General Theory of Employment, Interest and Money?" https://www.britannica.com/topic/The-General-Theory-of-Employment-Interest-and-Money

9. Landis, Austin, "One year on, Biden admin. has dispensed most of $1.9 trillion COVID relief fund," Spectrum News NY1, Mar 11, 2022, https://www.ny1.com/nyc/all-boroughs/news/2022/03/11/american-rescue-plan-one-year-90-percent-obligated

10. Werner, Richard & Lee, Kang-Soek, "Reconsidering Monetary Policy: An Empirical Examination of the Relationship Between Interest Rates and Nominal GDP Growth in the U.S., U.K., Germany and Japan," Ecological Economics, Volume 146, April 2018, pp. 26-34, https://www.sciencedirect.com/science/article/pii/S0921800916307510

11. Yamaguchi, Kaoru, Public Money System, "Public Money vs. Debt-Money System Structures," http://www.muratopia.org/Yamaguchi/Public-Money.html

12. Del Negro, Macro & Schorfheide, Frank, "DSGE Model-Based Forecasting," Federal Reserve Bank of New York, March, 2012, https://www.newyorkfed.org/research/staff_reports/sr554.html

13. Kumhof, Michael & Benes, Jaromir, *The Chicago Plan Revisited,* International Monetary Fund, Working Paper, https://www.imf.org/external/pubs/ft/wp/2012/wp12202.pdf

14. Kumhof, Michael & Benes, Jaromir, *The Chicago Plan Revisited,* p. 7

15. Bank of England, "Michael Kumhof Senior Research Advisor -- Research Hub," https://www.bankofengland.co.uk/research/researchers/michael-kumhof

16. Smith, Adam, *The Wealth of Nations,* Great Books, University of Chicago Press, 1952.

17. Menger, Carl, *The Origin of Money*, Oxford University Press, 1892, Introduction.

18. Graeber, David, *Debt – The First 5,000 Years,* Melville House, Brooklyn, N.Y., 2011.

19. Ridgeway, William., *The Origin of Metallic Weights and Standards*, Cambridge, 1892.

20. Zarlenga, Stephen, *The Lost Science of Money,* American Monetary Institute, Valatie, New York, 2002.

21. Einzig, Paul, *Primitive Money,* New York: Pergamon, 1966.

22. Laum, Bernhard, *Heiliges Geld*, J.C.B. Mohr, Tübingen, 1924.

23. Quiggen, A. Hingston, *A Survey of Primitive Money,* Methune, London, 1949.

24. Del Mar, Alexander, *History of Monetary Systems*, Charles H. Kerr & Co, Chicago, 1895, reprint Forgotten Books, p.60.

25. Zarlenga, Stephen, *The Lost Science of Money,* American Monetary Institute, Valatie, New York, 2002, Introduction & Chapter 1.

26. Kumhof, Michael & Benes, Jaromir, *The Chicago Plan Revisited,* International Monetary Fund, Working Paper, p.12

10. A Plea to the Economics Profession

1. Moore, Barrington, *Social Origins of Dictatorship and Democracy: Lord and Peasant in the Making of the Modern World,* Beacon, Boston, 1966, p. 523.
2. Macleod, Henry D, *The Theory and Practice of Banking,* London, Longman Greens & Co., 1906, Vol. 2, pp. 311, 408.
3. Werner, Richard A., "A lost century in economics: Three theories of banking and the conclusive evidence," International Review of Financial Analysis, Sept 8, 2015, https://www.sciencedirect.com/science/article/pii/S1057521915001477
4. Werner, Richard, *How do banks create money, and why can other firms not do the same? An explanation for the coexistence of lending and deposit-taking,* International Review of Financial Analysis Volume 36, December 2014, p. 71-77, https://www.sciencedirect.com/science/article/pii/S1057521914001434
5. Warren, Katie, Business Insider, May 23, 2019, "One brutal sentence captures what a disaster money in America has become," https://www.businessinsider.com/bottom-half-of-americans-negative-net-worth-2019-5
6. Steverman, Ben, Bloomberg Businessweek, May 23, 2019, "The Wealth Detective Who Finds the Hidden Money of the Super Rich," https://www.bloomberg.com/news/features/2019-05-23/the-wealth-detective-who-finds-the-hidden-money-of-the-super-rich?srnd=premium
7. Piketty, Thomas & Saez, Emmanuel, *Income Inequality in the United States, 1913–1998,* The Quarterly Journal of Economics, February 2003, https://eml.berkeley.edu/~saez/pikettyqje.pdf
8. Federal Elections Commission, "Citizens United v. FEC," United States of America, https://www.fec.gov/legal-resources/court-cases/citizens-united-v-fec/
9. Federal Reserve Bank of St. Louis, "H. R. 7230 A BILL PROVIDING FOR GOVERNMENT OWNERSHIP OF THE TWELVE FEDERAL RESERVE BANKS AND FOR OTHER PURPOSES, HEARINGS BEFORE THE COMMITTEE ON BANKING AND CURRENCY HOUSE OF REPRESENTATIVES, SEVENTY-FIFTH CONGRESS THIRD SESSION," https://fraser.stlouisfed.org/files/docs/historical/federal%20reserve%20history/Govt_ownership_HR7230.pdf
10. H. R. 7230 A BILL PROVIDING FOR GOVERNMENT OWNERSHIP OF THE TWELVE FEDERAL RESERVE BANKS..., p. 3.
11. H. R. 7230 A BILL PROVIDING FOR GOVERNMENT OWNERSHIP OF THE TWELVE FEDERAL RESERVE BANKS..., p. 6.
12. H. R. 7230 A BILL PROVIDING FOR GOVERNMENT OWNERSHIP OF THE TWELVE FEDERAL RESERVE BANKS..., p. 22.
13. Zarlenga, Stephen, *Lost Science of Money,* American Monetary Institute, 2002, Valatie, New York, pp. 664-665.
14. National Emergency Employment Defense Act (NEED Act), Sec. 314.
15. Federal Reserve Act, Board of Governors of the Federal Reserve System, "Section 31, Reservation of Right to Amend," https://www.federalreserve.gov/aboutthefed/section31.htm
16. Bondarenko, Peter, "Macroeconomics," Encyclopedia Britannica, https://www.britannica.com/topic/macroeconomics

17. Auerbach, Robert D. 2008. *Deception and Abuse at the Fed.* University of Texas Press, p. 142.
18. Klein, Naomi, *The Shock Doctrine: The Rise of Disaster Capitalism.* New York: Henry Holt, 2007, p. 204.
19. Madrick, Jeff. 2014. *Seven Bad Ideas.* New York: Alfred A. Knopf, p. 164-188.
20. Klein, Naomi, *The Shock Doctrine: The Rise of Disaster Capitalism.* New York: Henry Holt, 2007.
21. First World and Third World are Cold War Era terms. The First World referred to Western capitalist democracies (NATO), aligned against the Soviet Bloc, China, Cuba, North Korea and Vietnam which were considered the Second World, although I do not recall them ever being called the Second World. The Third World referred to the poor, unaligned and developing world, now often referred to as the Global South.
22. Auerbach, Robert D. 2008. *Deception and Abuse at the Fed.* University of Texas Press, p. 142.
23. Auerbach, pp.142-143.
24. Grim, Ryan, Huffpost, 10/ 23,/ 2009, updated 5/13/2013, "Priceless: How The Federal Reserve Bought The Economics Profession," https://www.huffpost.com/entry/priceless-how-the-federal_n_278805
25. The Intercept, "Ryan Grim", https://theintercept.com/staff/ryangrim/
26. Grim, Ryan, "Priceless...."
27. Grim, Ryan, "Priceless...."
28. Grim, Ryan, "Priceless...."
29. Grim, Ryan, "Priceless...."
30. Grim, Ryan, "Priceless...."
31. Heckman, James & Moktan, Sidharth, Institute for New Economic Thinking, Oct 2, 1018, "Tyranny of the Top Five," https://www.ineteconomics.org/perspectives/blog/the-tyranny-of-the-top-five-journals
32. Heckman, James & Moktan, Sidharth, "Tyranny of the Top Five."
33. American Economic Association, ASSA 2017 Annual Meeting, "The Curse of the Top 5," https://www.aeaweb.org/webcasts/2017/curse
34. Heckman, James & Moktan, Sidharth, "Tyranny of the Top Five."
35. National Center for Education Statistics, "Trends in Student Loan Debt for Graduate School Completers," May 2018, https://nces.ed.gov/programs/coe/indicator_tub.asp
36. Warren, Katie, Business Insider, May 23, 2019, "One brutal sentence captures what a disaster money in America has become," https://www.businessinsider.com/bottom-half-of-americans-negative-net-worth-2019-5
37. Steverman, Ben, Bloomberg Businessweek, May 23, 2019, "The Wealth Detective Who Finds the Hidden Money of the Super Rich," https://bloom.bg/3HVKr8r
38. Aschheim, Joseph & Tavlas, George, "Academic Exclusion: the Case of Alexander Del Mar," European Journal of Political Economy, March 2004, pp. 31-60.
39. Del Mar, Alexander, *History of Money in America,* Burt Franklin, 1900, New York, p. 96.
40. Del Mar, Alexander, (1895), *History of Monetary Systems,* reprint: New York, A.M. Kelley, 1978, p. 60.

41. The author retrieved these figures from the university websites in 2019: Harvard 224 economics courses, MIT 118, Stanford 147. With the Corona Virus Pandemic it appears the schools are currently not offering all the programs they did in earlier years.

42. Egnatz, Nick, "Challenging the Economics Profession," Alliance For Just Money, Nov 2, 2019, https://www.monetaryalliance.org/challenging-the-economics-profession/

43. Rutgers University, "Financial and Monetary History of the United States," Economics 444:01 Fall 2016, Professor Eugene N. White, https://economics.rutgers.edu/downloads-hidden-menu/undergraduate/syllabi/fall-2016/1332-fall2016white444-01/file

44. Harvard University, "Browsing within Economics," My. Harvard, https://shorturl.at/agQX1

45. Stanford University, "Courses," 2022-23 Econ courses, Department of Economics, https://shorturl.at/qvzZ3

46. Massachusetts Institute of Technology, "Economics (Course 14)," MIT Course Catalogue, Bulletin 2022-2023, http://catalog.mit.edu/subjects/14/

47. NEED Act, "National Emergency Employment Defense Act," https://www.monetary.org/wp-content/uploads/2013/01/HR-2990, https://www.congress.gov/bill/112th-congress/house-bill/2990/text

48. Zarlenga, Stephen, *Lost Science of Money*, American Monetary Institute, Kinderhook, N.Y., 2002.

49. McLeay, Michael, Radia, Amar, Thomas, Ryland of the Bank's Monetary Analysis Directorate, Bank of England, Quarterly Bulletin 2014 Q1, "Money creation in the modern economy," https://www.bankofengland.co.uk//media/boe/files/quarterly-bulletin/2014/money-creation-in-the-modern-economy

50. Werner, Richard A., "A lost century in economics: Three theories of banking and the conclusive evidence," International Review of Financial Analysis, Sept 8, 2015, https://www.sciencedirect.com/science/article/pii/S1057521915001477

51. Yamaguchi, Kaoru, *Workings of A Public Money System of Open Macroeconomies – Modeling the American Monetary Act Completed – (A Revised Version)*, 2011, Doshisha University, http://www.muratopia.org/Yamaguchi/doc/DesignOpenMacro.pdf

52. Kumhof, Michael & Benes, Jaromir, *The Chicago Plan Revisited*, International Monetary Fund, Working Paper, https://www.imf.org/external/pubs/ft/wp/2012/wp12202.pdf

53. Huber, Joseph, Split-*circuit reserve banking – functioning, dysfunctions and future perspectives*, Real-World Economics Review, Issue #80, 2017, http://www.paecon.net/PAEReview/issue80/Huber80.pdf

54. Krischer, Hayley, "Stand Up to Hurtful Family Members," Web MD, https://www.webmd.com/balance/features/stand-up-to-hurtful-family-members#:~:text=First%20things%20first%3A%20Shunning%20and,is%20to%20break%20the%20cycle.

55. McLeay et al, "Money creation in the modern economy."

56. Turner, Adair, *Credit, Money and Leverage: What Wicksell, Hayek and Fisher Knew and Modern Macroeconomics Forgot,* Presentation to Stockholm School of Economics (Part 3), Sept 2013, YouTube, app. 14 minute mark, https://www.youtube.com/watch?v=XoHs7vCdl3E

57. McLeay et al, "Money creation in the modern economy."

58. Zarlenga, Stephen, *The Lost Science of Money,* American Monetary Institute, Valatie, N.Y., 2002

59. Wolf, Martin, Financial Times, April 24, 2014, "Strip private banks of their power to create money," https://www.ft.com/content/7f000b18-ca44-11e3-bb92-00144feabdc0

60. Agility PR Solutions, "Top Ten Indiana Newspapers by Circulation," August 2020, bit.ly/3VWdmiA

61. "Fund infrastructure work with NEED Act," NWI Times, October 24, 2014, bit.ly/3NU0J5w

62. "NEED Act erases big steel's call for worker concessions," NWI Times, September 3, 2015, https://www.nwitimes.com/news/opinion/columnists/guest-commentary/guest-commentary-need-act-erases-big-steel-s-call-for/article_efe67721-18d7-5aad-9459-d6db3a8f3b49.html

63. "Gary could fulfill development needs with the NEED Act," NWI Times, May 13, 2016, https://bit.ly/3qhVxi4

64. NEED Act, National Emergency Employment Defense Act, https://www.monetary.org/wp-content/uploads/2013/01/HR-2990. https://www.congress.gov/bill/112th-congress/house-bill/2990/text

65. Egnatz, Nick, "Challenging the Economics Profession," Alliance For Just Money, Nov 2, 2019.

66. Sklansky, Jeffrey, "A new public digital dollar could be a big boost to American democracy," Washington Post, July 21, 2021, https://www.washingtonpost.com/outlook/2021/07/21/new-public-digital-dollar-could-be-big-boost-american-democracy/

67. Kasperky, "What is cryptocurrency and how does it work?" kaspersky.com.

68. Criddle, Cristina, "Bitcoin consumes 'more electricity than Argentina,'" BBC News, Feb 10, 2021, bbc.com/news/technology-56012952

69. Positive Money, "How Banks Create Money," https://positivemoney.org/how-money-%20works/how-banks-%20create-money/

11. Student Initiatives in the Fight for Monetary Reform

1. International Student Initiative for Pluralism in Economics, "Open Letter," http://www.isipe.net/open-letter/

2. Rethinking Economics, "An Exploration of Our Economic Futures," July 27-29, 2021, bit.ly/42pzKDn

3. "An Exploration of Our Economic Futures," Rethinking Economics, July 27-29, 2021.

4. Egnatz, Nick, "Challenging the Economics Profession," Alliance For Just Money, Nov 2, 2019.

5. Neoliberal means fiscal austerity, deregulation, free trade, privatization and a reduction in government spending (Investopedia) or to put it another way free market capitalism with a minimum of government interference.
6. Email conversation with Lino Zeddies.
7. Zeddies, Lino, "What's wrong with economics?" Lino Zeddies Blog, Feb 4. 2015.
8. Zeddies, Lino, "What's wrong with economics?" Lino Zeddies Blog, Feb 4. 2015.
9. Zeddies, Lino, "What's wrong with economics?" Lino Zeddies Blog, Feb 4. 2015.
10. Zeddies, Lino, "What's wrong with economics?" Lino Zeddies Blog, Feb 4. 2015.
11. McLeay, Michael, Radia, Amar, Thomas, Ryland of the Bank's Monetary Analysis Directorate, Bank of England, Quarterly Bulletin 2014 Q1, "Money creation in the modern economy," p. 14.
12. Werner, Richard A., "A lost century in economics: Three theories of banking and the conclusive evidence," International Review of Financial Analysis, Sept 8, 2015, https://www.sciencedirect.com/science/article/pii/S1057521915001477
13. Rethinking Economics, https://www.rethinkeconomics.org/

12. PRESIDENT BIDEN, PUBLICLY CREATED MONEY, AND THE DEBT-CEILING CRISIS

1. Steverman, Ben, "The Wealth Detective Who Finds the Hidden Money of the Super Rich," Bloomberg Businessweek, May 23, 2019, Referencing economist Gabriel Zucman's work, https://bit.ly/3C0RLvZ
2. NEED Act, "National Emergency Employment Defense Act," https://www.monetary.org/wp-content/uploads/2013/01/HR-2990, https://www.congress.gov/bill/112th-congress/house-bill/2990/text
3. "American Monetary Reform Act of 2022," https://www.monetaryalliance.org/wp-content/uploads/American-Monetary-Reform-Act.pdf
4. United States Code, "Title 3101. Public debt limit," https://www.govinfo.gov/content/pkg/USCODE-2008-title31/html/USCODE-2008-title31-subtitleIII-chap31-subchapI-sec3101.htm
5. Bailey, Kirk, "What is the U.S. Debt Ceiling?" Dummies: A Wiley Brand, Jan 19, 2023, Political Science, https://www.dummies.com/article/academics-the-arts/political-science/what-is-the-u-s-debt-ceiling-187249/
6. Bailey, Kirk, "What is the U.S. Debt Ceiling?" Dummies: A Wiley Brand, Jan 19, 2023, Political Science.
7. Bailey, Kirk, "What is the U.S. Debt Ceiling?" Dummies: A Wiley Brand, Jan 19, 2023, Political Science.
8. Constitution Annotated, "Public Debt Clause", 14th Amendment Section 4, https://constitution.congress.gov/browse/essay/amdt14-S4-1-1/ALDE_00000849/#:~:text=S4.-,1.1%20Public%20Debt%20Clause,rebellion%2C%20shall%20not%20be%20questioned.

9. Kogan, Richard, "Debt Limit Default Is Default, Even Under a 'Prioritization' Scheme," Center on Budget and Policy Priorities, Feb 6, 2023, https://www.cbpp.org/research/federal-budget/debt-limit-default-is-default-even-under-a-prioritization-scheme

10. U.S. Government Publishing Office, "Oath of Office," Ben's Guide to the U.S. Government, https://bensguide.gpo.gov/j-oath-office

11. Burman, Leonard & Gale, William G., "7 things to know about the debt limit," Brookings Institute, Jan 19, 2023, https://www.brookings.edu/2023/01/19/7-things-to-know-about-the-debt-limit/

12. Kogan, Richard, "Debt Limit Default Is Default, Even Under a 'Prioritization' Scheme," Center on Budget and Policy Priorities, Feb 6, 2023.

13. Government Book Talk, "The All-in-One Guide to All Federal Assistance Programs,"
Government Printing Office, https://govbooktalk.gpo.gov/2014/03/27/the-all-in-one-guide-to-all-federal-assistance-programs/

14. Mercer, Marsha, "States Strive to Help SNAP Recipients Cope with Lower Benefits," The Pew Charitable Trust, Feb 28, 2023, https://www.pewtrusts.org/en/research-and-analysis/blogs/stateline/2023/02/28/states-strive-to-help-snap-recipients-cope-with-lower-benefits

15. Rosenbaum, Dottie, Berg, Katie & Hall, Lauren, "Temporary Pandemic SNAP Benefits Will End in Remaining 35 States in March 2023," Center on Budget and Policy Priorities, Feb 6, 2023, https://www.cbpp.org/research/food-assistance/temporary-pandemic-snap-benefits-will-end-in-remaining-35-states-in-march

16. Sullivan, Becky, "What SNAP recipients can expect as benefits shrink in March," NPR, WBEZ Chicago, March 7, 2023, https://www.npr.org/2023/03/07/1161417967/snap-benefits-food-stamps

17. Social Security Administration, "Monthly Statistical Snapshot, February 2023," released March 2023, https://www.ssa.gov/policy/docs/quickfacts/stat_snapshot/

18. Ross, Jean, "Congress Must Raise the Debt Ceiling," Center for American Progress, March 22, 2023, https://www.americanprogress.org/article/congress-must-raise-the-debt-ceiling/

19. Picchi, Aimee, "Debt ceiling: Here's what could happen if lawmakers don't raise the country's borrowing limits," CBS News, Jan 19, 2023, https://www.cbsnews.com/news/debt-ceiling-2023-debt-limit-default-what-could-happen/

20. Brookings Institution, "Wendy Edelberg," https://www.brookings.edu/experts/wendy-edelberg/#:~:text=Edelberg%20received%20a%20Ph.,Studies%20at%20the%20Brookings%20Institution.

21. Harvard Kennedy School of Government, "Louise Sheiner," https://www.hks.harvard.edu/about/louise-sheiner

22. Edelberg, Wendy & Sheiner, Louise, "How worried should we be if the debt ceiling isn't lifted?" Brookings, Jan 25, 2023, https://www.brookings.edu/2023/01/25/how-worried-should-we-be-if-the-debt-ceiling-isnt-lifted/

23. Cornell Law School, "31 U.S. Code § 5112 - Denominations, specifications, and design of coins," https://www.law.cornell.edu/uscode/text/31/5112

24. Sheffey, Ayelet & Kaplan, Juliana, "Janet Yellen says 'it's not a given that the Fed would' accept a $1 trillion platinum coin to save the US from economic catastrophe," Business Insider, Jan 23, 2023, https://www.businessinsider.com/will-the-us-mint-platinum-coin-yellen-dismisses-debt-ceiling-2023-1

25. National Archives, "The Constitution of the United States: A Transcription," America's Founding Documents, https://www.archives.gov/founding-docs/constitution-transcript

26. Ewing, Giselle Ruhiyyih, "Biden signs the debt ceiling bill," Politico, June 3, 2023, https://www.politico.com/news/2023/06/03/biden-signs-debt-ceiling-bill-00100093